Machine Learning: Concepts, Tools and Techniques

Machine Learning: Concepts, Tools and Techniques

Edited by
Ivy Wright

| STATES |
ACADEMIC PRESS
www.statesacademicpress.com

Published by States Academic Press,
109 South 5th Street,
Brooklyn, NY 11249, USA

ISBN: 978-1-63989-336-2

Cataloging-in-Publication Data

Machine learning : concepts, tools and techniques / edited by Ivy Wright.
     p. cm.
Includes bibliographical references and index.
ISBN 978-1-63989-336-2
1. Machine learning. 2. Machine theory. 3. Artificial intelligence. I. Wright, Ivy.
Q325.5 .E44 2022
006.31--dc23

For information on all States Academic Press publications
visit our website at www.statesacademicpress.com

Contents

Preface

This book has been an outcome of determined endeavour from a group of educationists in the field. The primary objective was to involve a broad spectrum of professionals from diverse cultural background involved in the field for developing new researches. The book not only targets students but also scholars pursuing higher research for further enhancement of the theoretical and practical applications of the subject.

The study of computer algorithms that improve automatically through experience and by the use of data is referred to as machine learning. It is considered to be a part of artificial intelligence. Data mining is a related area of study, focusing on exploratory data analysis through unsupervised learning. Performing machine learning involves creating a model. Some of the different types of models that are used and researched for machine learning systems are artificial neural networks, decision trees, support vector machines, regression analysis, Bayesian networks and genetic algorithms. There are many applications for machine learning such as agriculture, banking, economics, marketing, medical diagnosis, telecommunication, software engineering, time series forecasting and bioinformatics. As this field is emerging at a rapid pace, the contents of this book will help the readers understand the modern concepts and applications of the subject. It provides comprehensive insights into the field of machine learning. This book is a collective contribution of a renowned group of international experts.

It was an honour to edit such a profound book and also a challenging task to compile and examine all the relevant data for accuracy and originality. I wish to acknowledge the efforts of the contributors for submitting such brilliant and diverse chapters in the field and for endlessly working for the completion of the book. Last, but not the least; I thank my family for being a constant source of support in all my research endeavours.

Editor

Using Sentiment Analysis and Machine Learning Algorithms to Determine Citizens' Perceptions

Sherrene Bogle

Abstract

This chapter analyzes the opinions expressed by individuals on four topical Jamaican issues and classifies them by emotions, feelings and polarity. The four trending topics on Twitter analyzed are the decriminalization of marijuana in Jamaica, Kaci Fennell's placing in Miss Universe, the Riverton Landfill fire and Barack Obama's working visit to Jamaica. The data pulled from Twitter for each topic was mined using three different classification algorithms to identify the accuracy of the data classified based on the polarity. The classifiers identified which polarity reflected what opinion is more dominant of the three; which are negative, positive or neutral. Sentiment analysis tools classified the opinions of Jamaican Twitter users with over 70% accuracy. Among three classification algorithms used, J48 decision tree received highest accuracy for the four topics tested and maintained the lowest error rate. For the decriminalization of marijuana, Kaci Fennell's placing in the Miss Universe competition and President Obama's visit, the accuracy was just over 70% and the mean absolute error (MAE) was less than 0.3. The methodology of the study provides a blueprint which can be utilized by managers and other decision making stakeholders to determine consumers' perception.

Keywords: Barack Obama, Jamaica, sentiment analysis, machine learning, Twitter

1. Introduction

Sentiment analysis uses linguistic and textual assessment, such as natural language processing to analyze word use, word order, and word combinations and thus to classify sentiments, often into the categories of positive, negative, or neutral polarity. Data gathered through sentiment analysis is believed to provide detailed information about something to which direct access did not previously exist: public opinion and feeling [1]. This research performs sentiment analysis by monitoring and analyzing local trending topics that create island country [2]. The aim of the study is to analyze the opinions and emotion expressed by citizens based on these topical issues and classifies them by emotions, feelings and polarity. It utilizes three machine learning algorithms to classify citizens perceptions namely decision tree J48, PART and naive bayes; and identifies the accuracy of the data classified based on the polarity. The classifiers identified the polarity reflected and which opinion is more dominant of the three (negative, positive or neutral). Research was undertaken on four topical issues in Jamaica: (1) The decriminalization of marijuana in Jamaica (2) Kaci Fennell's placing in the Miss Universe competition (3) The Riverton Landfill fire and (4) Barack Obama's working visit to Jamaica.

2. Methodology

The Sentiment analysis process consists of four main steps outlined in [3]: Data Acquisition, Data Pre-processing, Data Classification and Data Analysis.

2.1. Data acquisition

In this study, the twitter R package was used with RStudio to extract tweets which were subsequently used to create charts and classify data into emotions and polarity. Installation of packages such as install.packages ("twitteR", "ROAuth", "plyr") were required. The searchTwitter() function, found in the R library was used to obtain tweets on selected topics. Hashtags, single and double quotes were parameters accepted by the searchTwitter() function as a means of searching the Twitter API for tweets related to the keywords used in the search, for example temp = searchTwitter("#Jamaica Marijuana") would download tweets with the hashtag Jamaica Marijuana. It allows queries against the indices of recent or popular tweets and behaves similarly to, but not exactly like the search features available in Twitter mobile or web clients, making it very effective and easy to use in searching Twitter.

The population comprised of a corpus eleven thousand two hundred and five (11,205) tweets that were extracted from Twitter between January and April 2015. A search was done on Twitter to extract tweets on Jamaican topics that were not older than 2 weeks.

2.2. Data pre-processing

The corpus was also used offline where it was analyzed using machine learning and spreadsheet tools during pre-processing, classification and the post processing of the data. A function built into RStudio was then used to remove unwanted characters, texts, punctuations and numbers from the text files created as a result of the extracted data from Twitter. After successfully searching Twitter and obtaining the number of tweets required, the tweets were 'cleaned' using RStudio's cleaning function.

2.3. Data classification

RStudio provided two functions that analyzed the tweets and classified them into polarity (negative, neutral and positive) and emotion (joy, anger, fear, surprise). Analysis was done both on tweets (not re-tweeted) as well as re-tweets. After compiling the polarity function to classify the tweets into negative, positive and neutral polarities, the team observed that a number of tweets were classified incorrectly. This was a result of R's inability to understand the Jamaican dialect and RStudio's limited dictionary of words. Classifying tweets into emotions proved to be another challenge as majority of the tweets for the different topical issues returned a result of "unknown" for the emotion associated with the tweet. Both these tools, which are essential components of the sentiment analysis research being conducted, were somewhat ineffective in describing and classifying the data that was collected from Twitter.

2.4. Data analysis

The WEKA software was used offline to analyze data during pre- processing, classification and the post processing. In order to process the data gathered from the Twitter API, the file type or dataset was formatted to a file extension of .arff (attribute file format) and this file extension is generated from a.csv (comma-separated values) file which separates each attribute by a comma. The .arff file is an ASCII text file that describes a list of instances sharing a set of attributes.

A spreadsheet application was another useful tool in the sentiment analysis research conducted. This tool allowed one to inspect the comma-separated values files and also create graphs and tables.

3. Results

This section outlines the classification of tweets downloaded for each of the four topical issues. It shows how sentiment analysis of tweets can be used to explore the citizens perceptions on the topical issues selected. **Figure 1** below shows the summary and classification of such tweets.

Citizens from varying demographics express their opinions on Twitter on several topical issues. The four step methodology was executed and tweets were classified by the machine learning algorithms as shown in **Figure 1**. Barack Obama's visit to Jamaica represented the fourth bar among the quartet of tweets, received 2583 positive tweets and 658 negative tweets and the highest total tweets among the 4 topics investigated.

The next section will present results on polarity of topical issues for tweets and no-retweets.

3.1. Polarity of topical issues

A typical approach to sentiment analysis is to start with a lexicon of positive and negative words and phrases [4]. Polarity describes whether a word seems to evoke something positive

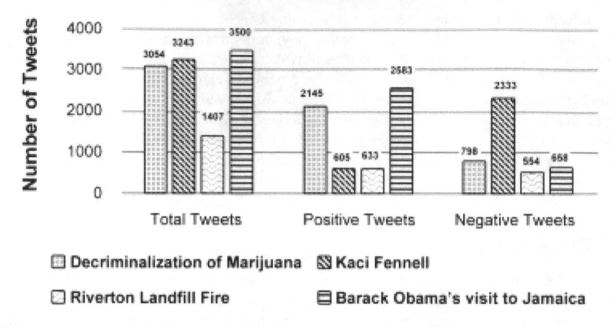

Figure 1. Bar chart depicting the number of tweets collected on each topical issue.

or something negative. For example, *beautiful* has a positive polarity and *horrid* has a negative polarity. Examples of tweets that represent a positive polarity include:

Eg. 1: "Jamaica legalizes medical marijuana and decriminalizes recreational use."

Eg. 2: "the jamaican cabinet approves a bill to legalise use of small amounts of marijuana which will be examined in the senate this week."

Examples of tweets classified as having a negative polarity include:

Eg. 1: "what nbc didn't show kaci fennell miss jamaica"

Eg. 2: "miss jamaica says the miss universe pageant "went exactly as it should""

3.1.1. The decriminalization of marijuana in Jamaica

As depicted in **Figure 2**, majority (2145) tweets of the three thousand and fifty four (3054) tweets collected on the decriminalization of marijuana in Jamaica were positive. This demonstrates that the Jamaican citizens on the Twitter social media platform support the decision by government to decriminalize marijuana (*Cannabis sativa*) in Jamaica. However, seven hundred and ninety eight (798) Jamaicans on Twitter expressed negative sentiments toward the government's decision to decriminalize marijuana in Jamaica.

3.1.1.1. No-retweets

The graph above depicts the results obtained from analysis of tweets that were not retweeted, as in these tweets were posted by the original author. **Figure 3** shows that three hundred and forty six (346) tweets were negative and four hundred and seven (407) were positive.

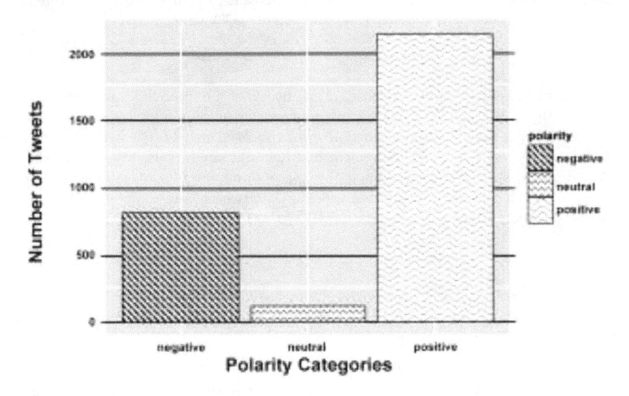

Figure 2. Sentiment polarity of tweets obtained on the decriminalization of marijuana in Jamaica.

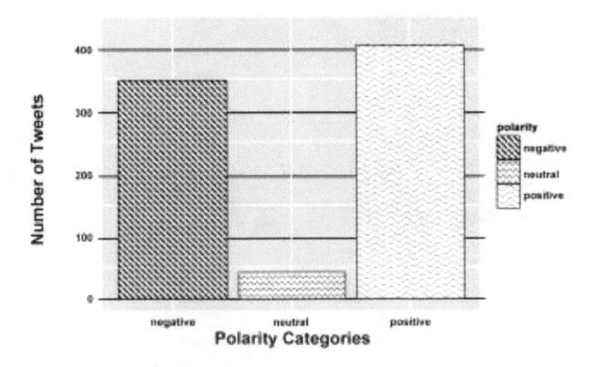

Figure 3. Sentiment polarity of no-retweets obtained on the decriminalization of marijuana in Jamaica.

3.1.1.2. Retweets

Among retweets for the topic, there were four hundred and fifty three (453) tweets were negative and one thousand seven hundred and thirty eight (1438) were positive.

3.1.2. Kaci Fennell's placing in Miss Universe

As depicted in **Figure 4** above, majority (2333) tweets of the three thousand two hundred
and forty three (3243) tweets collected on Kaci Fennell's placing in the Miss Universe competition were negative. Upon examination of the tweets collected the negative tweets were
expressions of anger and disappointment that Kaci did not win the Miss Universe competition or that she did not receive a higher placing than the fifth place ranking that she
received. On the contrary, six hundred and five (605) tweets were classified as positive by
the RStudio application.

3.1.2.1. No-retweets

The graph above depicts the results obtained from analysis of tweets that were not retweeted,
as in these tweets were posted by the original author. **Figure 5** shows that seven hundred and
ninety (790) tweets were negative and three hundred and ninety nine (399) were positive.

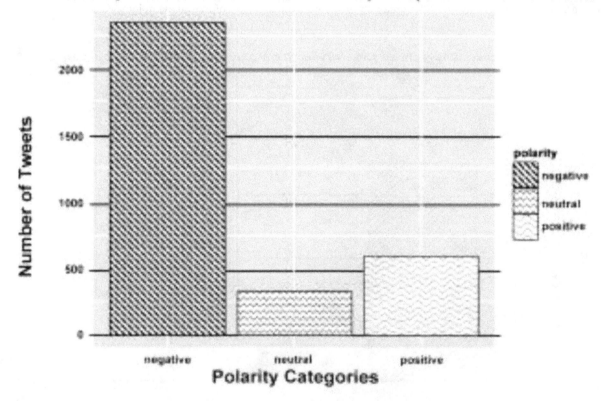

Figure 4. Sentiment polarity of tweets obtained on Kaci Fennell's placing in Miss Universe.

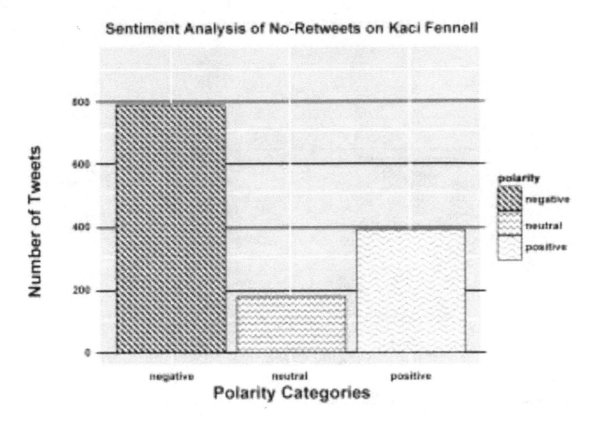

Figure 5. Sentiment polarity of no-retweets obtained on Kaci Fennell's placing in Miss Universe.

3.1.2.2. Retweets

Among retweets for the topic, one thousand five hundred and thirty (1530) tweets were negative and two hundred and forty (240) were positive.

3.1.3. Riverton Landfill fire

Figure 6 shows five hundred and fifty four (554) tweets of the one thousand four hundred and seven (1407) tweets collected on the Riverton Landfill fire in the Riverton community were negative. Smoke penetration from the fire was observed within a 20 mile radius from the landfill and further at times based on the wind direction. The fire lasted for 2 weeks and at least 29 critical air pollutants was detected [5]. The tweets classified as negative were Jamaicans expressing their anger toward the maintenance of the landfill and the effects of the fire on nearby communities. Six hundred and thirty three (633) tweets were classified as being positive.

3.1.3.1. No-retweets

The graph above depicts the results obtained from analysis of tweets that were not retweeted, as in these tweets were posted by the original author. **Figure 7** shows that two hundred and forty five (245) tweets were negative and three hundred and five (305) were positive.

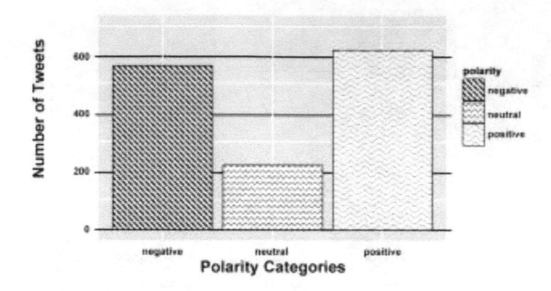

Figure 6. Sentiment polarity of tweets obtained on the Riverton Landfill fire in Jamaica.

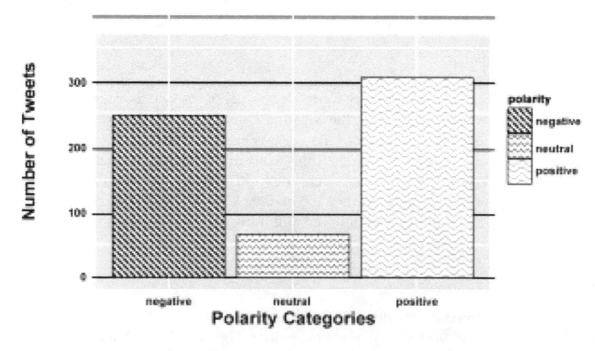

Figure 7. Sentiment polarity of no-retweets obtained on the Riverton Landfill fire in Jamaica.

3.1.3.2. Retweets

Of the retweets, three hundred and eleven (311) tweets were negative and three hundred and twenty eight (328) were positive.

3.1.4. Barack Obama's visit to Jamaica

Figure 8 shows that the majority (2583) tweets of the three thousand five hundred and one (3500) tweets collected on Barack Obama's visit to Jamaica were positive. This demonstrates that the Jamaican citizens on Twitter social supported the visit of the President to Jamaica. However, six hundred and fifty eight (658) Jamaicans on Twitter expressed negative sentiments toward Barack Obama's visit to Jamaica. There was a movement suggesting the success of visit of his visit was dependent on whether he offered or announced a Presidential Pardon to the country's first national hero Marcus Garvey, civil rights activist in Jamaica and the USA, who allegedly was falsely convicted of mail fraud in the USA. Failure to grant a pardon to the civil rights activists spurred some of the negative tweets. Hence, *anger* appears on the word cloud in **Figure 9**, generated by RStudio.

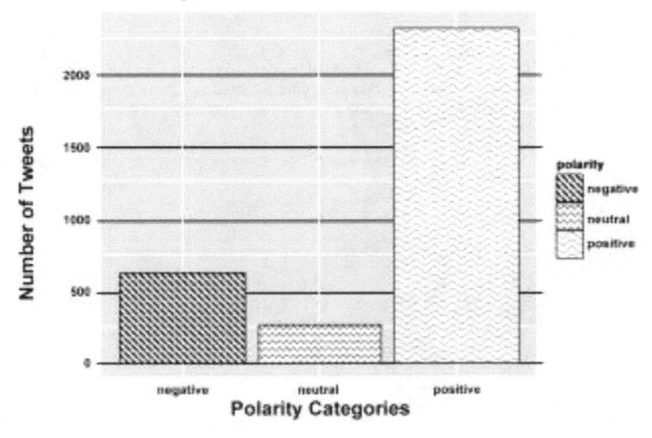

Figure 8. Sentiment polarity of tweets obtained on Barack Obama's visit to Jamaica.

Figure 9. Word cloud showing frequently tweeted words associated with Barack Obama's visit to Jamaica.

3.1.4.1. No-retweets

Figure 10 depicts the results obtained from analysis of tweets that were not retweeted, as in these tweets were posted by the original author. It shows that nine hundred and seventy one (971) tweets were positive and three hundred and twenty two (322) were negative.

3.1.4.2. Retweets

From the analysis of tweets that were retweeted by users who shared similar sentiments of tweets posted by other Twitter users there were three hundred and thirty seven (337) tweets were negative and one thousand six hundred and twelve (1612) were positive.

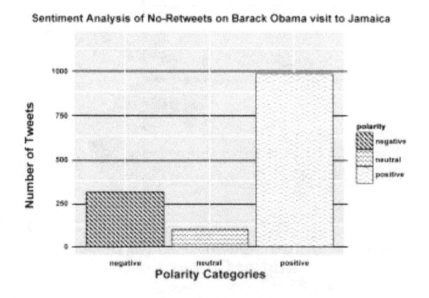

Figure 10. Sentiment polarity of no-retweets obtained on Barack Obama's visit to Jamaica.

3.2. Emotions of topical issues

This section will present information on emotions expressed for each topic, with no-retweets. In everyday speech, emotion is viewed as one's state of mind and instinctive response and are intertwined with mood, temperament, personality and disposition. Emotions are elicited by significant events that are significant when they touch upon one or more of the concerns of the subject. Emotions thus result from the interaction of an event's actual or anticipated consequences and the subject's concerns [6]. In this research several emotions were highlighted: anger, fear, joy, sadness, surprise and disgust. However, due to RStudio's incapability to classify some of the tweets into emotions many tweets were classifieds "unknown".

3.2.1. No-retweets

Tweets posted by authors were of mixed emotions, varying from anger to joy. As depicted in the **Figures 11–14**, RStudio encountered difficulty in classifying the emotions associated with majority of the tweets. As a result of this, majority of the tweets for the decriminalization of marijuana in Jamaica were classified as "unknown" in **Figure 11**. Many factors including the use of the Jamaican creole and the use of sarcasm may have contributed to R's difficulty in determining the emotions of the tweets. This was noticed for the emotions depicted on the other topical issues selected (**Figure 11**).

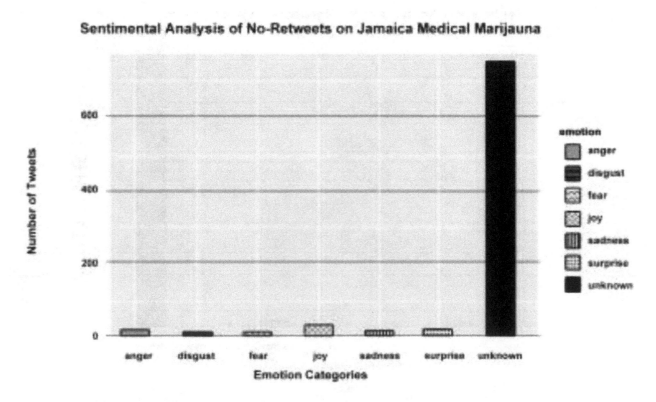

Figure 11. Sentiment emotion of no-retweets obtained on the decriminalization of marijuana in Jamaica.

3.2.2. Retweets

The tweets that were retweeted by Twitter users for the decriminalization of marijuana in Jamaica were of joy and sadness.

3.3. Kaci Fennell's placing in Miss Universe

3.3.1. The decriminalization of marijuana in Jamaica

In **Figure 12**, apart from the tweets that were classified as unknown, it can be seen that tweets expressing anger, joy and surprise recorded the highest numbers. Tweets posted by authors were of mixed emotions, with joy and anger representing the more frequent emotions expressed.

3.3.2. Retweets

The tweets that were retweeted by Twitter users for Kaci Fennell's placing in the Miss Universe event were mostly of joy and anger.

3.4. Riverton Landfill fire

As depicted in **Figure 13**, the emotions discovered for the Riverton Landfill fire varied, more so than the other topical issues that was selected. The tweets analyzed resulted in emotions of anger, disgust, joy, sadness and surprise.

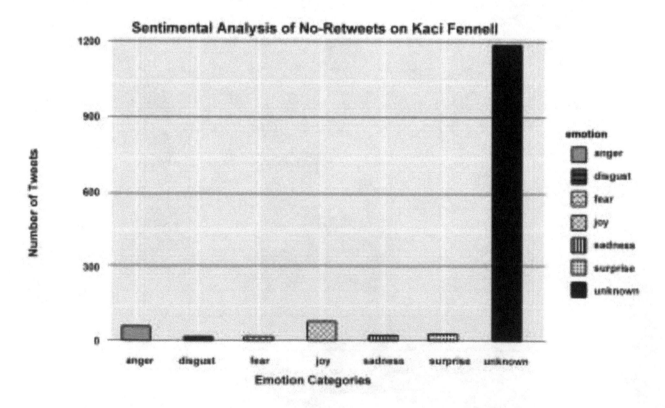

Figure 12. Sentiment emotion of no-retweets obtained on the Kaci Fennell's placing in Miss Universe.

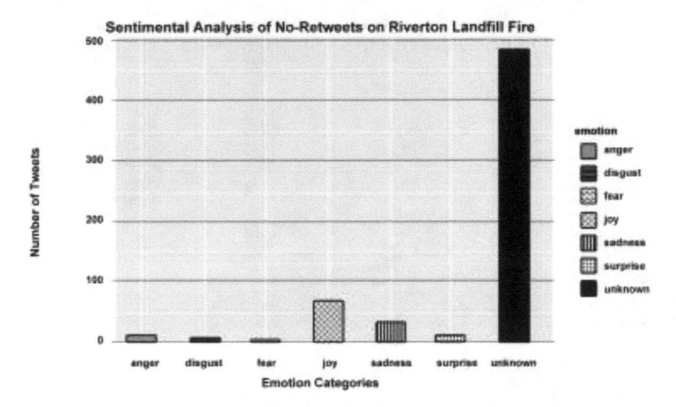

Figure 13. Sentiment emotion of no-tweets obtained on the Riverton Landfill fire.

3.4.1. No-retweets

Tweets posted by authors were of mixed emotions, with joy and sadness representing the more frequent emotions expressed.

3.4.2. Retweets

The tweets that were retweeted by Twitter users on the Riverton Landfill fire were mostly of joy, sadness, disgust and anger.

3.5. Barack Obama's visit to Jamaica

As shown in **Figure 14**, there was difficulty in classifying the emotions associated with majority of the tweets. As a result of this, majority of the tweets for the Barack Obama's visit to Jamaica were classified as "unknown". Many factors including the use of the Jamaican creole and the use of sarcasm may have contributed to R's difficulty in determining the emotions of the tweets. This was noticed for the emotions depicted on the other topical issues selected. Other emotions expressed were of joy and surprise.

3.5.1. No-retweets

Tweets posted by authors were of mixed emotions, varying from joy to surprise to fear.

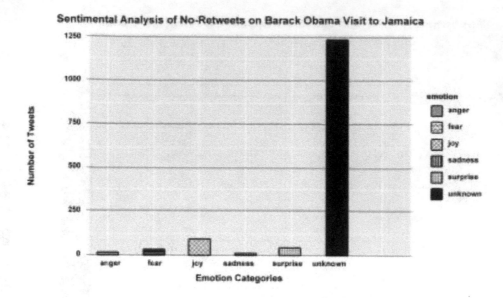

Figure 14. Sentiment emotion of no-retweets obtained on Barack Obama's visit to Jamaica.

3.5.2. Retweets

The tweets that were retweeted by Twitter users for Barack Obama's visit to Jamaica were of joy and surprise.

Sample tweets: This section shows samples of tweets and their sentiment classification for each of the four topical issues (**Tables 1–4**).

Decriminalization of marijuana in Jamaica	
Tweet	**Polarity**
"Jamaica passes law that decriminalizes small amounts of pot. legislation also creates licensing agency to regulate medical"	Positive
"Jamaica decriminalizes marijuana, reminds rest of world it isn't legalized"	Neutral
"in other words, don't get too crazy. weed wasn't legal before, and now it's just less illegal."	Negative

Table 1. Examples of Twitter posts with expressed opinions on the decriminalization of marijuana in Jamaica.

Kaci Fennell's placing in Miss Universe	
Tweet	**Polarity**
"we continue to be proud of kaci fennel"	Positive
"miss jamaica universe kaci fennell will play mass with tribe for carnival 2015 come monday and Tuesday"	Neutral
"miss jamaica kaci fennell 'robbed' of miss universe crown"	Negative

Table 2. Examples of Twitter posts with expressed opinions on Kaci Fennell's placing in Miss Universe.

Riverton Landfill fire

Tweet	Polarity
"said fire would be out by weekend it's not yet Friday"	Positive
"adding to the confusion gleaner when will riverton dump fire be extinguished odpem heads give conflicting deadlines"	Neutral
"a number of schools closed early again today because of rivertondump smoke incl hydel schools amp st patricks primary"	Negative

Table 3. Examples of sample Twitter posts with expressed opinions on the Riverton Landfill fire.

Barack Obama's visit to Jamaica

Tweet	Polarity
"that moment after barack obama said wah gwaan jamaica"	Positive
"barack obama is in jamaica hes just said this"	Neutral
"chronixx upset at barack obamas jamaica visit calls him a waste man bash government"	Negative

Table 4. Examples of Twitter posts with expressed opinions on President Barack Obama's visit to Jamaica.

4. Conclusion

This chapter presented information on how sentiment analysis can be used to extract subjective information from a social media website such as Twitter. It provides researchers with an opportunity to collect deep, rich, readily available qualitative information from a large group of participants in an unobstructed real world environment. Despite several potential uses of sentiment analysis, the literature highlights some general challenges that can be faced when using it with Twitter, such as the noisy nature of Twitter's one hundred and forty (140) character long expressions.

4.1. Significance of the research

Many organizations have taken the initiative to use the tools available through sentiment analysis because of the benefits. The sentiment analysis approach presented in this chapter can be very useful for entities and organizations interested in gathering and understanding the opinions of stakeholders who are Twitter users. This is further facilitated by the availability of Twitter data and posts through Twitter's privacy policy. This study is significant as it presents the results of topical issues being discussed in the country to the public.

This method can be used by companies for marketing research, to aid campaigns and allow stakeholders to understand customer perceptions and thus improve service delivery. Sentiments derived from citizens tweets has even used in forecasting stocks. In Ref. [7], the sentiments marijuana tweets were used to predict stock prices of pharmaceutical companies.

4.2. Recommendations for further research

Overall, the tools available to conduct sentiment analysis on social media sites including Twitter are readily available, but had limitations when used in a Jamaican context. The results received were incorrect at times, which could be as a result of RStudio's inability to understand the Jamaican dialect (patois) that was used in some of the tweets and even the use of sarcasm in some of the tweets presented.

To improve the classification of tweets, in terms of classifying tweets into polarity and emotion, a dictionary of Jamaican words and expressions could be created and then included in the RStudio application. Through the use of this dictionary, in addition to the dictionary already included in RStudio, classification will be improved and misclassification will be deterred when sentiment analysis is used in the Jamaican context.

4.3. Summary

Results indicate that the opinions of Jamaicans on Twitter varied and that many Jamaicans shared the sentiments of others, evidenced by the number of retweets discovered. Among three classification algorithms used, J48 received highest accuracy for the four topics tested and maintained the lowest error rate. The accuracy was just over 70% and the mean absolute error (MAE) was less than 0.3 for the decriminalization of marijuana, Kaci Fennell's placing in the Miss Universe competition and President Obama's visit. For Riverton Landfill fire, the MAE was higher at 0.38 with a comparatively lower accuracy of 55% and precision of 61%. For the decriminalization of Marijuana 72% of the tweets analyzed were positive while for Kaci Fennell's placing in the Miss Universe event 71% of tweets analyzed were of negative sentiments. There was a marginal difference between positive and negative views obtained on the Riverton Landfill fire. Finally, 73% of the tweets collected on President Obama's visit to Jamaica showed positive sentiments, which can be interpreted that many Jamaicans were appreciative of his visit to the island.

Acknowledgements

The author wishes to acknowledge the following students who participated in downloading and classifying the tweets: Jordan Wayne Daley, Kleyon-Paul White, Miguel Robinson, Rickone Powell and Nicholas Jarrett.

Author details

Sherrene Bogle

Address all correspondence to: sbogle@utech.edu.jm; sherrene.bogle@gmail.com

University of Technology, Jamaica, Kingston, Jamaica

References

[1] Kennedy H. Perspectives on sentiment analysis. Journal of Broadcasting & Electronic Media. 2012 Oct 1;**56**(4):435-450

[2] Jamaica Information Service. President Barack Obama Arrives in Jamaica [Internet]. 2015. Available from: http://jis.gov.jm/president-barack-obama-arrives-jamaica/

[3] Bogle S, Bogle V, Anderson T. Sentiment analysis of consumers' perceptions on social media about the main mobile providers in Jamaica. World Academy of Science, Engineering and Technology, International Journal of Biomedical and Biological Engineering. 2016;**2**(1):355

[4] Wilson T, Wiebe J, Hoffmann P. Recognizing contextual polarity in phrase-level sentiment analysis. In: Proceedings of the Conference on Human Language Technology and Empirical Methods in Natural Language Processing. Association for Computational Linguistics. Vancouver, Canada. 2005 Oct 6. pp. 347-354

[5] Frijda NH, Manstead AS, Bem S, editors. Emotions and Beliefs: How Feelings Influence Thoughts. Cambridge University Press; 2000 Oct 12

[6] March Fire at Riverton Dump [Internet]. 2015. Available from: http://m.jamaicaobserver.com/news/Report--March-fire-at-Riverton-dump-most-detrimental-in-history_18885503 [Accessed: 11-09-2017]

[7] Bogle SA, Potter WD. SentAMaL-a sentiment analysis machine learning stock predictive model. In: Proceedings on the International Conference on Artificial Intelligence (ICAI). The Steering Committee of The World Congress in Computer Science, Computer Engineering and Applied Computing (WorldComp). 2015. p. 610. ISBN: 1601324057

2

Classification of Malaria-Infected Cells using Deep Convolutional Neural Networks

W. David Pan, Yuhang Dong and Dongsheng Wu

Abstract

Malaria is a life-threatening disease caused by parasites that are transmitted to people through the bites of infected mosquitoes. Automation of the diagnosis process will enable accurate diagnosis of the disease and hence holds the promise of delivering reliable healthcare to resource-scarce areas. Machine learning technologies have been used for automated diagnosis of malaria. We present some of our recent progresses on highly accurate classification of malaria-infected cells using deep convolutional neural networks. First, we describe image processing methods used for segmentation of red blood cells from wholeslide images. We then discuss the procedures of compiling a pathologists-curated image dataset for training deep neural network, as well as data augmentation methods used to significantly increase the size of the dataset, in light of the overfitting problem associated with training deep convolutional neural networks. We will then compare the classification accuracies obtained by deep convolutional neural networks through training, validating, and testing with various combinations of the datasets. These datasets include the original dataset and the significantly augmented datasets, which are obtained using direct interpolation, as well as indirect interpolation using automatically extracted features provided by stacked autoencoders. This chapter ends with a discussion of further research.

Keywords: deep learning, convolutional neural network, autoencoders, data augmentation, classification, wholeslide images, malaria

1. Introduction

Malaria is a widespread disease that has claimed millions of lives all over the world. According to the World Health Organization, approximately 438,000 deaths result from 214 million infections in 2015 [1]. Endemic regions with widespread disease include Africa and South-East Asia. In these and other parts of the world where malaria mortality is significant, necessary resources such as reliable prevention, healthcare, and hygiene are far from adequate [1]. In most cases, the only available method of malaria diagnosis is manual examination of the microscopic slide [2]. In order to provide reliable diagnosis, extensive experience and training are required. Unfortunately, such specialized human resources are very often limited in rural areas where malaria has a marked predominance. Also, manual microscopy is subjective and suffers from a lack of standardization. This problem is further exacerbated by the large size of microscopic wholeslide images, which require a lengthy scanning.

1.1. The need for an automated malaria diagnosis process

The issues associated with manual diagnosis present the case for automation of the malaria diagnosis process. The automation of the diagnosis process will ensure accurate diagnosis of the disease and hence holds the promise of delivering reliable health-care to resource-scarce areas. Hence, rural areas suffering from lack of specialized infrastructure and trained man-power can benefit greatly from automated diagnosis. Automating the diagnosis of malaria involves adapting the methods, expertise, practices, and knowledge of conventional micros-copy to a computerized system structure [3]. Early detection of malaria is essential for ensuring proper diagnosis and increasing chances of cure. In consideration of the severity and the number of fatalities claimed by this disease, it is rational to accept potential small implemen-tation errors introduced by an automated system. An automated system consists of stream-lined image processing techniques for initial filtering and segmentation and suite of pattern recognition and/or machine learning algorithms directed toward robustly recognizing infected cells in a light or wholeslide microscopic image [4]. Previous studies have shown that the degree of agreement between clinicians on the severity of the disease in a given patent's sample is very low. Hence, a computer-assisted system as a decision support system can be paramount to faster and reliable diagnosis. It can help provide a benchmark and standardized way of measuring the degree of infection of the disease [5].

1.2. Wholeslide images for computer-aided malaria infection classification

Among recent works on computer-aid diagnosis, two types of images have found prevalent use: light microscopic images and wholeslide images. The former has been in existence since a longer time frame compared to the latter, which has come into popular adoption recently. Because of recent advancements in computing power, improved cloud-based services and robust algorithms have enabled the widespread use of wholeslide images. For conventional light microscopy, the patient tissue image is acquired by means of incision and then examined under a light microscope. A diagnostic conclusion is arrived upon based interpretation of multiple slide samples [6]. This type of examination does not provide a good sensitivity and specificity for malaria diagnosis [7]. With an aim to standardize slide interpretations, wholeslide images were introduced. The wholeslide image is obtained by scanning an entire slide in one pass. The final image consists of several component images obtained by scanning the areas under the respective fields of sight of the microscope and stitched together. The most widely used methods of scanning include tile scanning and line scanning. In tile scan, the component images are obtained in the form of 512 × 512 tiles. In the line scan method, the component images are generated in a strip-scan fashion.

The file sizes of the wholeslide images are governed by the objective of the lens while scanning. Wholeslide images scanned 40× objective give rise to substantially large file size, for instance, approximately 2 GB. Magnification beyond the maximum level can result in pixelation [8]. Wholeslide images can be decomposed into a pyramid structure of different resolutions. The image at each magnification level is broken down into smaller constituent tiles and stored in respective folders. The image pyramid allows for real-time viewing of wholeslide images. The zoom levels are precalculated and stored in the metadata associated with the file [9]. Each tile can be viewed and analyzed individually. **Figure 1** shows an illustration [10]. The process of

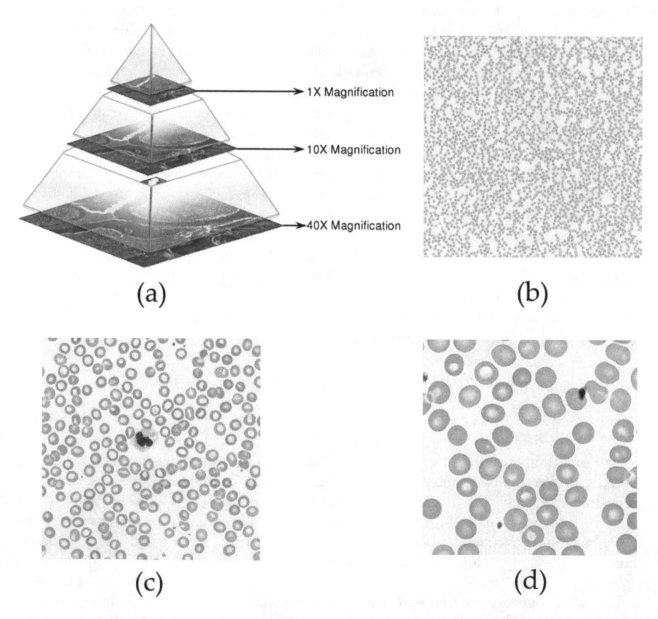

Figure 1. (a) Image pyramid of the DeepZoom structure. Example image tiles at various DeepZoom pyramid resolutions (b) Level 14, (c) Level 15, and (d) Level 16. Each tile image is 258 × 258, and magnification is 100×.

examining a wholeslide image is termed as "virtual microscopy", since analysis and examination can be performed through compatible software virtually on the computer. The DeepZoom structure is favorable in terms of storage and transmission. This arrangement of the original wholeslide image allows for smooth loading and panning using multiresolution images. Initially upon loading, a low-resolution version of the image is displayed. The higher resolution details get blended into the image as they become available. Thus, while viewing the image in DeepZoom, the user experiences a blurred image to sharp image transition. In terms of transmission, the DeepZoom structure is bandwidth efficient. Since, initially, a coarse low-resolution version is transmitted, the bandwidth overhead is reduced. At each level, each tile can be worked on individually [11].

1.3. Classification of malaria-infected red blood cells using deep learning

There has recently been an increasing amount of studies devoted to the application of computer vision and machine learning technologies to the automated diagnosis of malaria. Among the most recent related work [12–16], an automated analysis method was presented in [14] for detection and staging of red blood cells (RBCs) infected by the malaria parasite. In order to classify RBCs, three different types of machine learning algorithms were tested for prediction accuracy and speed as RBC classifiers. In [12], the authors built a low-cost automated digital microscope coupled with a set of computer vision and classification algorithms. Support vector machine (SVM) has been applied to detect malaria-infected cells using provided handcrafted features. In our prior work [17], we sought the best features from a set of 76 features organized into five categories extracted from the input data, in order to optimize SVM-based classification of wholeslide malarial smear images. We found that the binary SVM classifier yielded a superlative accuracy of 95.5% if the feature-selection is based on Kullback-Leibler distance. In contrast, deep learning has appeared as a genre of machine learning algorithms, which attempt to solve problems by learning abstraction in data following a stratified description paradigm based on non-linear transformation architectures. Recent advances in deep machine learning provide tools to automatically classify images and objects with (and occasionally exceeding) human-level accuracy. A key advantage of deep learning is its ability to perform semi-supervised or unsupervised feature extraction over massive datasets.

Deep learning has found exciting new applications in biomedicine [18], genomic medicine [19], bioinformatics [20], and medical imaging analysis [21–28]. However, there has been very sparse work on applying deep learning methods to computer-assisted malaria infection detection. In [16] were described point-of-care diagnostics using microscopes and smartphones, where deep convolutional neural network (CNN) was employed to identify image patches suspected to contain malaria-infected RBCs. The detection accuracy is similar to the results achieved with deep learning [15], where a CNN (with three convolutional layers and two fully connected layers) achieved a precision of 95.31% using images from dedicated microscope cameras [16]. Nevertheless, deep learning methods typically involve the calculation of tens of thousands of parameters, which in turn require large training datasets that may not be readily available. Thus, many commonly used machine learning methods such as support vector machine can outperform deep learning methods when experimental data is scarce. When the datasets are not sufficiently large, one of the major challenges with training deep CNNs is to deal with the risk of overfitting. When training error is low but the test error is high, the model fails to learn a proper generalization of knowledge contained in data [18]. There are ways to regularize the deep network, such as randomized pruning of excessive connectivity, but overfitting is still a threat with small image datasets, especially with unbiased data.

In this chapter, we present some of our recent progresses on highly accurate classification of malaria-infected cells using deep convolutional neural networks. We will discuss the procedures of compiling a pathologists-curated image dataset for training deep neural network, as well as data augmentation methods used to significantly increase the size of the dataset, in light of the overfitting problem associated with training deep convolutional neural networks. In the other section, we describe image processing methods used for segmenting red blood cells from wholeslide images.

2. Cell image pre-processing and compilation of dataset for deep learning

The images used in this work were wholeslide images provided in the PEIR-VM repository built by the University of Alabama in Birmingham. The original whole slide image data contain significant amount of redundant information. In order to achieve good classification accuracy, image segmentation and de-noising are needed to extract only blood cells and remove those redundant image pixels simultaneously. Several effective image processing techniques were used to accurately segment tiles into individual cells.

2.1. Image pre-processing tasks

Most image tiles may easily be visualized as having no malaria-infected cells, so preselection of noninfected tiles can be used to significantly reduce overall processing runtime. Given the contrast between the darkly purple/blue-stained nuclei of malaria and the light pink color of normal cells, pixel color information is used for preliminary selection of "infected" tiles. In order to estimate the color of infected cells, we conducted statistical analysis on the collected cell pixels. The maximal and minimal RGB values of infected cells were selected as two thresholds for "suspect" tiles. Considering the risk of excluding infected cells, we expanded the selected RGB value range to include more tiles. In this work, 24,648 of the original 85,094 tiles (29%) were marked as suspect and require further analysis.

For the suspected tile, thresholding is performed on the binarized image using Otsu's method. An example is shown in **Figure 2**. We can see that noise not only exists in the image background but also inside RBCs. A series of morphological steps were applied to fill the isolated dots and holes to finally obtain the individual cell samples.

In our work, only RBCs will provide features in the wholeslide image to the following classification. Therefore, we only keep RBCs and remove everything else using a combination of morphological operations. After all RBCs are processed, we then obtain all clean RBC samples for further classification. **Figure 3** shows some normal and infected RBC samples.

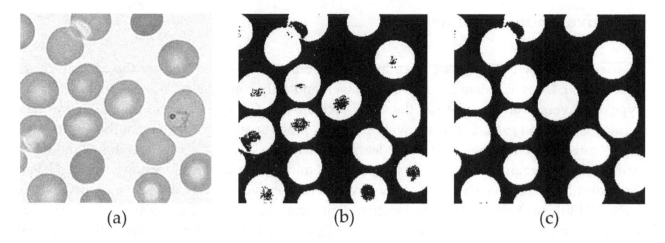

(a) (b) (c)

Figure 2. Steps of image pre-processing. (a) An image tile of interest; (b) Otsu thresholded image; and (c) morphologically filled image.

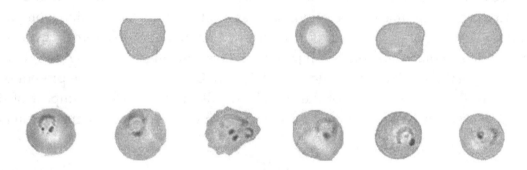

Figure 3. Some example segmented red blood cell images. (Upper row) normal cells and (lower row) infected cells.

2.2. Construction of an image dataset

There is no sufficiently large, high-quality image dataset of pathologically annotated cell images available to fully train multiple-layer neural networks. The only reasonably large, publicly available dataset in [16] we are aware of contains only 2703 images. However, these images were taken from thick blood smears, showing blurry patches rather than extractable RBCs found in high-resolution wholeslide images scanned from thin blood smears. Therefore, we worked with a team of pathologists to construct a dataset. After the data preprocessing, we randomly selected a large number of cell images and provided them to pathologists at the University of Alabama at Birmingham. The entire whole slide image dataset have been divided into four segments evenly. Each of four pathologists is assigned with two segments so that each cell image will be viewed and labeled by at least two experienced pathologists. One cell image can only be considered as infected and included in our final dataset if all the reviewers mark it positively whereas it will be excluded otherwise. The same selection rule also applies to the normal cells in our dataset.

3. Convolution neural network

Convolutional neural network is an artificial neural network inspired by the animal visual system [29]. Convolutional layer, pooling layer, and fully connection layer are the three main types of layers used to construct the CNN architecture. Compared to traditional neural networks, CNNs can extract features without losing much spatial correlations of the input. Each layer consists of neurons that have learnable weights and biases. The optimal model is achieved after feeding data into the network and minimizing the loss function at the top layer. Several different architectures of CNN have been proposed. In this work, we used LeNet-5. LeNet-5 [30] was first used in handwritten digit recognition and achieved an impressive error rate as low as 0.8%. **Figure 4** shows the architecture of the LeNet-5 convolutional neural network used for classification of the red blood cell images.

One of the major challenges of the research is that the current image dataset is still too small, which could lead to overfitting when used for training deep convolutional neural network. To this end, we consider data augmentation. More similar images can be added to the dataset by applying to the existing images operations such as rotation, translation, flip, zoom, and color perturbations. Other methods include data augmentation in the spatial domain by learning the statistical models of data transformation [31], as well as data augmentation through interpolation and extrapolation in the feature domain ([32, 33]). In the following, we present our work in augmenting the image dataset of the red blood cells and discuss the impact of the data augmentation on the image classification accuracies using deep convolutional neural network.

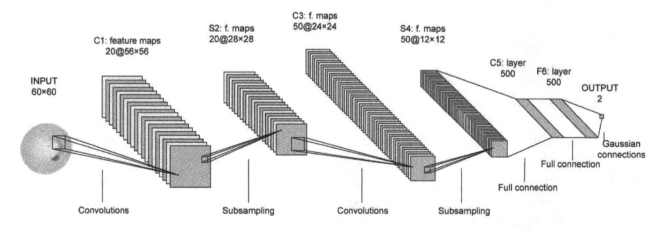

Figure 4. LeNet-5 convolutional neural network architecture. There are two convolution layers (C1 and C3), two subsampling (pooling) layers (S2 and S4), and two fully connected layers.

4. Image data augmentation

The set of infected red blood cell images has 800 images, each with size of $50 \times 50 \times 3$ (for red, green, and blue channels). Only the red channel pixel values were used. Since we want to evaluate the quality of the augmented data set, we used only half of the infected cell images (400 images) for data augmentation, with the remaining 400 images untouched. The same configuration applies to the set of normal red blood cell images, which contains 4000 images. Only half (2000 images) of the dataset were used for augmentation.

We first describe the algorithms for data augmentation by using image interpolation in the spatial domain (Section 4.1), and in the feature domain (Section 4.2), respectively. As a comparison, we then present some example read blood cell images to show the effect of image interpolation in the spatial and feature domains at the end of Section 4.2.

4.1. Image interpolation in the spatial domain

For any two images A and B in the dataset, we can generate a new image by finding a weighted average C. Specifically, the pixel at location (i, j) in C can be obtained by

$$C(i,j) = \min[A(i,j), B(i,j)] + k \times \{\max[A(i,j), B(i,j)] - \min[A(i,j), B(i,j)]\}, \tag{1}$$

where k is a weight ranging between 0 and 1. It can be seen that $C(i,j) = \min[A(i,j), B(i,j)]$ for $k = 0$; $C(i,j) = \max[A(i,j), B(i,j)]$ for $k = 1$. By varying the k values, for example, from 0 to 1 with a step size of 0.1, we can create 11 different images for any two input images. Assume the number of images in the dataset to be augmented is N, we can generate $\frac{11N(N-1)}{2}$ images, which can lead to a much enlarged dataset.

4.2. Image interpolation in the feature domain

To obtain the features of the red blood cell images, we used Hinton's autoencoder [34], which in essence is artificial neural network that performs unsupervised learning on the input data [35]. In the encoding phase, low-dimensional representations of the input data are learned through training the neural network. These learned representations are extracted features of the input image. The features can then be used to reconstruct the original data (decoding). The training algorithm will seek to optimize the neural network by minimizing the reconstruction loss as a cost function on sufficiently large amount of data. Moreover, a deep neural network can be constructed by concatenating multiple autoencoders. This would allow for a hierarchical representation of the data through a multilayer architecture. In [34], the Restricted Boltzmann Machine (RBM) was used as an autoencoder, which serves as a building block of a deep autoencoder network. Each RBM was pretrained and unrolled. Then, back propagation was carried out to fine-tune the entire stacked autoencoder based on cross entropy as the cost function.

In our implementation, the numbers of neurons in each of the four layers are 2500-1500-500-30. The maximum number of epochs for training the autoencoder was set to 1000, and back propagation was set to 500 iterations. **Figure 5** shows the architecture of the stacked autoencoders and autodecoders, where data interpolation is performed on the 30-point feature vectors. **Figure 6** shows some examples of reconstructed images.

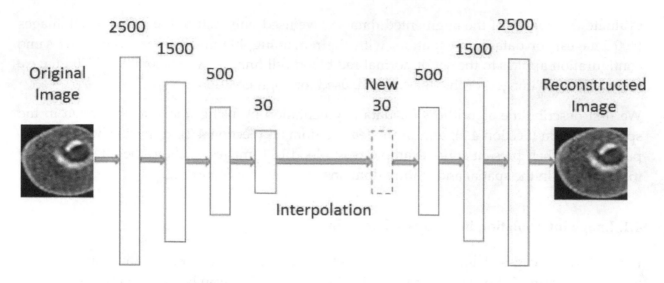

Figure 5. A four-layer stacked autoencoders and autodecoders used to extract the 30-point features of the input image in an unsupervised learning manner. After network training, interpolation of the input images is performed using their 30-point features. The resulting feature vector was then used to reconstruct the red blood cell image by the autodecoders.

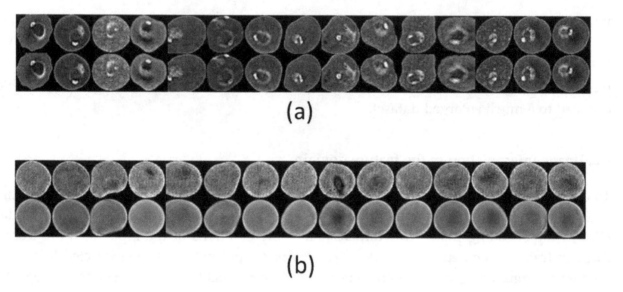

Figure 6. Original images (top row) and the reconstructed images (bottom row) using the stacked autodecoders. (a) Malaria-infected cells and (b) normal cells.

For any two images A and B in the dataset, two 30-point feature vectors F_A and F_B can be obtained by the stacked autoencoders that have been trained. Similar to the image interpolation in the spatial domain, we can generate a new 30-point vector F_C by finding a weighted average. Specifically, the pixel at location (i, j) in C can be obtained by

$$F_C = \min[F_A, F_B] + k \times \{\max[F_A, F_B] - \min[F_A, F_B]\}, \tag{2}$$

where k is a weight varied between 0 and 1 with a step size of 0.1. The newly generated feature vectors are then fed into the trained autodecoders to reconstruct the image $\overline{C}$ in the spatial domain.

4.3. Results of image interpolation

As a visual comparison of the effect of image interpolation in the spatial and feature domains, **Figure 7** shows the result of interpolating from two example red blood cell images.

4.4. Image classification using the original and augmented datasets

The original image dataset is split into two halves, as shown in **Table 1**. The first half (Dataset 1) was used for data augmentation. Using data augmentation methods discussed above, images of 400 infected cells were increased to 4000 cells, and images of 1000 normal cells were increased to 10,000 cells. Consequently, we created two datasets, one as the result of using spatial domain interpolation, the other as the result of using feature domain (via stacked autoencoders) interpolation, as shown in **Table 2**. Note that the samples for validation were randomly selected.

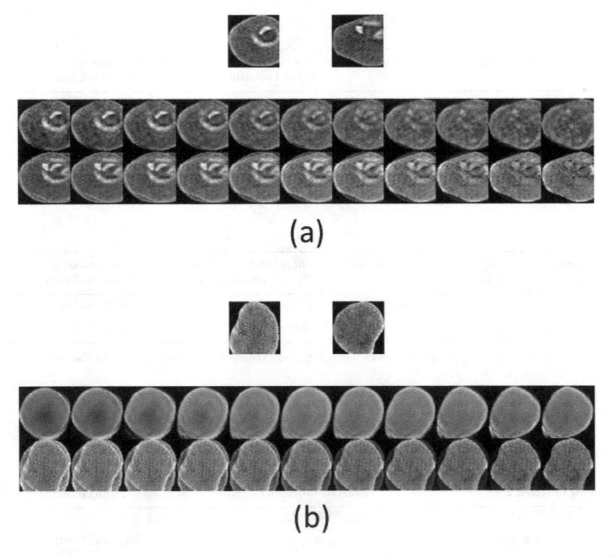

(a)

(b)

Figure 7. Result of interpolation using two example images. (a) Top row: two images of malaria-infected red blood cells used to generate a new image using interpolation. Middle row: 11 images obtained by interpolation using Eq. (1), where k is a weight varied between 0 and 1 with a step size of 0.1. Bottom row: 11 images obtained by interpolation in the feature domain using Eq. (2), where k is a weight varied between 0 and 1 with a step size of 0.1. (b) Similar to (a), images obtained by interpolation in the spatial (middle row) and the feature domain (bottom row).

We conducted various simulations based on the configuration shown in **Table 3**. For example, we used the augmented images in Dataset 3 to train the LeNet-5 convolutional neural network, and tested the original images in Dataset 2 using the trained network in order to classify the images into two categories: either infected or normal cells. Inversely, we trained the LeNet-5 using the original dataset and tested using the augmented datasets, in order to see how the trained classifier would perform on the augmented datasets.

Simulation results are shown in **Figures 8** and **9**.

It can be seen in **Figure 8** that training and validation using the augmented dataset provides fairly high accuracy (above 90%) when testing using the original dataset, implying the augmented data agree reasonably well statistically with the original data. Besides, feature domain interpolation seems to offer higher accuracy than spatial domain interpolation. Furthermore, the classification accuracies vary more significantly with the interpolation (mixing) coefficient k for spatial domain interpolation than for feature domain interpolation. For both interpolation

Original dataset	# of infected cells	# of normal cells	# of infected cells for training (T) and validation (V)	# of normal cells for training (T) and validation (V)
Dataset 1	400	1000	N/A	N/A
Dataset 2	400	1000	(T:320, V: 80)	(T: 800, V:200)

The first half (Dataset 1) was used for data augmentation. The second half (Dataset 2) was used for training and testing.

Table 1. The original image dataset is split into two halves.

Augmented dataset	# of infected cells	# of normal cells	# of infected cells for training (T) and validation (V)	# of normal cells for training (T) and validation (V)
Dataset 3	4000	10,000	(T:3200, V:800)	(T:8000, V:2000)
Dataset 4	4000	10,000	(T:3200, V:800)	(T:8000, V:2000)

Dataset 3 was obtained using the spatial domain interpolation and Dataset 4 was obtained using the feature domain (via stacked autoencoders) interpolation.

Table 2. The augmented image dataset from dataset 1 in **Table 1**.

Training (infected, normal)	Validation (infected, normal)	Testing (infected, normal)
Dataset 3 (3200, 8000)	Dataset 3 (800, 2000)	Dataset 2 (400, 1000)
Dataset 4 (3200, 8000)	Dataset 3 (800, 2000)	Dataset 2 (400, 1000)
Dataset 2 (320, 800)	Dataset 2 (80, 200)	Dataset 3 (4000, 10,000)
Dataset 2 (320, 800)	Dataset 2 (80, 200)	Dataset 4 (4000, 10,000)

Table 3. Several combinations of datasets used in training, validation and testing of the convolutional neural network.

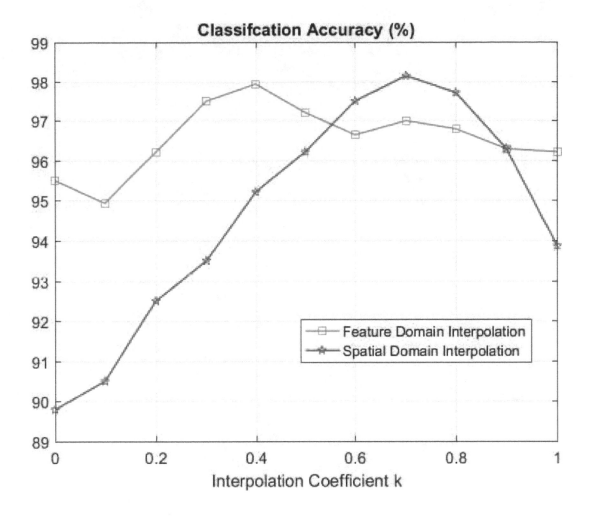

Figure 8. Classification accuracies as a function of the interpolation coefficient k in Eqs. (1) and (2), when we trained the LeNet-5 using the augmented datasets and tested the classifier using the original dataset. The augmented datasets are dataset 3 with spatial domain interpolation and dataset 4 with feature domain interpolation, respectively.

methods, there exists an optimal coefficient such that the classification accuracy reaches its maximum.

It can be seen in **Figure 9** that by using the classifier trained on the original dataset, we might get very low (below 80%) classification accuracy on the input images in the augmented dataset (obtained using interpolation in the spatial domain). This highlights the importance of using data augmentation in order to attain a more balanced estimation of the generalization ability of the classifier. This generalization ability seems to depend heavily on the varying new image samples that were interpolated using a different interpolation (mixing) coefficient from the original dataset (e.g., when $k = 0.7$, the accuracy can reach about 99%). **Figure 9** also shows that Dataset 4 (feature domain interpolation) seems to be a less challenging dataset than Dataset 3 (spatial domain interpolation), in that all accuracies are above 95%, possibly suggesting that mixing images using their features extracted by the stacked autoencoder would generate less diverse images than directly mixing images in the spatial domain.

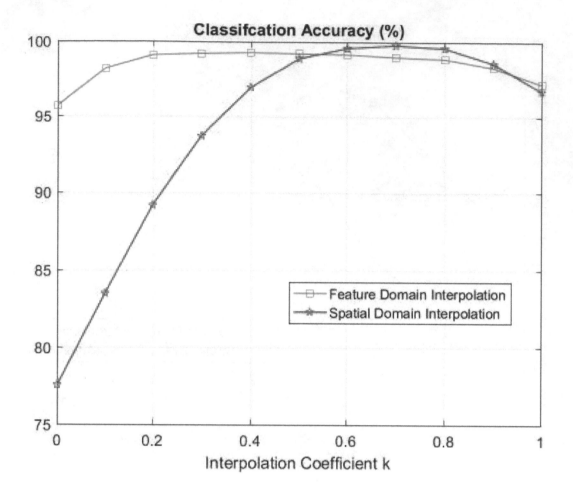

Figure 9. Classification accuracies as a function of the interpolation coefficient k in Eqs. (1) and (2), when we trained the LeNet-5 using the original dataset (dataset 2) and tested the classifier using the augmented datasets, where dataset 3 is with spatial domain interpolation and dataset 4 with feature domain interpolation.

5. Conclusions and further research

Malaria is a widespread disease that has claimed millions of lives all over the world. Automation of the diagnosis process will provide accurate diagnosis of the disease, which will benefit health-care to resource-scarce areas. We showed that the deep convolutional network based on LeNet-5 was capable of achieving very high classification accuracies for automated malaria diagnosis, by automatically learn the features from the input image data. We briefly described the workflow of classification of the red blood cell images, and discussed in details the data augmentation methods we proposed to deal with the issue with training deep convolutional neural networks with a small dataset. We then compared the classification accuracies associated with training, validating, and testing with various combinations of the original dataset and the significantly augmented datasets, which were obtained using direct interpolation in the spatial domain, as well as indirect interpolation using automatically extracted features provided by stacked autoencoders. This comparative study indicated that data augmentation in the feature domain seemed to be more robust in terms of preserving the high classification accuracies. We plan to expand the existing dataset by including more pathologist-curated cell images and further evaluate the effectiveness of the proposed data augmentation methods.

Author details

W. David Pan[1]*, Yuhang Dong[2] and Dongsheng Wu[2]

*Address all correspondence to: pand@uah.edu

1 Department of Electrical and Computer Engineering, University of Alabama in Huntsville, Huntsville, AL, USA

2 Department of Mathematical Sciences, University of Alabama in Huntsville, Huntsville, AL, USA

References

[1] Chan M. World Malaria Report. Geneva: World Health Organization; 2015

[2] Kettlehut MM et al. External quality assessment schemes raise standards: Evidence from the UKNEQAS parasitology subschemes. Journal of Clinical Pathology. 2003 Dec;56:927-932

[3] Tek FB. Computerised diagnosis of malaria [PhD Thesis]. University of Westminster; 2007

[4] Tek FB, Dempster AG, Kale I. Computer vision for microscopy diagnosis of malaria. Malaria Journal. 2009 Dec;8(1):1-14

[5] Mitiku K, Mengistu G, Gelaw B. The reliability of blood film examination for malaria at the peripheral health unit. Ethiopian Journal of Health Development. 2003;17(3):197-204

[6] Center for Devices and Radiological Health. Technical Performance Assessment of Digital Pathology Whole Slide Imaging Devices. Center for Devices and Radiological Health. Silver Spring, MD, USA: Food and Drug Administration; 2016

[7] World Health Organization. Microscopy. Available: http://www.who.int/malaria/areas/diagnosis/microscopy/en/

[8] Farahani N, Parwani AV, Pantanowitz L. Whole slide imaging in pathology: Advantages, limitations, and emerging perspectives. Pathology and Laboratory Medicine International. 2015 June;2015(7):23-33

[9] Cornish TC, Swapp RE, Kaplan KJ. Whole-slide imaging: Routine pathologic diagnosis. Advances In Anatomic Pathology. 2012 May;19(3):152-159

[10] Consortium for Open Medical Image Computing. ISBI Challenge on Cancer Metastasis Detection in Lymph Node. Available: http://grand-challenge.org/site/camelyon16/data/

[11] Microsoft Corporation. Deep Zoom. Available: https://msdn.microsoft.com/en-us/library/cc645050(VS.95).aspx

[12] Delahunt CB, Mehanian C, Hu L, McGuire SK, Champlin CR, Horning MP, et al. Automated microscopy and machine learning for expert-level malaria field diagnosis. In: Global Humanitarian Technology Conference (GHTC). 2015 IEEE; 2015. pp. 393-399

[13] Muralidharan V, Dong Y, Pan WD. Comparison of feature selection techniques for machine learning based automatic malarial cell recognition in wholeslide images. In: Proc. of IEEE International Conference on Biomedical and Health Informatics. Las Vegas, NV; 2016

[14] Park HS, Rinehart MT, Walzer KA, Chi JTA, Wax A. Automated detection of P. falciparum using machine learning algorithms with quantitative phase images of unstained cells. PLoS One. 2016;**11**(9):e0163045

[15] Sanchez CS. Deep Learning for Identifying Malaria Parasites in Images. MSc Thesis. Edinburgh, UK: University of Edinburgh; 2015

[16] Quinn JA, Nakasi R, Mugagga PKB, Byanyima P, Lubega W, Andama A. Deep convolutional neural networks for microscopy-based point of care diagnostics. CoRR. 2016; abs/1608.02989. Available from: http://arxiv.org/abs/1608.02989

[17] Muralidharan V, Dong Y, Pan WD. A comparison of feature selection methods for machine learning based automatic malarial cell recognition in wholeslide images. In: 2016 IEEE-EMBS International Conference on Biomedical and Health Informatics (BHI); 2016. pp. 216-219

[18] Mamoshina P, Vieira A, Putin E, Zhavoronkov A. Applications of deep learning in biomedicine. Molecular Pharmaceutics. 2016;**13**(5):1445-1454. PMID: 27007977. Available from:. DOI: 10.1021/acs.molpharmaceut.5b00982

[19] Leung MKK, Delong A, Alipanahi B, Frey BJ. Machine learning in genomic medicine: A review of computational problems and data sets. Proceedings of the IEEE. 2016 Jan;**104**(1): 176-197

[20] Min S, Lee B, Yoon S. Deep learning in bioinformatics. Briefings in Bioinformatics. 2017 Sep 1;**18**(5):851-869

[21] Greenspan H, van Ginneken B, Summers RM. Guest editorial deep learning in medical imaging: Overview and future promise of an exciting new technique. IEEE Transactions on Medical Imaging. 2016 May;**35**(5):1153–1159

[22] Shin HC, Roth HR, Gao M, Lu L, Xu Z, Nogues I, et al. Deep convolutional neural networks for computer-aided detection: CNN architectures, dataset characteristics and transfer learning. IEEE Transactions on Medical Imaging. 2016 May;**35**(5):1285-1298

[23] Lai M. Deep learning for medical image segmentation. CoRR. 2015;abs/1505.02000. Available from: http://arxiv.org/abs/1505.02000

[24] Tajbakhsh N, Shin JY, Gurudu SR, Hurst RT, Kendall CB, Gotway MB, et al. Convolutional neural networks for medical image analysis: Full training or fine tuning? IEEE Transactions on Medical Imaging. 2016 May;**35**(5):1299-1312

[25] Anthimopoulos M, Christodoulidis S, Ebner L, Christe A, Mougiakakou S. Lung pattern classification for interstitial lung diseases using a deep convolutional neural network. IEEE Transactions on Medical Imaging. 2016 May;**35**(5):1207-1216

[26] Twinanda AP, Shehata S, Mutter D, Marescaux J, de Mathelin M, Padoy N. EndoNet: A deep architecture for recognition tasks on laparoscopic videos. IEEE Transactions on Medical Imaging. 2016;PP(99):1-1

[27] Albarqouni S, Baur C, Achilles F, Belagiannis V, Demirci S, Navab N. AggNet: Deep learning from crowds for mitosis detection in breast cancer histology images. IEEE Transactions on Medical Imaging. 2016 May;**35**(5):1313-1321

[28] Wang D, Khosla A, Gargeya R, Irshad H, Beck AH. Deep learning for identifying metastatic breast cancer. Arxiv. 2016

[29] Hubel DH, Wiesel TN. Receptive fields and functional architecture of monkey striate cortex. The Journal of Physiology. 1968;**195**(1):215-243

[30] LeCun Y, Bottou L, Bengio Y, Haffner P. Gradient-based learning applied to document recognition. Proceedings of the IEEE. 1998;**86**(11):2278-2324

[31] Hauberg S, Freifeld O, Larsen ABL, Fisher J, Hansen L. Dreaming more data: Class-dependent distributions over diffeomorphisms for learned data augmentation. In: Proceedings of the 19th International Conference on Artificial Intelligence and Statistics (AISTATS), Cadiz, Spain; 2016. pp. 342-350

[32] Wong SC, Gatt A, Stamatescu V, McDonnell MD. Understanding data augmentation for classification: When to warp? In: 2016 International Conference on Digital Image Computing: Techniques and Applications (DICTA). IEEE; 2016. pp. 1-6

[33] DeVries T, Taylor GW. Dataset Augmentation in Feature Space. arXiv preprint arXiv: 170205538; 2017

[34] Hinton GE, Salakhutdinov RR. Reducing the dimensionality of data with neural networks. Science. 2006 Jul 28;**313**(5786):504-507

[35] Goodfellow I, Bengio Y, Courville A. Deep Learning. Cambridge, Massachusetts, USA: MIT Press; 2016

3

Machine Learning in Educational Technology

Ibtehal Talal Nafea

Abstract

Machine learning is a subset of artificial intelligence (AI) that helps computers or teaching machines learn from all previous data and make intelligent decisions. The machine-learning framework entails capturing and maintaining a rich set of information and transforming it into a structured knowledge base for different uses in various fields. In the field of education, teachers can save time in their non-classroom activities by adopting machine learning. For example, teachers can use virtual assistants who work remotely from the home for their students. This kind of assistance helps to enhance students' learning experience and can improve progression and student achievement. Machine learning fosters personalized learning in the context of disseminating education. Advances in AI are enabling teachers to gain a better understanding of how their students are progressing with learning. This enables teachers to create customized curriculum that suits the specific needs of the learners. When employed in the context of education, AI can foster intelligence moderation. It is through this platform that the analysis of data by human tutors and moderators is made possible.

Keywords: machine learning, artificial intelligence education, virtual assistant education sector

1. Introduction

Currently, technology is everywhere including the education sector, where it has proven to be of great importance for realizing the learning outcomes for students. Education is no longer just the teaching of text or requiring the student to memorize manuscripts. The instructional process, both inside and outside of the classroom, has become an activity with measurable goals and results. Over time, educational techniques have turned out to be a dynamic part of the inputs and outputs of the learning process. Moreover, these practices have grown into a vital part that plays a significant role in broadening the advancement of the components of the learning system, upgrading the rudiments of the curriculum, and making both more effective and resourceful.

These components are used in the process of planning, implementing, evaluating, following-up and developing objectives [1]. Machine learning has become a new frontier for higher education. Being one of the strongest newer technologies, machine learning plays the main rules in artificial intelligent and human interaction. Machine learning is the innovative tool being used to combat cancer, climate change, and even terrorism [2]. It is the new infrastructure for everything. Consequently, machine learning helps computers to find hidden insights without being programmed to do so. Moreover, machine learning works as a good predictive.

- In this chapter, machine learning technology is used as a principle of educational activities. There are different ways of using machine learning technology in education, such as in providing diverse learning options so a learner can discover what suits him/her best but in a manner where all individual variances between pupils are considered. Machine learning can also be used in review a lesson that was hard to understand [1]. Machine learning in education works in harmony with students' needs, and at a time and place that suits them best.

- Virtual assistance plays a crucial role in education and is a good forum for machine learning use. A virtual assistant can interact in a conversation with students [1]. This interaction involves conversational agents who assist students by using an application or website. The process works is quite simple with the student needing to input text. On the other hand, the agents execute the task and determine the appropriate response to the input before providing an easy response that the student can easily understand.

- Both machine learning and virtual assistants are used to interpret patterns and human interaction which supports deeper learning and provides users with fast and accurate data. This chapter proposes a new education framework that is powered by virtual assistance. It provides customized research for students. The suggested framework allows teachers to monitor their students' progress through their learning activities at any time. This is the best approach to training students to enhance their experience. The framework also helps teachers save time that is normally spent in preparing lectures, creating exams, document review, document creation, and light specific research. The proposed framework facilitates the leveraging of the most powerful technologies in improving the quality of education for both student and teacher. Another advantage associated with this framework of machine learning and virtual assistants is that it is less prone to the errors that usually encumber human operations. If an error occurs, the framework allows it to easily troubleshoot the problem and craft the appropriate resolution of the error.

2. Related works

With the recent increase in the spread and use of technology across the world, it has become common for various sectors to adapt technology for use in their respective fields. This applies the education sector as it does to any other field. Terms such as artificial intelligence (AI), deep learning, and machine learning are now commonly used in education and by education professionals. Indeed, in the educational field, AI is used in machine learning. That is, machine learning makes use of AI in its effort to teach machines how to look for different types of data.

2.1. Machine learning

Currently, education and learning remains largely focused on feeding students with information and hoping that it is retained. Accordingly, a student's intelligence is assessed by testing their ability to recall information previously taught. The problem is that this model ignores examining how well the students understand the information and how they apply it in real-life situations. This model has proven to be toxic over the years. More schools and education centers have begun to realize how use of machine learning can make work more efficient and easier and have started to adopt technology at an increasing rate. Indeed, machine learning can accommodate all kinds of students. In the long run, machine learning is bound to produce the following advantages:

Customized and personalized learning – Machine learning is flexible enough to cater to all students regardless of their learning speeds. By making use of algorithms that learn how the student consumes information, machine learning allows the learner to move ahead only after they have truly grasped the previous content. This process ensures that no student is overlooked or left behind. This is true even if they are the only one in class that has not yet understood the content. The machine learning system also allows teachers to individually monitor student and help them those areas where they are deficient. This contrasts with the traditional educational method, which focuses on a one-size-fits-all management where everyone in class is taught the same way. This type of learning can be found in the EdTech and MagicBox learning systems [3].

Analytics of content—Refers to a machine learning system where teachers instruct students by using machines. The machines are used to analyze the information teachers are using to teach and to determine whether the quality of the content meets the applicable standards. The machines are also used to help determine if the content taught to the students complies with the intellectual ability of each student. Since students are taught in accordance to their individual needs, their learning progress and understanding improve.

Grading—Machine learning systems are used to reduce the amount of time needed to grade student work. In addition, machines are used to increase the efficiency and accountability of the grading system. The system still allows for the larger portion of the grading to be performed by teachers. However, machines aid in the analysis of student information such as in the detection of plagiarism or cheating.

Simplification of tedious tasks—In the traditional method of learning, teachers spend a substantial amount of time in repetitive and tedious tasks, such as taking class attendance or gathering of class assignments. Machines can be used to automate these tasks and reduce the time or need for teachers to do them. Accordingly, teachers will have more time to focus on more important tasks such as making sure that their students fully understand the learning material.

Students' progress—By using machines, the teachers can monitor each student on a personal level and evaluate their learning progress, individually. Machines can also provide additional learning patterns of the students, which help teachers to determine the best ways of teaching the students.

As the above information makes clear, using machine learning in teaching brings numerous advantages to the table. It is therefore advisable for every school to adopt these types of learning platforms, such as the EdTech revolution program. With this, learning becomes easier, more efficient and customizable to each student's need [4]. By employing methods relating to digital learning, there is the possibility of collecting a wide range of data about the behaviour of the learner, especially in the learning activities. The measurements collected consist of variables like completion time, video views, group discussion activities and test results. Measurements of this nature are applicable in the context of feature engineering that leans on the machine learning algorithms. Experts argue that the algorithms can find a correlation between the specific behaviour exhibited by learners, regarding their learning performance [5]. It is this outcome that is used to determine the overall efficiency manifested by a particular machine program.

Recommender systems are the more obvious target of machine learning usage. The experience of this technology is illustrated by its use on some of the more prominent software platforms like Amazon and LinkedIn. Recently, Twitter has begun applying this technology to their platform. Researchers in the education sector consider recommender systems as the most utilized systems in modern times. In the context of human learning, recommender systems that are oriented to learning in a specific way have the capacity to assist learners properly identify the appropriate content [6]. In this regard, there is a guarantee of realizing the projected competence development objectives as far as machine-oriented education is concerned.

The advance in AI technology has allowed machine learning in education gain a considerable amount of support. In fact, machine learning should be credited for making AI a possible and fruitful endeavor in education. In achieving this result, machine learning has combined and utilized the aspects of mathematical algorithms. Researchers in the vast education field have tried to introduce the concept of machine learning into the mainstream schooling system. The goal has been to use machine learning as teaching assistants that can ease the job of human educators [7]. This approach aids in data provision of the students' performance, coupled with suggested actions geared towards making improvements to the student's learning experience.

The use of machine learning in tools related to education technology has been more significant in its overall applications. Experts have created a real-time platform capable of giving immediate feedback to learners. The same platform has harnessed the efficiency and effectiveness of online-based tutors. In fact, the platform has been credited with almost all the success that takes place on the Internet. The latest platforms are so sophisticated that they are capable of detecting and monitoring the reaction of the student concerning the concepts being taught. This approach is known to reduce the misunderstanding normally experienced during the learning process. The ability of these platforms to give early warning to tutors enables them to avoid mistakes that would have otherwise been made during the learning process [8]. Tutoring systems based on AI is an interesting and resourceful concept, to the extent that it employs substantial amounts of data that is coupled to machine learning, to offer guidance that is personalized and supplemental to the students. The feedback system provided by the AI tutoring systems is critical in tracking the learners' progress.

The adoption of machine learning technology has enhanced the concept of crowd-sourced tutoring. The goal of crowd-sourced tutoring is to provide assistance from private tutors, and in some cases, classmates who fill gaps in understanding by supplementing the content learned in class. Students using social networking sites for learning purposes, like Brainy, are enjoying the effectiveness of AI in the learning process. Most of the social networking sites that are education-oriented tend to employ AI algorithms which harness their networking features. The algorithms also bring a personal touch to the learning process, making it more appealing to the learner. In addition, AI increases the level of interactivity in these platforms, which is helpful in fostering the learning process.

Machine learning algorithm works by having machines use software applications that assist the machine to determine outcomes that are accurate. By using algorithms, the machines can receive data, analyze it and then produce an output that is within an acceptable range. Machine learning algorithms are divided into two major groups: supervised algorithms and unsupervised algorithms. For supervised algorithms, people input information together with the required results into the machine. With this, the machine can learn what is desired of it when a similar command is inputted. For unsupervised learning, the machines are not fed with the outcome that one would like [9].

In the education sector, machine learning algorithms have made normal operations easier, faster and more efficient when compared to when they are done manually. This has proven to be a game changer in education sector. One of the major benefits of its adoption has been to help identify each student's needs so that the teachers can differentiate between problems general to the class and those specific to individual students. Accordingly, through machine learning, no student is overlooked or left behind. Additionally, with machine learning, students are also given a platform from which they can voice their grievances so that the problems do not escalate beyond resolution. The machines help in the grading, by monitoring the scores of the students in their assignments and the tests. The machines also assist teachers by organizing the information being taught to students. The inclusion of machine learning in education has, therefore, made the education system more convenient for both teachers and students alike.

AI has enabled teachers and to a larger extension, schools, design textbooks and learning exercises that can achieve a high degree of customization to the needs of the user. Content Technologies, Inc. (CTI) is one of the major players in the industry. CTI tends to specialize on deep learning concepts to create custom textbooks [9]. This is achieved by inputting a syllabus into the engine of CTI. After that, the system absorbs the content to generate new patterns. It is then the work of algorithms to use the knowledge gained for the purposes of creating textbook materials.

3. The architecture of the virtual assistance framework

Since students have different styles of learning, it is necessary to use a variety of assistance to help increase the performance level of learning. Various machine learning algorithms and techniques, such as decision-making algorithms and techniques, can be implemented for allowing the virtual assistant to communicate with the students and teachers.

There are two main parts to the virtual assistants, namely, one for students and other for teachers. Students can answer one or more virtual assistant's questions. One or more sponsored links, related to the determined course, is then provided to the student. The sponsored links can be voice, audio data, displaying video or textual information. Exam training and test dates remainder are kinds of the virtual assistant that gets provided to learners. Also, the proposed system helps students to manage their teamwork project. After the session with the system, a student is provided with the feedback about his progress.

The system is also able to design presentations for specific learners. Notably, different students have different learning abilities; therefore, the system is able to compute a favorable learning style for each student. The teacher monitors the progress of each student through feedback about how each student performed in the sessions. This facilitates appropriate grading. Also, the virtual assistant is able to point out areas of the course that need to be explored further to enhance learning by providing additional reference materials to a topic. Also, the teacher is able to identify which students need extra help using the feedback provided by the system.

The proposed architecture is a reliable virtual assistant website that not only helps teachers and students to do their tasks in a shorter time but also allows them to coordinate their work.

4. Technical implementation

The underlying technical implementation of the virtual assistant system starts with creating use cases for the product. The identification of virtual assistants and the underlying technology are required for moving ahead with the implementation of the proposed website [10]. The following technical specifications have been identified for building the virtual assistant website:

Software used:

- BitVoicer: Speech recognition.

- Python 2.7: Coding language

- Eclipse, Geany or your preferred interface for coding on Python Virtual COM Port.

To facilitate interaction between the virtual assistant website and the user, a software known as Wit.ai is installed. Wit.ai offers a perfect combination of voice recognition, and subsequent machine learning in the context of developers. The software offers services that concentrate on converting verbal commands into text. Moreover, Wit.ai has the capability of understanding the commands that are said. The most sophisticated forms of Wit.ai can be programmed to understand commands whose prior understanding was scant or non-existent. This is crucial in the educational context since learners tend to understand at varying paces. The extensive capability of Wit.ai software to improve the interactivity of virtual assistant website can be verified by the fact that it has been incorporated by a number of notable social media networks, such as Facebook [10].

Clarifai is another service that can be added to the virtual assistant website to improve its interactivity. Clarifai is a service geared towards AI, and it possesses the ability to decode contents that is in an image and video format. Another strength associated with Clarifai is that it possesses a deep learning engine that improves with its usage [10]. The tool is of paramount importance when there is a need to make improvements in the AI prototype and grant it the capability of seeing and recognizing objects.

The virtual assistant experience with the users has been remarkable. All students who provided feedback regarding their interactions reported positive experiences. Fundamentally, the issue of the ease of interactivity, friendly user interfaces and responsiveness were reviewed. The first student reported that the system has a friendly user interface that is not complex, thus allowing a user to navigate through different sections of the system. The student added that the system was highly responsive in terms of answering questions. He recounted that, in the traditional class setting, he was afraid to ask questions in front of the other student. However, the virtual assistant offered personalized interaction where he could ask any questions, clarifications and point out his areas of weakness. The second student who experimented with the software also found it quite useful. He emphasized that he liked the fact that he was able to get immediate feedback on his questions. This was a vast improvement over the traditional way of waiting to talk to the teacher after class, when the teachable moment has already expired. Some instructors are always in a rush after finishing their classes. As such, they are unable to allocate ample time to explain specific concepts taught in class to the student. Therefore, the student misses out on these concepts that might cause low academic performance. In other cases, teachers recommend students with clarifications to get the assistance of their classmates. This hampers full understanding as one needs to develop a rapport with their fellow student to enhance learning, and others become intimidated. However, the virtual assistant allocates enough time and is able to answer all questions, providing detailed explanations. The third student said that she found it was an effective supplement to one teacher's extensive use of multiple choice exams. According to the student, while such exams might tell her whether or not she knows the answer to a question, they do not help her understand the logic underlying the answer. The virtual assistance was helpful in achieving that understanding. The fourth student also reported satisfaction with the system. Firstly, the student confessed to being a slow learner. This had really affected how she grasped concepts. Most of the times, she felt left behind in classwork and had no one to consult as she was shy about her condition. However, the system helped her to learn at her pace and recommended interactive learning model that allowed her ask for clarification after every 10 minutes of the learning session. She was enthusiastic to note that this has helped her understand most of the concepts taught in class and generally improve her grades. Lastly, a teacher who had made use of the assistance said it allowed her more time to figure out what her students actually understood and where they were having difficulties. By so doing, it helped her know which areas needed much attention to enhance understanding. She recounted that teaching a class of 30 students can sometimes be difficult to know who understood well, who needed extra attention on a specific topic and what learning model suited a specific group of students. The virtual assistant, according to the teacher, answers these questions. The system is able to compile interactive activities to address specific learning outcomes to indent whether the students understood the topic.

5. Conclusion

Machine learning with AI has opened incredible possibilities in various fields. This is especially the case in terms of the education sector and education-related fields. This means that future learning environments are likely to be highly personalized, with the ability to help learners realize their utmost potential in the most fulfilling way. There will be a steady adoption of machine learning in various areas of concern for educational technology. In the initial stages, its impact will not be clearly apparent or significant to the end user. Despite this, teachers have started to see how tasks can be simplified and more effectively completed through the employment and application of machine learning technologies. The advances made in adopting machine learning into education sector have significantly saved teachers' time in both the classroom and non-classroom-related activities. Stakeholders have welcomed this unprecedented benefit, as it makes learning easier and more appealing.

The future work on machine learning, especially in the education context, shall witness the development of more sophisticated AI tools. There are multiple prospects for designing complex chatbots that will improve the sophistication of virtual assistants. This development shall foster more human interactions that will replace emails and text messages. Already, plans are underway for developing online virtual assistants named "Amy" or "Andrew" at x.ai to schedule meetings with both tutors and learners. AI coupled with machine learning that incorporates deep learning and natural language processing is projected to go a level higher by incorporating more sophisticated systems laced with capabilities to adapt, learn and predict systems with utmost autonomy. The future works on these systems shall incorporate a combination of advanced algorithms and embedded massive data sets.

Author details

Ibtehal Talal Nafea

Address all correspondence to: inafea@taibahu.edu.sa

College of Computer Science and Engineering (CCSE), Taibah University, Medina, Kingdom of Saudi Arabia

References

[1] Lv Z, Li X. Virtual reality assistant technology for learning primary geography. In International Conference on Web-Based Learning. Springer International Publishing. ISO 690. 2015 November. pp. 31-40. DOI: 10.1007/978-3-319-32865-2_4

[2] Tomei LA. Learning Tools and Teaching Approaches through ICT Advancements. Hershey, PA: Information Science Reference; 2013

[3] Mulwa C, Lawless S, Sharp M, Arnedillo-Sanchez I, Wade V. Adaptive educational hypermedia systems in technology enhanced learning: A literature review. In Proceedings of the 2010 ACM Conference on Information Technology Education. ACM. ISO 690. 2010 October. pp. 73-84

[4] Bhat AH, Patra S, Jena D. Machine learning approach for intrusion detection on cloud virtual machines. International Journal of Application or Innovation in Engineering & Management (IJAIEM). 2013;**2**(6):56-66

[5] Lafond D, Proulx R, Morris A, Ross W, Bergeron-Guyard A, Ulieru M. HCI dilemmas for context-aware support in intelligence analysis. Dalhousie Medical Journal. 2014

[6] Lisetti C, Amini R, Yasavur U. Now all together: Overview of virtual health assistants emulating face-to-face health interview experience. KI – Künstliche Intelligenz. 2015;29(2):161-172. DOI: 10.1007/s13218-015-0357-0

[7] Bell B. Supporting educational software design with knowledge-rich tools. In Authoring Tools for Advanced Technology Learning Environments. Springer Netherlands. 2003. pp. 341-375

[8] Haynes M, Anagnostopoulou K. Supporting educational software design with knowledge-rich tools. In Authoring Tools for Advanced Technology Learning Environments. Springer Netherlands. 2003. pp. 341-375

[9] Brinson JR. Learning outcome achievement in non-traditional (virtual and remote) versus traditional (hands-on) laboratories: A review of the empirical research. Computers & Education. 2015;87:218-237. DOI: 10.1016/j.compedu.2015.07.003

[10] Padró L, Stanilovsky E. Towards wider multilinguality. In: Proceedings of the 8th International Conference on Language Resources and Evaluation. 2012

4

Sentiment-Based Semantic Rule Learning for Improved Product Recommendations

Dandibhotla Teja Santosh and
Bulusu Vishnu Vardhan

Abstract

Crucial data like product features and opinions that are obtained from consumer online reviews are annotated with the concepts of product review opinion ontology (PROO). The ontology with instance data serves as background knowledge to learn rule-based sentiments that are expressed on product features. These semantic rules are learned on both taxonomical and nontaxonomical relations available in PROO ontology. These rule-based sentiments provide important information of utilizing the relationship among the product features 'as-a-unit' to improve the sentiments of the parent features. These parent features are present at the higher level near the root of the ontology. The sentiments of the related product features are also improved. This approach improves the sentiments of the parent features and the related features that eventually improve the aggregated sentiment of the product. The result is either the change in the position of the product in the list of similar products recommended or appears in the recommended list. This helps the user to make correct purchase decisions.

Keywords: recommender system, product feature, feature sentiment, ontology, rule-based sentiments, purchased decision

1. Introduction

Traditional machine learning algorithms experience the data and learn the hypothesis. Tree and rule-based algorithms learn the hypothesis using the attribute-value pairs from the input data. Machine cannot go beyond the task of identifying features and opinions from the reviews as it never possess prior knowledge to understand the relationships among the attributes and context specific constraints that are available among the product features and opinions.

Semantic web ontology helps to overcome this problem. Ontology [1] encodes the relationships among the concepts of features and opinions with inequality constraints, semantic characteristics, and cardinality restrictions. This ontology is used as background knowledge on the product reviews. The knowledge mined from the ontology is expressed in the form of semantic rules. These semantic rules emphasize the target sentiment expressed on the product feature. Machines are able to classify the product reviews automatically with exact sentiments learned on the product feature.

Sentiment analysis [2] plays a vital role in understanding the opinions from online reviews. It helps to understand the views of the people on the product, to take quick purchase decisions on the product, and to improve the availability of the product in the market. Online reviews affect the emotion of the readers. Measuring the effect of the sentiment on the semantic rules in the form of knowledge spread is performed to understand whether positive reviews of the product spread faster than negative reviews. The kind of emotions that are more representative on various e-commerce sites about the product is also well identified. Furthermore, the type of sentiment expressed in reviews based on temporal changes on the features of the product is determined in a proper manner.

2. Literature survey

The recommender systems (RS) are the information filtering systems which deal with the large amount of information that is dynamically generated based on user's preferences, interests, and observed behaviors. These traditional recommender systems fall into three categories. They are collaborative filtering-based RS, content-based RS, and knowledge-based RS.

The collaborative recommender systems are the most popular and widely implemented systems. These systems aggregate ratings from the set of users on the item and recommend it. It also identifies the users who are similar with the user from whom recommendations are to be provided. Resnick et al. developed [3] a system called GroupLens to help people to find articles they are most interested in. Stavrianou and Brun developed [4] an application to recommend products based on the opinions and suggestions written in the online product reviews.

The content-based recommender systems learn the user profile based on the product feature where the user has targeted. Lang developed [5] a system called NewsWeeder which uses the words of the text as the features. Zhou and Luo developed [6] a content-based recommender system that views customer shopping history to recommend the similar products based on the similarity between the product features.

The knowledge-based recommender systems provide the entity suggestions based on the deductions from user's needs and preferences. These systems have the knowledge about how a particular product meets the customer requirement based on the factual data. The user profile is also required to provide good product recommendations to the user. Case-based reasoning (CBR) is a kind of knowledge-based recommender system. Kolodner used [7] CBR to recommend the restaurants based on the user's choice of features. Burke used [8] the FindMe system to recommend the online products. Stefan et al. worked [9] on user log data to mine the product preferences based on the like or dislike information available in the log.

Sentiment-based product recommendations have gained research importance in the recent times. The knowledge discovered in terms of product features and opinions from online product reviews among the category of products are useful to the customer in personalized recommendations. These feature-level sentiments are aggregated to form the product sentiment. Chen and Wang proposed [10] a novel explanation interface that fuses the feature sentiment information into the recommendation content. They also provided the support for multiple products comparison with respect to similarity using the common feature sentiments. Gurini et al. proposed [11] friends recommendation technique in Twitter using a novel weighting function which is called sentiment-volume-objectivity (SVO) that considers both the user interests and sentiments. Xiu et al. proposed [12] a recommender system that recognizes the sentiment expressions from the reviews, quantified with the sentiment strength and appropriately recommend products according to customer needs. Recently, Dong et al. developed [13] a product recommendation strategy that combines both similarity and sentiments to suggest products.

The utilization of ontologies for better product recommendations is an emerging research area. Uzun and Christian developed [14] a semantic extension to FOKUS recommender system. This extension is capable of integrating contextual and semantic information in the recommendations. Hadi Khosravi and Mohamad Ali introduced [15] a semantic recommendation procedure using ontology on online products based on the usage patterns of the customers.

The works on ontology-based recommender systems [14, 15] was neither concentrated on utilizing the depth information of the domain feature nodes from the ontology tree nor on height of the ontology tree. These properties act as supervised weights in improving the sentiment of the feature and thereby help in improving the recommendations.

3. Improving product recommendations using semantic sentiments

The recommender system proposed in this work is a knowledge-based recommender system that encapsulates the product catalog knowledge in the form of classes in the ontology and product functional knowledge in the form of facts in the ontology. The user profile is created as and when the user navigates the web pages for the products. The user profile is indexed with the product information from the ontology.

The principal objective of recommending products using sentiments learned from the ontology is to utilize the taxonomical and non-taxonomical constraints mined from ontology for sentiments. The detailed procedures expressed in algorithmic form for learning taxonomical constraints and non-taxonomical constraints are presented below.

Input: PROO {Ontology}

Output: machine interpretable rule {A→B}

EXTRACT_TAXONOMICAL_CONSTRAINT (Ontology)

{

    for each concept with hierarchy from Ontology

      {

        contentconstraint = false;

```
        if(parent_of(superconcept, subconcept))

            contentconstraint = true;

            write(parent_of(superconcept, subconcept) →
    target_class(subconcept));

            else if(parent_of(superconcept1, subconcept1) ∧
    parent_of(superconcept2, subconcept2))

                subconcept1 ←superconcept2;

            contentconstraint = true;

            write(parent_of(superconcept1,subconcept2) ∧
    datatype_property(superconcept1,rel(int)) →
    target_class(subconcept2));

        }}
```

Algorithm for extracting taxonomical constraints from ontology

Algorithm for extracting taxonomical constraints runs as follows: given the PROO ontology, all the super concept and sub concept hierarchies are identified. Super concept node is called parent and sub concept node is called child. The rules are then obtained as of the predicate on the hierarchy as the relation between parent and child concepts leading to target class. Content constraint is initialized to the false value in the beginning. It is then changed to true value after taxonomical constraints are obtained. The Algorithm also tests for descendant child nodes in the hierarchy. A descendant node is a node which is derived from the ancestor node. An ancestor node is the parent node in the given hierarchy. All the child nodes for a given parent are known as descendant nodes. The intermediate parent node is devised as another child node to satisfy the descendant property. At this level, the content constraint value is changed to true. The rules are then obtained as of the predicate on the hierarchy as the relation between parent, newly created child and the datatype property leading to target class.

Input: PROO {Ontology}

Output: machine interpretable rule {A→B}

EXTRACT_NONTAXONOMICAL_CONSTRAINT (Ontology)

```
{

for each node in Ontology

    {

        contentconstraint = false;

        if(object_property(node_i, node_j))

            contentconstraint = true;

            write (object_property(node_i, node_j) →
    target_class(node_i));
```

else if(object_property(node$_i$, node$_j$) ^
[datatype_property(node$_i$,rel(int)) v
datatype_property (node$_j$,rel(int))])

> contentconstraint = true;

write(object_property(node$_i$,node$_j$)^datatype_property(node$_j$,rel(int))
→ target_class(node$_j$));

write(object_property(node$_i$,node$_j$)^datatype_property(node$_i$,rel(int))
→ target_class(node$_i$));   }}

Algorithm for extracting nontaxonomical constraints from ontology

Algorithm for extracting nontaxonomical constraints runs as follows: given the ontology, all the related class nodes that are bound with the object properties are identified. Content constraint is initialized to the false value in the beginning. It is then changed to true value once related class nodes are obtained. The rules are then obtained with the object property as the relation between the related classes leading to the target class. The Algorithm also tests the relation between related classes and datatype properties. The related class node and the datatype property are associated using the conditions that are imposed on the ontology. This is identified by the algorithm. The content constraint value is changed to true. The rules are then generated from the relation between object property and the datatype property leading to the target class.

The PROO ontology concepts namely Opinion and Feature and the properties namely ObjectPart and ObjectPartFeature are used in generating the machine interpretable rules on target sentiment class. These articulate that they are the features to acquire positively oriented sentiment when the opinion strength on these features has a value greater than or equal to 2.5. The corresponding class hierarchies and the related classes of the PROO ontology are presented in **Figure 1**.

The sentiments of the product features that are present near to the root of the ontology are to be improved. The features located at the higher level near the root of the ontology are considered to be more important as compared with the lower level features [16]. The product features that are present near the ontology root are the parent features obtained from the taxonomical constraints and the other features present at the same level as the parent features. Other features are obtained from the non-taxonomical constraints. In order to achieve this goal, a framework is presented in **Figure 2**.

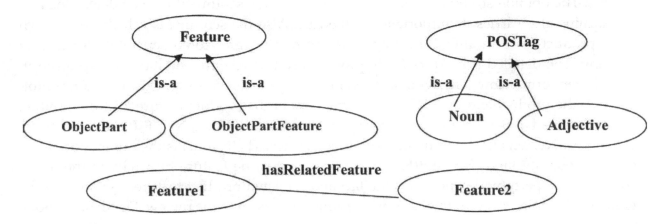

Figure 1. Class hierarchies and related classes in PROO.

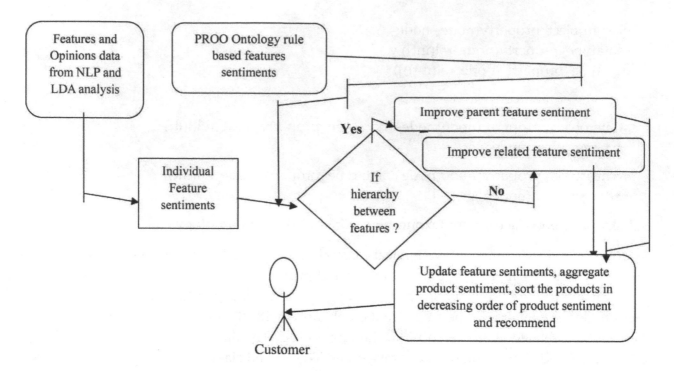

Figure 2. Model for improving the sentiments of the product features.

The framework is composed of main component. The improvement of sentiments of the product features using the knowledge mined from the PROO ontology for improved product recommendations is shown in a diagram as under. The first two modules, i.e., the development of PROO ontology and semantic data mining the PROO ontology, were already carried out by the researchers in their work in [17]. The proposed main component of improving the sentiments of the product features using the knowledge mined from the PROO ontology for better product recommendations is described below with the algorithm pseudo-code.

3.1. Improving the product recommendations using rule-based sentiments from ontology

The rule-based sentiments mined from the PROO ontology specify the relations between the parent feature and the child feature. It also reveals the relations among the related product features. The opinion strength of the feature for which the sentiment is to be determined by the machine also carries its importance in the rule. Also the sentiments calculated for each of the product features after extracting from the reviews are stored separately for further mapping. The detailed procedure for improving product recommendations is expressed in step-by-step form below. The symbols used in the steps are as follows: O is the PROO ontology. P_i is the product and i = 1,2,3,... The sentiment of the product feature F_j of the product P_i is represented as Sentiment(F_j,P_i) where j = 1,2,3,... The Pos(F_j,P_i), Neg(F_j,P_i), and Neu(F_j,P_i) are the positive, negative, and neutral product features. The count() is the number of occurrences of polarity kind. Parentof($F_{jkparent\_node}$, $F_{jkchild\_node}$) is the feature hierarchy in the ontology. Objectproperty($node_a$, $node_b$) is the fact about related product features. Strength(node, rel(int)) is the opinion strength of the feature which is present in the review. Depth of the node in the ontology and the height of the ontology are the ontology tree measures. The asterisk '*' in the steps represents the multiplication operator.

1. Retrieve the similar products from the ontology based on the user-searched product. The common features of retrieved products and the searched product are called as 'k-common features.'

2. For each of the k-common features, calculate the sentiment using the count of positive mentions and count of negative mentions on the features as:

$$\text{Sentiment}(F_j, P_i) = \text{count}(\text{Pos}(F_j, P_i)) - \text{count}(\text{Neg}(F_j, P_i))$$

$$\text{count}(\text{Pos}(F_j, P_i)) + \text{count}(\text{Neg}(F_j, P_i)) + \text{count}(\text{Neu}(F_j, P_i))$$

3. Retrieve taxonomical and non-taxonomical sentiment rules on the product features from ontology.

4. Map Rule_Positive_Sentiment = [0.001 ... 1] and Rule_Negative_Sentiment = [−1 ... −0.001].

5. For each k-common feature among all the similar products in ontology,

if (parentof($F_{jkparent\_node}$, $F_{jkchild\_node}$) == true)

{

    if (Sentiment($F_{jkparent\_node}$, P_i) < Sentiment($F_{jkchild\_node}$, P_i))

    {

    Sentiment($F_{jkparent\_node}$, P_i) = Sentiment($F_{jkparent\_node}$, P_i) +
[Sentiment($F_{jkchild\_node}$, P_i) * depth of the $F_{jkchild\_node}$];

    New_Sentiment($F_{jkparent\_node}$, P_i) = Sentiment($F_{jkparent\_node}$, P_i);

    }

    if (Sentiment($F_{jkchild\_node}$, P_i) == Sentiment($F_{jkparent\_node}$, P_i))

        Continue;

}

else if (objectproperty($node_a$, $node_b$) ^ strength(node, rel(int)) == true)

    {

    if(Sentiment($F_{jknodea}$, P_i) <= 0)

    {

    Sentiment($F_{jknodea}$, P_i) = Sentiment($F_{jknodea}$, P_i) + height of the
ontology/100; /**Since to have small change in the score**/

    New_Sentiment($F_{jknodea}$, P_i) = Sentiment($F_{jknodea}$, P_i);

}

if(Sentiment($F_{jknodeb}$, P_i) < = 0)

{

Sentiment($F_{jknodeb}$, P_i) = Sentiment($F_{jknodeb}$, P_i) + height of the ontology/100; **/*Since to have small change in the score*/**

New_Sentiment($F_{jknodeb}$, P_i) = Sentiment($F_{jknodeb}$, P_i);

6. Sort the products in the descending order based on the enhanced sentiments of the k-common features.

7. Recommend products.

The explanation of the steps is as follows: given the product to be searched by the end user in the E-Commerce site, all the similar products are recommended. Initially, the algorithm retrieves all the similar products data from the ontology based with respect to the user-searched product. The common product features of retrieved products and the searched product are called as 'k-common features'. Next for each of the k-common features, the corresponding sentiment is calculated by using the number of positive mentions and number of negative mentions on the features. Whenever a neutral mention is identified, it is also counted and used in the sentiment calculation. Then the taxonomical and non-taxonomical sentiment rules on the product features are retrieved from the ontology. The target sentiment instances Positive and Negative are mapped to the minimum and maximum sentiment scores of the product features to create a sentiment range. Following discussions are the examples to clarify how the improved product recommendations are returned to the customer when a search for the product takes place. The dataset details for which the examples discussed were presented in **Table 1** which was presented in section V.

The product 'Samsung Galaxy j7 prime' has one of the taxonomical features as battery and battery life respectively. The number of positive mentions and negative mentions on the battery are 6 and 0. There are no neutral mentions. The number of positive and negative mentions on the battery life is 1 and 0. There are no neutral mentions. The sentiment scores obtained after calculation for battery and battery life are 1 and 1 respectively. The opinion strengths for battery and battery life obtained from review dataset are 3 and 3. By applying these features as instances in the taxonomical sentiment rule, the semantic sentiment learned is positive. The sentiment scores of battery and battery life are now mapped to Positive sentiment label.

Document attributes	Values
Number of review documents	300
Minimum sentences per review	9
Maximum sentences per review	15

Table 1. Reviews dataset details.

The product 'Samsung Galaxy j7 prime' has one of the non-taxonomical features as RAM and performance respectively. The number of positive and negative mentions on the RAM is 6 and 5. There are no neutral mentions. The number of positive and negative mentions on the performance is 6 and 2. There are no neutral mentions. The sentiment scores obtained after calculation for RAM and performance are 0.09 and 0.1 respectively. The opinion strengths for RAM and performance obtained from review dataset are 2.5 and 2.5. By applying these features and opinion strength values as instances in the non-taxonomical sentiment rule, the semantic sentiment learned is positive. The sentiment scores of RAM and performance are now mapped to Positive sentiment label.

The similar products are retrieved from the ontology by querying on the 'similarTo' object property for the corresponding instance values for the customer-searched product. Now for each k-common feature among all the retrieved products in ontology, whenever there exists any taxonomical constraints and when the sentiment of the parent feature node in the ontology is less than the sentiment of the child feature node then the sentiment of the parent feature node is updated by adding the weighted sentiment of the child feature node. The weight is the depth of the child feature node present in the ontology. This kind of analysis is possible as specified by [6], who say that the importance of the feature is determined by the depth of the feature in the ontology. This analysis views the taxonomical features 'as-a-unit.' Whenever the sentiment of the parent feature node is equal to the sentiment of the child feature node, then no update is carried out on these nodes.

Once all the taxonomical constraints are analyzed, the non-taxonomical constraints are also analyzed. The non-taxonomical constraints are analyzed to learn the related features and the contribution to their sentiment values. When the sentiments of the related nodes are less than or equal to zero, the sentiments of the related nodes are updated by adding the ratio. The ratio is 1/100th of the height of the ontology to make the score present in the sentiment range. The height of the ontology is added to the existing sentiment score as the related nodes are present at any level in the ontology other than the root.

The product 'Samsung Galaxy j7 prime' has sentiment scores obtained after calculation for battery and battery life is 1 and 1 respectively. There is no update in the sentiment value for either of the features. This is because the sentiment values for parent feature (battery) and child feature (battery life) which fall under taxonomical constraints are equal.

The product 'Samsung Galaxy j7 prime' has sentiment scores obtained after calculation for screen and display is 1 and 0 respectively. There is an update in the sentiment value for feature 'display'. This is because the sentiment value of display is equal to zero. The updated sentiment value for the feature 'display' is 0.03. The product features screen and display fall under non-taxonomical constraints.

Finally, the products are sorted in the descending order of the enhanced sentiments. The sorted list is provided as the product recommendations to the customer.

4. Design decisions in the implementation of ontology

The description logic (DL) is used in reasoning the instances of ontology. DL is the math behind the constructs of the ontology. The engineered PROO ontology has DL expressivity level *ALCIN(D)*. ALCIN(D) is attribute logic with complement, role inverse, unqualified number restriction and datatype. This ontology is robustly scalable and the rules learned from it are computationally solvable in polynomial running time, i.e., PTIME. The target sentiment which is learned as the rule consequent on the object properties of PROO ontology is decidable as the rules are deductible in the PTIME. Also the learned rules are DL-safe as these rules are restricted to known instances of the ontology.

There were some issues encountered at the time of PROO ontology development. This PROO ontology development was based on design decisions taken at two stages. The two stages were namely the design decisions made before the ontology development and, the decisions made at the time of ontology development.

The first design decision before the development of ontology was on the scope of the ontology to represent the appropriate knowledge for conceptualization. In the product reviews domain, the PROO ontology was intended to support the new customers in retrieving the object information from a large number of reviews by reasoning on object property ontology path. The second design decision was on adhering to the development of a formal ontology so as to reason the ontology for making meaningful conclusions. The PROO ontology was developed using the formal Web Ontology Language (OWL) constructs. The third design decision was whether to annotate the product features and opinions extracted from the reviews as instances to the concepts of the ontology or not.

The design decision taken during the development of ontology was to choose the required superclass-subclass taxonomies in the ontology. The taxonomies created in the development of PROO ontology were the hierarchy of the product features and the PoS word class tags. For some queries on PROO ontology, it was observed that the information retrieved is incorrect. The same instance that was used in analyzing the different product reviews has led to the former mentioned problem.

5. Evaluation of results

The datasets that were used in the feature specific sentiment classification and knowledge-based product recommendations were the collection of electronic device reviews from Amazon. The electronic devices were Iphone 6 s plus, oppo f1 plus and Samsung galaxy j7 prime smartphones. These products were named as P1, P2 and P3, respectively. The selection of reviews was considered in such a way as each review contains the mention of the product features. **Table 1** presents the details of the datasets used for this experiment.

The reviews preprocessing was carried out by eliminating stop words and non-English words. The negation words which were present by the adjective in review sentences were handled with care. For such review sentences, the sentiment orientation of the word was determined by flipping the actual sentiment. The product features and opinions extracted on the considered mobile phone reviews using NLP-based language model and LDA-based language model are collected. PROO ontology is engineered and annotated with the collected product features and opinions. Only one product type for the rule-based sentiments analysis as the PROO ontology is developed for a class of mobile phones of different manufacturers.

ILP rules are also extracted from PROO ontology. The rule predecessor is learned by forming a conjunction of PROO ontology classes and the relevant properties which relate to these classes. The class instances and the property values are reasoned for extracting the target sentiment class instance which is the rule consequent. The generated rules cover the positive instances of the product feature. The assessment of the generated rules is envisioned with area under receiver operating characteristic curve (AUC).

The AUC is a measure to showcase the reviews covered in either of the two sentiment groups (good/bad) available from the dataset. The parameters of the receiver operating characteristic (ROC) curve are the target class label and the ranking attribute. The target instance considered is good for the sentiment class and the ranking attribute is considered as opinion strength. An accuracy of 86.7% of ROC area coverage is obtained. The k-common features identified after the customer searched for Iphone 6 s plus are tabulated in **Table 2**. The value of k found is 17. The similar products are Oppo f1 plus and Samsung galaxy j7 prime.

k-Common features
Phone
ROM
Battery
Performance
OS
Brand
Network connectivity
Camera
Price
Build quality
Touch
Screen
Battery life
Camera quality
Appearance
Display
RAM

Table 2. List of k-common features.

The algorithm calculates sentiments for all the three cellular products on 17 features. Now the algorithm gets all the taxonomical and nontaxonomical constraints for learning feature sentiments from the ontology in the form of rules. In this work, the height of the PROO ontology is 3 and the depth of the child feature node in the ontology tree for taxonomical sentiments is 2. In order to evaluate the sentiments of the k-common features for recommending products, similarity metrics namely cosine similarity [18] and Better [19] are considered.

The small number for k-common features restricts the ability to compare the products during retrieval. This leads to a problem called 'sparsity problem'. This problem is common in collaborative filtering systems.

An empirical analysis is carried out to understand the impact of small k values on product recommendations. The scatter plot for the percentage of products with different k values with the searched product is presented in **Figure 3**.

It is observed from the above figure that at k value of 1, the product recommendations are not possible as all the products have same similarity value. It is also observed that a single product is not recommended with the available k features as the products are competing with respect to the sentiments on these k features. From k = 2 through 17, the product recommendations has started.

In order to know the product recommendations for small k values, the cosine similarity values for k values 1, 2, and 3 without and with ontology are tabulated in **Table 3**.

An important observation is made **Table 3**. It is that the cosine similarity values without and with ontology for small values of k are same. The influence of taxonomical and nontaxonomical constraints on the product recommendations is reflected from the k value of 4.

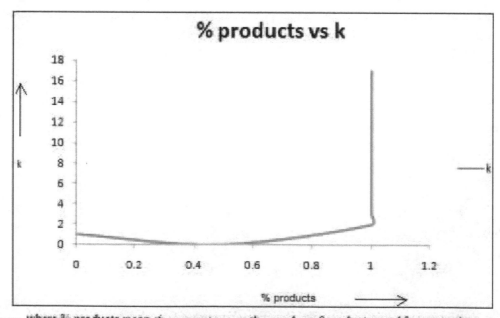

where % products mean the percentage on the number of products used for comparing 'k' common product features

Figure 3. Scatter plot for the percentage of products with different k values.

	Without ontology		With ontology	
k	Cosine(P1,P2)	Cosine(P1,P3)	Cosine(P1,P2)	Cosine(P1,P3)
1	1	1	1	1
2	0.86	0.89	0.86	0.89
3	0.69	0.94	0.69	0.94

Table 3. Cosine similarity values for small k.

Different values for 'k' provide the useful understanding about the products comparison for eventual recommendations. The variations in the number of k-common features on the similar products using sentiments without ontology and with ontology are tabulated in **Table 4**.

The higher better values in relative comparison with the search product specify that the product is on the top of the recommendation list. The lower cosine values in relative comparison with the search product specify that the product is on the top of the recommendation list. The sentiments of k-common features on the three products in the absence of ontology are displayed in **Figure 4**.

The product similarity with the sentiment data on the similar products without the support of ontology is displayed in **Figure 5**.

The sentiments of k-common features on the three products in the presence of ontology are displayed in **Figure 6**.

The product similarity with the sentiment data on the similar products with the support of ontology is displayed in **Figure 7**.

The product recommendations based on the Cosine similarity measures with and without ontology support for different 'k' values are specified in **Table 5**.

From the results in **Table 5**, it is observed that without the support of ontology for different values of 'k' (4,8,12) the cosine similarity returned the similar products as recommendations in the same order (product P2 comes first in the list and then the product P3) by using the sentiments on k-features. The product with higher cosine value between two similar products is

k	Without ontology				With ontology			
	Better (P1,P2)	Cosine (P1,P2)	Better (P1,P3)	Cosine (P1,P3)	Better (P1,P2)	Cosine (P1,P2)	Better (P1,P3)	Cosine (P1,P3)
4	−0.0275	0.87	−0.0075	0.79	−0.0275	0.75	−0.0075	0.95
8	−0.0006	0.61	−0.08938	0.45	−0.00063	0.33	−0.08938	0.52
12	0.0370	0.54	0.044583	0.51	0.037083	0.54	0.025874	0.51
17	0.0997	0.29	0.058235	0.48	0.099705	0.29	0.035866	0.49

Table 4. Better and cosine similarity measures statistics for analyzing similarities between products.

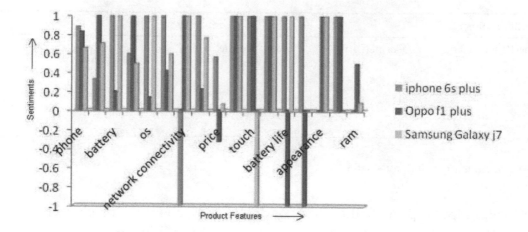

Figure 4. Sentiments of k-common features of similar products in the absence of ontology.

shown as first product in the recommendations list. For k value of 17, the order in the product recommendations is changed. This is because the product P3 has higher cosine value and P2 has lower cosine value when compared with the searched product.

When ontological knowledge is utilized in the product recommendations analysis, the sentiments of the taxonomical features [(battery, battery life) and (camera, camera quality)] are not changed as the sentiments of the parent features are greater than the sentiments of the child features in the taxonomy. The sentiments of the non-taxonomical features [in the work the related features are (RAM, mobile performance), (brand, price), and (screen, display)] are improved in the similar products of k-common features by using the recommendation algorithm. It is observed that the order of product recommendations after improving the sentiments of the related features is changed for two k values (for values 4 and 8). This is because the related sentiments of product P3 have improved so they show higher cosine value than the product P2. This shows the improvement in the product recommendations.

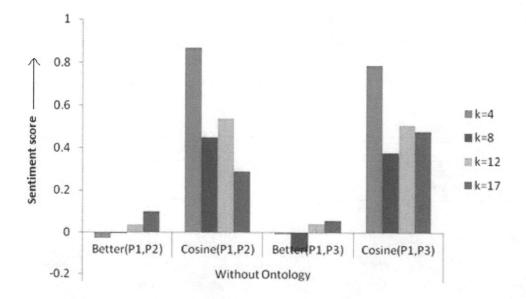

Figure 5. Products comparison with the searched product in the absence of ontology.

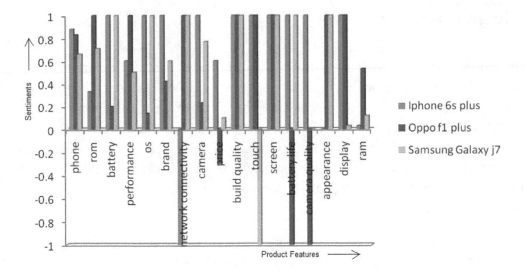

Figure 6. Sentiments of k-common features of similar products in the presence of ontology.

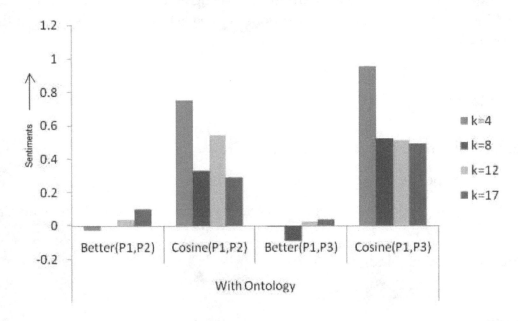

Figure 7. Products comparison with the searched product in the presence of ontology.

Searched product in E-Commerce site: Iphone 6 s plus		
k **(No. of common product features)**	**Product recommendations order–without ontology** **(product1, product2)**	**Product recommendations order–with ontology** **(product1, product2)**
4	Oppo f1 plus, Samsung Galaxy j7	Samsung Galaxy j7, Oppo f1 plus
8	Oppo f1 plus, Samsung Galaxy j7	Samsung Galaxy j7, Oppo f1 plus
12	Oppo f1 plus, Samsung Galaxy j7	Oppo f1 plus, Samsung Galaxy j7
17	Samsung Galaxy j7, Oppo f1 plus	Samsung Galaxy j7, Oppo f1 plus

Table 5. Product recommendations.

6. Conclusions and future work

The sentiment-based semantic rule learning for improved product recommendations is presented. The role of semantic rules in sentiment learning is discussed. The influence of sentiments on semantic rules is also discussed. The algorithms for learning taxonomical and non-taxonomical constraints are explained and results are tabulated. Also the algorithm for improving product sentiments using the learned taxonomical and nontaxonomical constraints for product recommendations is explained and results are tabulated. The design decisions in the implementation of PROO ontology are discussed. Several observations from the experiment are also discussed.

Future scope of work is in the lines of learning the intentions of the reviewers using the advanced machine learning algorithms and bigger datasets. The influence of the intentions on new customers and on the product manufacturers by quantifying the effect of intention on information diffusion in social media are to be investigated. The classification performance of the machine learning model on the intentions is to be examined for discovering the actual intention of the reviewer.

Author details

Dandibhotla Teja Santosh[1]* and Bulusu Vishnu Vardhan[2]

*Address all correspondence to: tejasantoshd@gmail.com

1 School of Technology, GITAM, Rudraram, Patancheru, Sanga reddy, Hyderabad Campus, India

2 JNTUHCEM, Manthani, India

References

[1] Horrocks I. 2009. Ontologies and the Semantic Web. ACM. 2009

[2] Liu B. Sentiment analysis and subjectivity. Handbook of Natural Language Processing. 2010;2:627-666

[3] Resnick P, Iacovou N, Suchak M, Bergstrom P, Riedl J. GroupLens: An Open Architecture for Collaborative Filtering of Netnews. In Proceedings of CSCW '94, Chapel Hill, NC. 1994

[4] Stavrianou A, Brun C. Expert recommendations based on opinion mining of user-generated product reviews. Computational Intelligence. 2015;31(1):165-183

[5] Lang K. Newsweeder: Learning to filter netnews. Proceedings of the 12th International Conference on Machine Learning; 1995

[6] Zhou J, T Luo, F Cheng. Modeling learners and contents in academic-oriented recommendation framework. Dependable, Autonomic and Secure Computing (DASC), 2011 IEEE Ninth International Conference on. IEEE, 2011

[7] Kolodner J. Case-Based Reasoning. Morgan Kaufmann; 2014

[8] Burke RD, Hammond KJ, Yound BC. The FindMe approach to assisted browsing. IEEE Expert. 1997;**12**(4):32-40

[9] Holland S, Ester M, Kießling W. Preference Mining: A Novel Approach on Mining User Preferences for Personalized Applications. European Conference on Principles of Data Mining and Knowledge Discovery. Berlin, Heidelberg: Springer; 2003

[10] Chen G, Chen L. Recommendation based on contextual opinions. International Conference on User Modeling, Adaptation, and Personalization. Springer International Publishing; 2014

[11] Gurini DF et al. Analysis of sentiment communities in online networks. Proceedings of the International Workshop on Social Personalization & Search, co-located at SIGIR; 2015

[12] Li X, Wang H, Yan X. Accurate recommendation based on opinion mining. Genetic and Evolutionary Computing. Springer International Publishing; 2015. 399-408

[13] Dong R et al. Combining similarity and sentiment in opinion mining for product recommendation. Journal of Intelligent Information Systems. 2016;**46**(2):285-312

[14] Uzun A, Christian R. Competence Center FAME. Exploiting Ontologies for better Recommendations. GI Jahrestagung. 2010;(1)

[15] Farsani HK, Nematbakhsh MA. Designing a catalog management system—An ontology approach. Malaysian Journal of Computer Science. 2007;**20**(1):35

[16] Agarwal B et al. Sentiment analysis using common-sense and context information. Computational Intelligence and Neuroscience 2015;**2015**:30

[17] Teja SD, Vardhan BV. PROO ontology development for learning feature specific sentiment relationship rules on reviews categorisation: A semantic data mining approach. International Journal of Metadata, Semantics and Ontologies. 2016;**11**(1):29-38

[18] Huang A. Similarity measures for text document clustering. Proceedings of the Sixth New Zealand Computer Science Research Student Conference (NZCSRSC2008), Christchurch, New Zealand; 2008

[19] Dong R et al. Opinionated product recommendation. International Conference on Case-Based Reasoning. Berlin Heidelberg: Springer; 2013

5

Hardware Accelerator Design for Machine Learning

Li Du and Yuan Du

Abstract

Machine learning is widely used in many modern artificial intelligence applications. Various hardware platforms are implemented to support such applications. Among them, graphics processing unit (GPU) is the most widely used one due to its fast computation speed and compatibility with various algorithms. Field programmable gate arrays (FPGA) show better energy efficiency compared with GPU when computing machine learning algorithm at the cost of low speed. Finally, various application specific integrated circuit (ASIC) architecture is proposed to achieve the best energy efficiency at the cost of less reconfigurability which makes it suitable for special kinds of machine learning algorithms such as a deep convolutional neural network. Finally, analog computing shows a promising methodology to compute large-sized machine learning algorithm due to its low design cost and fast computing speed; however, due to the requirement of the analog-to-digital converter (ADC) in the analog computing, this kind of technique is only applicable to low computation resolution, making it unsuitable for most artificial intelligence (AI) applications.

Keywords: machine learning, hardware accelerator, model compression, analog computing, GPU, FPGA, ASIC

1. Introduction

Machine learning (ML) is currently widely used in many modern artificial intelligence (AI) applications [1]. The breakthrough of the computation ability has enabled the system to compute complicated different ML algorithm in a relatively short time, providing real-time human-machine interaction such as face detection for video surveillance, advanced driver-assistance systems (ADAS), and image recognition early cancer detection [2, 3]. Among all those applications, a high detection accuracy requires complicated ML computation, which comes at the cost of high computational complexity. This results in a high requirement on the hardware platform. Currently, most applications are implemented on general-purpose compute engines, especially graphics processing units (GPUs). However, work recently reported

c

from both industry and academy shows a trend on the design of application specific integrated circuit (ASIC) for ML, especially in the field of deep neural network (DNN). This chapter gives an overview of the hardware accelerator design, the various types of the ML acceleration, and the technique used in improving the hardware computation efficiency of ML computation.

2. Recent development on deep learning hardware accelerator

2.1. GPU/FPGA-based accelerator in datacenter

Over the past decades, graphics processing units (GPUs) have become popular and standard in training deep-learning algorithms or convolutional neural networks for face, object detection/recognition, data mining, and other artificial intelligence (AI) applications. GPUs offer a wide range of hardware selections, a high-performance throughput/computing power, and a stable but ever-expanding ecosystem. The GPU architecture is usually implemented with several mini graphics processors. Each graphics processor has its own computation unit and local cache which fits for the matrix multiplication. A shared high-speed bus is included in multiple mini processors to enable fast data exchange among mini processors. In addition, it also acts as a bridge to connect the main CPU and multiple mini graphics processors.

Taking NVIDIA's DGX-1 as an example [4], DGX-1 has eight Tesla P100-SXM2 GPUs conforming to Pascal architecture. Each GPU has 56 multiprocessors with 64 CUDA cores per multiprocessor. This makes each GPU equipped with 3584 CUDA cores. The GPU and memory clock frequencies are 1.3 GHz and 700 MHz, respectively. The GPU has 4096-bit memory bus width, 16 GB global memory, and 4 MB L2 cache. **Figure 1** shows the system-level topology of DGX-1. The network of NVLink interconnect is wired so that any two GPUs can hop away from less than one another GPU. The GPU cluster is connected to a switch (PLX) with a PCIe × 16

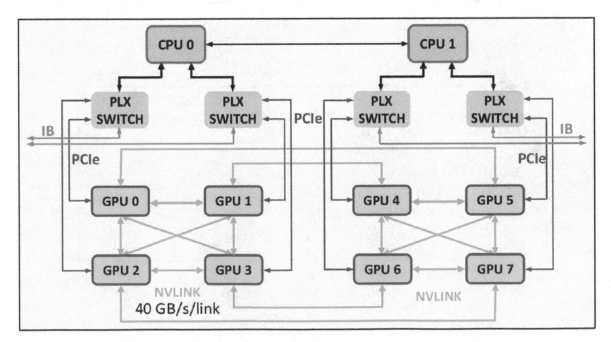

Figure 1. Diagram of NVIDIA DGX-1 system-level topology.

interconnect. The maximum bandwidth of NVLink interconnect with Tesla P100 is reported at 160 GB/s. In a clustering or multicore parallel computation scenario, the communication inter-connect performance becomes the bottleneck to achieving high throughput, low latency, and high energy efficiency. **Figure 2(a)** and **(b)** shows that DGX-1 GPU outperforms comparable Intel CPU (KNL) in power efficiency and computing throughput for two different batch sizes when running CLfarNet.

The GPU offers significant computation speed due to a lot of parallel processing cores. How-ever, a relatively large power consumption is also requested for the computation and data movement. In addition, a high-speed interconnect interface is required to support the fast data exchange. Thus, compared with other techniques, GPU offers power computation ability at the expense of high design cost (unit price) and power consumption.

As the industry matures, field programmable gate arrays (FPGAs) are now starting to emerge as credible competition to GPUs for implementing CNN-based deep learning algorithms. Microsoft

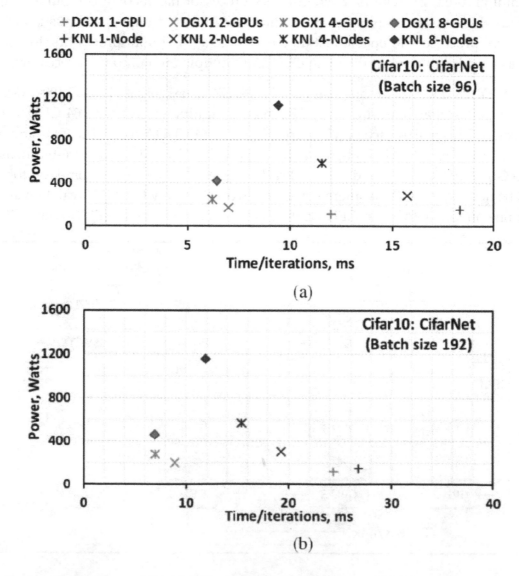

Figure 2. Power and performance of CifarNet/Cifar 10 with batch sizes (a) 96 and (b) 192.

Research's Catapult Project garnered quite a bit of attention in the industry when it contended that using FPGAs could be as much as 10 times more power efficient compared to GPUs [5]. Although the performance of single FPGA was much lower than comparable-price GPUs, the fact that power consumption was much lower could have significant implications for many applications where high performance may not be the top priority. **Figure 3(a)** shows a logical view of FPGAs in cloud-scale application and **Figure 3(b)** shows how the FPGA-based accelerator fits into a host server.

As **Figure 3(b)** shows, the FPGA-based machine learning accelerator typically involves hardware blocks such as DRAM, CPUs, network interface controller (NIC), and FPGAs. The DRAMs act as a large buffer to store the temporary data while the CPU is in charge of managing the computation, including sending instructions to FPGAs. The FPGA is programmed to fit the ML algorithm. Since the ML algorithm is optimized at a hardware level through FPGA programming, a high data access efficiency is obtained compared with regular GPU computation which does not have any hardware optimization on the corresponding ML algorithms.

Although the FPGA reduces the power consumption in computing through optimizing the ML algorithms on the hardware design, the overall efficiency is still much lower compared with the ASIC for single kind of algorithms. Compared with the ASIC, the programmability introduced by the FPGA also brings complicated logic which increases the hardware design cost. In addition, the speed of the FPGA is usually limited to 300 MHz, which is 4–5× times lower than a typical ASIC [6].

2.2. ASIC-based CNN accelerator at edge

2.2.1. Introduction

In the HPC or datacenter, hardware accelerator solutions are dominated by GPU and FPGA solution. State-of-the-art machine-learning computation mostly relies on the cloud servers.

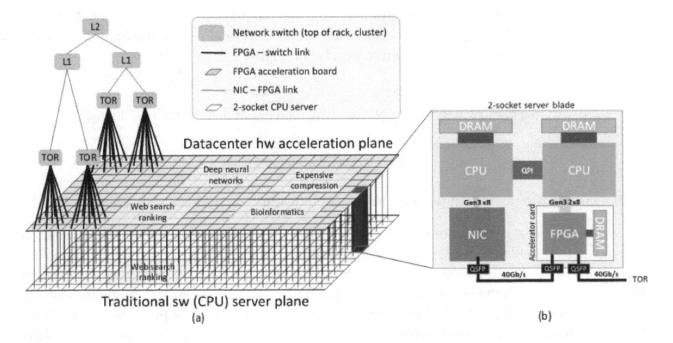

Figure 3. (a) De-couples programmable hardware plane, (b) server plus FPGA schematic.

However, high-power consumption makes this approach limited in many real application scenarios. Since cloud-based AI applications on portable devices require network connection capability, the quality of network connection affects user experience. Furthermore, the network and communication latency is not acceptable for real-time AI applications. In addition, most of IoT AI applications have a strict power and cost constrain, which could support neither high-power GPU nor transmitting a large amount of data to cloud servers.

To address the abovementioned issues, several edge-based AI processing schemes were introduced in [7–9]. The edge-based AI processing scheme targets utilizing the localized data at the edge side and avoids network communication overhead. Currently, most localized AI processors focus on processing convolutional neural network (CNN) which is widely used for computation vision algorithms and requests a lot of computing resources.

2.2.2. CNN accelerator layer function definition

The state-of-art convolutional neural networks commonly include three different computational layers: convolution layer, pooling layer, and fully connected layer. Convolution layer is the most computation intensive part of the neural network, with pooling layer inserted between two convolution layers with the function of reducing intermediate data size and remapping feature maps. Fully connected layer is usually the last layer of the CNN to predict labels of input data, which is memory bandwidth limited, rather than computation resource limited.

The primary role of a convolution layer is to apply convolution function to map the input (previous) layer's images to the next layer. Data from each input layer are composed of multiple channels as a three-dimensional tensor. One set of regional filter windows is defined as one filter or weight. The results run through inner product computation by the filter weight and input data. Output feature is defined by using the filter or weight to scan and accumulate different input channels. After interproduct computation, a separated bias vector (the same dimension as output feature number) will be added in each final result. The analytical representation of convolution layer is shown in Eq. (1) and **Figure 4**.

$$O[o][m][x][y] = B[o] + \sum_{k=1}^{M} \sum_{i=1}^{K} \sum_{j=1}^{K} I[o][k][\alpha x + i][\alpha y + j] \times W[m][k][i][j]$$

$$1 \leq o \leq N, 1 \leq m \leq M, 1 \leq x, y \leq S_o \tag{1}$$

O, B, I, and **W** are the output features, biases, input features, and filters, respectively.

In addition to the convolution layer, pooling layer is to compress important information through a group of local image pixel data in each input channel. There are two types of pooling operations: max pooling and average pooling. For max pooling operation, the output of pooling layer collects the maximum of pixel data in the local group window, while for average pooling operation, the output of pooling layers calculates the mean of pixel data in the local group window. The representations of these two pooling operations are defined as Eqs. (2) and (3). **Figure 5** is an example of the max pooling function.

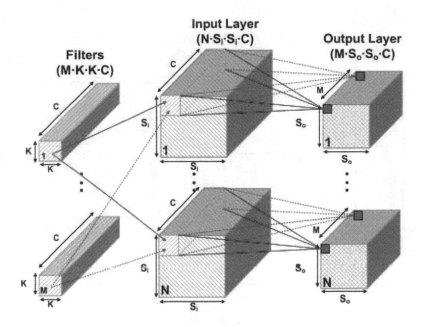

Figure 4. Concept of computation of CONV layer.

$$O_{avg}[r][c] = avg \begin{bmatrix} I[r][c] & \cdots & I[r][c+K-1] \\ \vdots & \ddots & \vdots \\ I[r+K-1][c] & \cdots & I[r+k-1][c+K-1] \end{bmatrix} \quad (2)$$

$$O_{max}[r][c] = max \begin{bmatrix} I[r][c] & \cdots & I[r][c+K-1] \\ \vdots & \ddots & \vdots \\ I[r+K-1][c] & \cdots & I[r+k-1][c+K-1] \end{bmatrix} \quad (3)$$

Here I[r][c] represents the input channel's data at the position (r,c) and the kernel size of the pooling window is K.

2.2.3. CNN accelerator architecture overview

Today's CNN accelerator architecture can mainly separate into two categories. The central computation architecture and the sparse computation architecture. **Figure 6** is a typical central

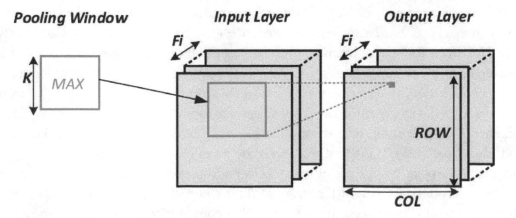

Figure 5. Example of computation of a max pooling layer.

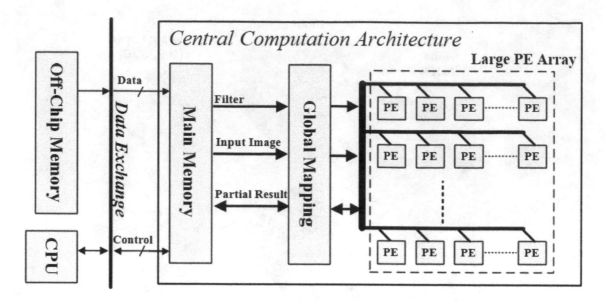

Figure 6. Central computation architecture of the CNN accelerator.

computation architecture that reports in 2015 [10]. The central computation architecture has one large PE array. Multiple filters will be sent out into the PE array to enable parallel computation. The output result of each filter will be gathered at the PE array's output to feedback to the memory for next layer computation. This large PE array in the central computation architecture provides a benefit to computing large kernel-sized CNN; however, it needs to reconstruct the array when computing the small kernel-sized CNN.

On the other hand, a sparse computation architecture is made of many parallel small convolution units that fit for small-sized kernel [11]. **Figure 7** is one of such implementations. The computing unit (CU) Engine Array is made of 16 3 × 3 kernel-sized convolution units. It provides a benefit to compute small kernel-sized convolution operations and simplify the data flow. However, the computing unit is only supported for 3 × 3 convolution. So when computing a kernel size that is larger than 3 × 3, a kernel decomposition technique is proposed in the following section.

2.2.4. Kernel decomposition technique

The filter's kernel size in a typical CNN network can range from a very small size (1 × 1) to a very large size (11 × 11). A hardware engine needs design to support various sized convolutional operation. However, for sparse architecture, the computation units are not separated into many small blocks. Each block consists of a small-sized processing engine array and can only support small-sized convolution, making each block hard to process large convolution. To minimize the hardware resource usage, a filter decomposition algorithm is proposed to compute any large kernel-sized (>3 × 3) convolution through using only 3 × 3-sized CU [11]. The algorithm is separated into three steps: (1) It first examines the kernel size of the filter. If the original filter's kernel size is not an exact multiple of three, zero padding weights will be added in the original filter's kernel boundary to extend the original filter's kernel size to be a multiple of three. The added weights are all zero to keep the extended filter convolution result to be same as the original one. (2) The extended filters will be decomposed into several 3 × 3-sized filters. Each filter will be

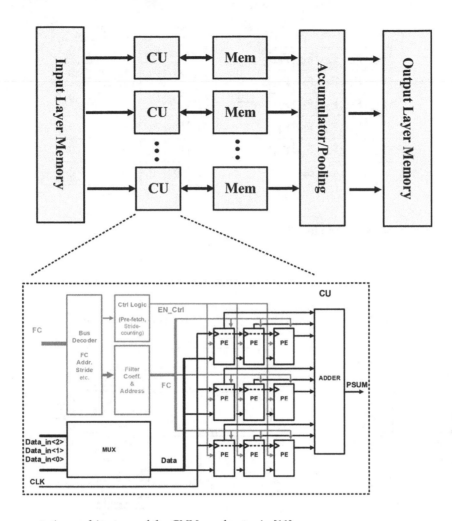

Figure 7. Sparse computation architecture of the CNN accelerator in [11].

assigned a shift address based on its top left weight's relative position in the original filter and each decomposed filter will be computed individually. (3) The output result of each decomposed filter will be summed together based on its shift address to generate the final output. The mathematical derivation of this decomposition technique is also explained in [11].

Figure 8 is an example of decomposing a 5×5 filter into four 3×3 filters using this technique. One row and column zero padding are added in the original filter. The decomposed filters F0, F1, F2, F3's shift address are (0,0), (0,3), (3,0), (3,3). **Figure 9** shows the detailed procedure.

2.3. Model compression

In addition to the hardware architecture level development, model compression is also reported as a way to improve the hardware computation efficiency of the machine learning. Ref [12] reported a methodology to prune the neural network and achieve up to $35\times$ to $49\times$ model parameters reduction. The procedure is shown in **Figure 10**. The original network will be pruned and retrained several times to achieve parameters reduction. After that, quantization is implemented with clustered weights to achieve additional parameter size reduction. Finally, Huffman encoding is added into the final weights to achieve further model size reduction.

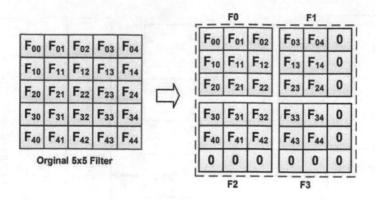

Figure 8. A 5 × 5 Filter decomposed into four 3 × 3 sub-filter.

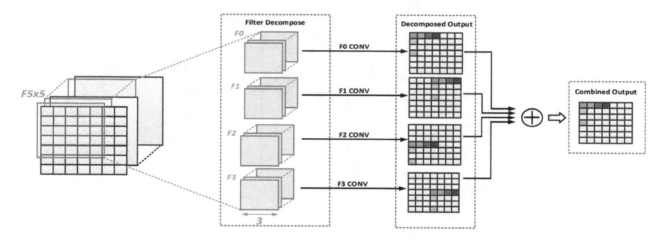

Figure 9. Filter decomposition technique to compute a 5 × 5 filter on the 7 × 7 image. The 5 × 5 filter is decomposed into four separated 3 × 3 filters F0, F1, F2, F3, and generating four sub-images. The sub-images are summed together to generate the final output. Same color's pixels in each sub-image will be added together to generate the corresponding pixels in the output image.

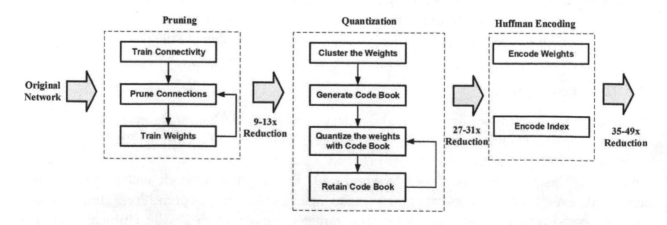

Figure 10. Neural network compression reported in Ref [12].

Due to the rapid increment of the deep learning model size, model compression becomes more and more important for machine-learning hardware acceleration, especially for the edge-side user case. In addition, the fixed-point data format is also used in many deep learning applications to reduce the computation cost [13].

2.4. Analog computing

In addition to the traditional digital accelerator design, analog computing is also becoming one of the trends to improve the processor computation ability in solving machine learning problems. Here, we use the charge-trapping transistors (CTTs) technique as an example to introduce analog computing [14]. The complementary metal oxide semiconductor (CMOS)-compatible feature of the CTTs makes them very promising devices to implement large-sized computation using analog methodology.

As the scaling of transistors is reaching its manufacturing limit, the computation throughput using current architectures will also inevitably saturate. Recent research reports the development of analog computing engines. Compared to traditional digital computation, analog computing shows tremendous advantages regarding the power, design cost, and computation speed. Among many analog computing systems, memristor-based ones have been widely reported [14]. Recently, more promising charge-trapping transistors (CTTs)

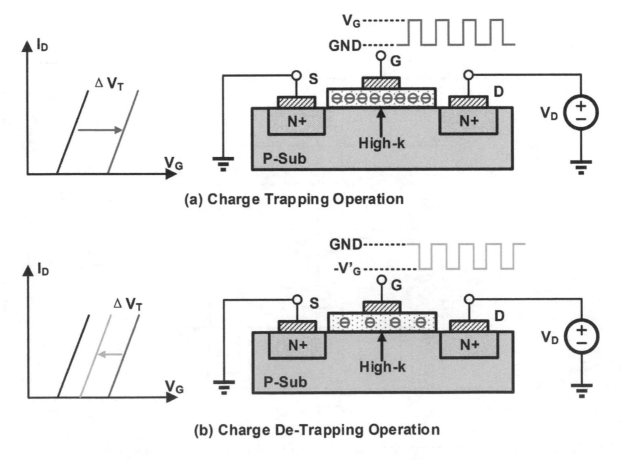

Figure 11. A schematic showing the basic operation of CTT device (equally applicable to FinFET-based CTTs): (1) charge trapping operation, (2) charge de-trapping operation.

were reported to be used as digital memory devices with reliable trapping and de-trapping behavior. Different from other charge-trapping devices such as floating-gate transistors, transistors with an organic gate dielectric, and carbon nanotube transistors, CTTs are manufacturing ready and fully CMOS compatible in terms of process and operating. IT shows that more than 90% of the trapped charge can be retained after 10 years even when the device is baked at 85°C [15].

A schematic of the basic operation of a CTT device is depicted in **Figure 11**. The device threshold voltage, VT, is modulated by the charge trapped in the gate dielectric of the transistor. VT increases when positive pulses are applied to the gate to trap electrons in the high-k layer and decreases when negative pulses are applied to the gate to de-trap electrons from the high-k layer. CTT devices can be programmed by applying logic-compatible voltages.

A memristive computing engine based on the charge-trapping transistor (CTT). The proposed memristive computing engine consists of 784 by 784 CTT analog multipliers and achieves $100\times$ power and area reduction compared to the conventional digital approach. Through implementing a novel sequential analog fabric (SAF), the mixed-signal interfaces are simplified and it only requires an 8-bit analog-to-digital converter (ADC) in the system. The top-level system architecture is shown in **Figure 12**. A 784 by 784 CTT computing engine is implemented using TSMC 28 nm CMOS technology and occupies 0.68mm^2 as shown in **Figure 13**. It achieves 69.9 TOPS with 500 MHz clock frequency and consumes 14.8 mW.

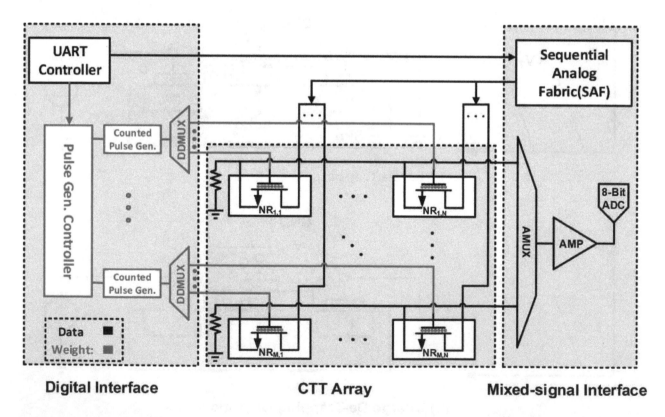

Digital Interface   **CTT Array**   **Mixed-signal Interface**

Figure 12. Top-level system architecture of the proposed memristive computing engine, including CTT array, mixed-signal interfaces including tunable low-dropout regulator (LDO), analog-to-digital converter (ADC), and novel sequential analog fabrics (SAF).

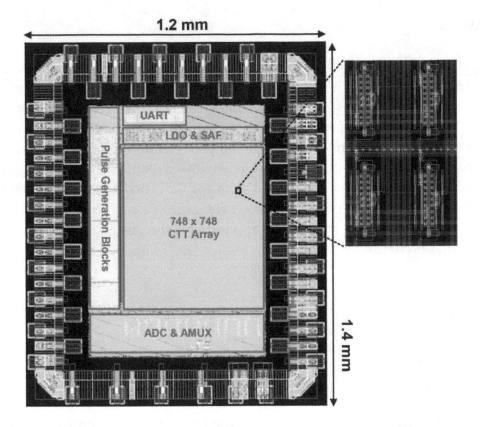

Figure 13. Layout view in TSMC 28 nm CMOS technology.

Compared with the traditional digital processor, analog-based computing processor achieves much less power as well as large area reduction in the design. **Table 1** is a comparison of the computation ability between the analog processor and digital processor. As it shows, analog processor achieved more than 100 times computing speed with 1/10 times area consumption compared to digital processor.

Even the analog computing shows advantages in the computation speed and design cost, a low computing resolution limits its application in most ML algorithms. Due to the design challenges of the ADC in the analog processor, the processor can only handle computation resolution that is less or equal to around 10 bits, making it not suitable for most AI applications.

Merits	Digital [16]	This work
Process	Standard 28 nm FD-SOI CMOS	Standard 28 nm CMOS
Core Area (mm^2)	5.8	0.68
Power (mW)	41	14.8
Clock Speed	200–1175 MHz	500 MHz
Peak MACs #	0.64 K	69.9 K
SRAM Size	128 KB	0
Non-Volatile	No	Yes

Table 1. Comparison table between analog computing and digital computing in Ref [14].

3. Conclusion

In this chapter, various computation hardware platforms for machine learning algorithms are discussed. Among them, GPU is the most widely used one due to its fast computation speed and compatibility with various algorithms. FPGA shows better energy efficiency compared with GPU when computing machine learning algorithm at the cost of low speed. Finally, different ASIC architectures are proposed to support certain kinds of the machine learning algorithms such as a deep convolutional neural network with model compression technique to improve hardware performance. Compared with the GPU and FPGA, ASIC shows the best energy efficiency and computation speed, however, at the cost of reconfigurability to various ML algorithms. Depending on the specific applications, the designers should select the most suitable computation hardware platform.

Author details

Li Du* and Yuan Du

*Address all correspondence to: dl1989113@ucla.edu

Hardware Architecture Research Engineer, Kneron Inc., Research Scientist, UCLA, Los Angeles, USA

References

[1] LeCun Y, Bengio Y, Hinton G. Deep learning. Nature. May 2015;**521**:436-444

[2] Krizhevsky A, Sutskever I, Hinton GE. ImageNet classification with deep convolution neural networks. Proceeding of Advances in Neural Information Processing Systems. 2012;**25**:1097-1105

[3] Silver D et al. Mastering the game of go with deep neural networks and tree search. Nature. Jan. 2016;**529**(7587):484-489

[4] Gawande NA, Landwehr JB, Daily JA, Tallent NR, Vishnu A, Kerbyson DJ. Scaling deep learning workloads: NVIDIA DGX-1/Pascal and intel knights landing. In: IEEE International Parallel And Distributed Processing Symposium Workshops (IPDPSW); Lake Buena Vista. 2017 pp. 399-408

[5] Putnam A. The configurable cloud – accelerating hyperscale datacenter services with FPGA. In: IEEE 33rd International Conference on Data Engineering (ICDE); San Diego. 2017. p. 1587

[6] Chang AXM, Culurciello E. Hardware accelerators for recurrent neural networks on FPGA. In: IEEE International Symposium on Circuits and Systems (ISCAS); MD, Baltimore. 2017. pp. 1-4

[7] Sim J, Park J-S, Kim M, Bae D, Choi Y, Kim L-S. A 1.42TOPS/W deep convolution neural network recognition processor for intelligent IoE systems. In: Proceeding of IEEE International Solid-State Circuits Conference (ISSCC). Jan/Feb. 2016. pp. 264-265

[8] Bong K, Choi S, Kim C, Kang S, Kim Y, Yoo HJ. 14.6 A 0.62mW ultra-low-power convolutional-neural-network face-recognition processor and a CIS integrated with always-on haar-like face detector. IEEE International Solid-State Circuits Conference (ISSCC); San Francisco. 2017. pp. 248–249

[9] Desoli G et al. 4.1 A 2.9TOPS/W deep convolutional neural network SoC in FD-SOI 28nm for intelligent embedded systems. In: IEEE International Solid-State Circuits Conference (ISSCC); San Francisco. 2017. pp. 238–239

[10] Chen YH, Krishna T, Emer J, Sze V. 14.5 Eyeriss: An energy-efficient reconfigurable accelerator for deep convolution neural networks. In: IEEE International Solid-State Circuits Conference (ISSCC); San Francisco. 2016. pp. 262–263

[11] Du L et al. A reconfigurable streaming deep convolutional neural network accelerator for internet of things. IEEE Transactions on Circuits and Systems I: Regular Papers. 2017; **99**:1-11

[12] Han S, Mao H, Dally W. Deep compression: Compressing DNNs with pruning, trained quantization and huffman coding. 2015. arxiv:1510.00149v3

[13] Du Y et al. A streaming accelerator for deep convolutional neural networks with image and feature decomposition for resource-limited system applications. Sep. 2017. arXiv:1709.05116 [cs.AR]

[14] Du Y et al. A memristive neural network computing engine using CMOS-compatible Charge-Trap-Transistor (CTT). Sep 2017. arXiv:1709.06614 [cs.ET]

[15] Shin S, Kim K, Kang SM. Memristive computing- multiplication and correlation. In: IEEE International Symposium on Circuits and Systems; Seoul. 2012. pp. 1608-1611

[16] Desoli G et al. 14.1 A 2.9TOPS/W deep convolutional neural network SoC in FD-SOI 28nm for intelligent embedded systems. In: IEEE International Solid-State Circuits Conference (ISSCC); San Francisco. 2017. pp. 238-239

6

Regression Models to Predict Air Pollution from Affordable Data Collections

Yves Rybarczyk and Rasa Zalakeviciute

Abstract

Air quality monitoring is key in assuring public health. However, the necessary equipment to accurately measure the criteria pollutants is expensive. Since the countries with more serious problems of air pollution are the less wealthy, this study proposes an affordable method based on machine learning to estimate the concentration of $PM_{2.5}$. The capital city of Ecuador is used as case study. Several regression models are built from features of different levels of affordability. The first result shows that cheap data collection based on web traffic monitoring enables us to create a model that fairly correlates traffic density with air pollution. Building multiple models according to the hourly occurrence of the pollution peaks seems to increase the accuracy of the estimation, especially in the morning hours. The second result shows that adding meteorological factors allows for a significant improvement of the prediction of $PM_{2.5}$ concentrations. Nevertheless, the last finding demonstrates that the best predictive model should be based on a hybrid source of data that includes trace gases. Since the sensors to monitor such gases are costly, the last part of the chapter gives some recommendations to get an accurate prediction from models that consider no more than two trace gases.

Keywords: urban air pollution prediction, heterogeneous data sources, hybrid models, low-cost approach, real-time traffic monitoring, meteorological and chemical features

1. Introduction

Over the last century, the global human population has augmented more than four times. Most of the recent growth is accredited to the urban areas in the less developed parts of the world [1]. This has resulted in 80% of global cities and 98% of cities in low- and middle-income countries to exceed the recommendations for air quality [2]. Apart from economic losses, reduced visibility, and climate change, ambient air pollution costs millions of premature deaths annually, mostly due to anthropogenic fine particulate matter ($PM_{2.5}$—particles with aerodynamic diameter less than 2.5 μm) [3]. In the case of business-as-usual, the global atmospheric chemistry models suggest that the contribution of outdoor air pollution to premature mortality could double by 2050 [4].

Even though the concentrations of $PM_{2.5}$ are 2–5 times higher in the developing countries, most of the air quality studies and measurements are concentrated in the developed countries [2, 5]. This is often due to the investments required to launch and support a reliable air quality monitoring station or network. High accuracy, standard air quality reference method equipment costs can range from $6000 to $36,000 per sensor [6], excluding the costs for maintenance, calibration and accessories, resulting in a price of a functional air quality monitoring station well over $100,000. Meteorological equipment is also essential for the evaluation of air quality, as high UV radiation, high winds, precipitation, or extreme temperatures can cause serious health concerns. Meteorological station, depending on accuracy requirements, can cost from $1000 to over $7000; although, the accuracy differences are not too great between the tiers (not including the lowest level equipment). Dynamic and nonhomogeneous urban systems contain different pollution sources, infrastructures, varying terrains, requiring more than one station for a comprehensive evaluation of air pollution conditions, consequently excluding poorer cities.

The question of economic limitations has recently been brought to attention resulting in the introduction of the lower cost sensors (<$500) or bundled platforms ($5000–10,000) to the market. Based on the comparative studies, evaluating sensor performance (fit for air quality monitoring), some air criteria pollutants compare quite well with the standard air quality reference methods, while some show lower correlation [6–8]. In addition, in some cases, adding a PM sensor to the platform increases costs significantly.

Recently, a different approach aims at using machine learning to estimate particulate pollution [9, 10]. This study proposes to evaluate the reliability for predicting air quality through a machine-learning approach and from data sources with a different scale of affordability. It focuses on the case study of Quito, the capital city of Ecuador, because it is a model example of complex terrain rapidly growing in mid-size cities in developing world with air pollution issues and economic limitations (e.g., poor quality fuel). In addition, Quito has many years of environmental data collection that can be used for data mining.

2. Machine-learning approach

2.1. Prediction by multiple regression

In regression, features derived from a dataset are used as input of the regression model to predict continuous valued output. This kind of prediction is obtained by learning the relationship between the input x and the output y. The simplest case of a regression model is a simple regression, in which a single feature is used to estimate the value of the output. This relationship is acquired by fitting a linear or nonlinear curve to the data. In order to correctly fit the curve, it is necessary to define the goodness-of-fit metric, which allows us to identify the curve that fits better than the other ones. The optimization technique used in regression, and in several other machine-learning methods, is the gradient descent algorithm. In the case of a simple linear regression, the objective is to find the value of the slope and the intercept of the line that minimizes the goodness-of-fit metric. The residual sum of squares (RSS), also called sum of squared errors of prediction, is used to calculate this cost. The RSS adds up the squared difference between the estimated relationship between x and y (regression model) and the actual values of y (y_i), as described in Eq. (1)

$$RSS(w_0, w_1) = \sum_{i=1}^{N} (y_i - [w_0 + w_1 x_i])^2 \tag{1}$$

where N is the number of observations, x_i are the input values, and the coefficients w_0 and w_1 are the intercept and slope of the linear regression, respectively. For simplification, Eq. (1) is commonly rewritten as follows:

$$RSS(w_0, w_1) = \sum_{i=1}^{N} (y_i - \hat{y}_i(w_0, w_1))^2 \tag{2}$$

where $\hat{y}_i(w_0, w_1)$ is the predictive value of observation yi, if a linear regression defined by w_0 and w_1 is used. In the case of a multiple regression model, more than one input (or feature) is considered to predict the output. The generic equation of such a model can be written as follows:

$$y_i = \sum_{j=0}^{D} w_j h_j(\vec{x}_i) + \varepsilon_i \tag{3}$$

where D is the number of features, $h_j(\vec{x}_i)$ are functions of the inputs (represented as a vector) that are weighted by different coefficients w_j, and ε_i is the error. Thus, the RSS is generically defined by Eq. 4 as

$$RSS(\vec{w}) = \sum_{i=1}^{N} (y_i - \hat{y}_i(\vec{w}))^2 \tag{4}$$

where $\vec{w}$ is a vector of the weights (or coefficients) of the whole parameters of the fit. The best regression model is the function that provides the smallest RSS. The model is obtained after a split of the dataset into two independent sets: a training set and a test set. The training set is used to build the model, and the calculation of the RSS is performed over the test set, only. The gradient descent is an iterative method that minimizes the RSS metric. It takes multiple steps to eventually provide the optimal solution as described in Algorithm 1. At first, all the parameters are initialized to be zero at the first iteration (t = 1). Then, the algorithm repeats while the magnitude of the RSS does not converge. The internal part of the loop calculates the partial derivative (partial[j]) for each feature of the multiple regression model, and then, the gradient step takes the jth coefficient at time t and subtracts the step size (η) times that partial derivative. Once the algorithm cycled through all the features of the model, the t counter is incremented and the convergence condition is tested to decide whether the program must loop through or not. When the minimum is reached (RSS ≤ ε), the respective values of the regression coefficients are used as the model parameters to form the predictions.

Algorithm 1. Gradient descent algorithm for multiple regression.

1: init $\vec{w}^{(1)} = 0$, t = 1

2: while $\| \nabla\ RSS(\vec{w}^{(t)}) \| > \varepsilon$.

3:　　　for j = 0, …, D

4:　　　　　partial[j] = $-2\sum_{i=1}^{N} h_j(\vec{x}_i)(y_i - y_i(\vec{w}^{(t)}))$

5:　　　　　$\vec{w}_j^{(t+1)} \leftarrow \vec{w}_j^{(t)} - \eta\,\text{partial}[j]$

6:　　　t ← t + 1

In addition, the final regression models of this study are obtained after an attribute selection using the M5 method, which steps through the attributes removing the one with the smallest standardized coefficient until no improvement is observed in the estimate of the error given by the Akaike information criterion (AIC) [11].

$$AIC = N\,ln\left(\frac{RSS}{N-D}\right) + 2D \qquad (5)$$

where N is the number of observations (or instances), and D is the number of features (or attributes). The selected model is the model that gets the lowest AIC.

All the models presented in the manuscript are obtained after a normalization of the value of the variables, in order to avoid a dominance of the variables with the highest intrinsic values. The used method to evaluate the model accuracy is a 10-fold cross-validation. The regression modeling is performed with Pandas and scikit-learn machine-learning library for Python.

2.2. Cumulative modeling method

Air pollution data ($PM_{2.5}$) were collected in central Quito over a period of 2 months in June and July of 2017 by the city Secretariat of the Environment. Belisario (alt. 2835 m.a.s.l, coord.78°29′24″ W, 0°10′48″ S) measurement station was setup following the criteria of the Environmental Protection Agency of the United States (USEPA). For $PM_{2.5}$ concentration data Thermo Scientific FH62C14-DHS continuous ambient particulate monitor 5014i was used based on beta rays' attenuation method (EPA No. EQPM-0609-183). For all the data 1 hour averages were calculated, resulting in 1118 instances.

In this work, we present several regression models to provide a reliable estimation of the current level of $PM_{2.5}$ from data collection methods of different levels of affordability. In Section 3, we describe a prediction of $PM_{2.5}$ concentrations based on real-time traffic monitoring, only. This type of data does not cost anything to the user as it is based on publicly available worldwide traffic data. Section 4 describes a prediction that adds meteorological factors on top of the traffic data. Most of the meteorological equipment is not as costly as air quality sensors, thus still presenting a viable option for the prediction of $PM_{2.5}$ concentrations. Subsequently, Section 5 describes a prediction that includes traffic data, meteorological factors and trace gas concentrations. This way we build from the simplest to the most complex model, increasing the equipment costs with every step and improving the prediction performance. Finally, we finish our study by proposing the best simple model based on a feature selection method, letting us to reduce the costs significantly, but still producing a high performance.

3. Prediction from real-time traffic monitoring

We propose a method to extract data from Google Maps Traffic, in which a simple request to the website enables us to build a database regarding the traffic in the city and, consequently, the level of urban air pollution.

3.1. Dataset

3.1.1. Data acquisition

3.1.1.1. Screenshot

A request to Google Maps Traffic is performed by the use of the library selenium for Python. A screenshot is carried out each 10 minute in a specific zone of Quito, which is centered on the neighborhood of Belisario. The exact coordinates of the geographic area of interest are −0.181661, −78.4987077, which is 1.2 km southwest from the center of the traffic map. Two kinds of images are stored: the one with traffic (**Figure 1a**) and the another without traffic (**Figure 1b**). It is necessary to save these two different types of pictures in order to proceed with the next step that consists of isolating the traffic information only (**Figure 1c**).

3.1.1.2. Background subtraction

A technique of background subtraction is used to eliminate picture information that is not related to traffic (**Figure 1**). The background removal is carried out through the process as follows [12]:

- Memorize the background image (picture without traffic).

- Check every pixel in the frame. If it is different from the corresponding pixel in the background image, it is a foreground pixel (traffic information). If not, it is a background pixel.

To get a clean image of the traffic, it is necessary to define a distance threshold of brightness when comparing the background image to the traffic + background images (see Algorithm 2). For every pixel, if the absolute difference of brightness between the image with traffic and the background image is lower than the threshold (empirically defined at 30), then the corresponding pixels are considered identical. In this case, the pixels are colored white

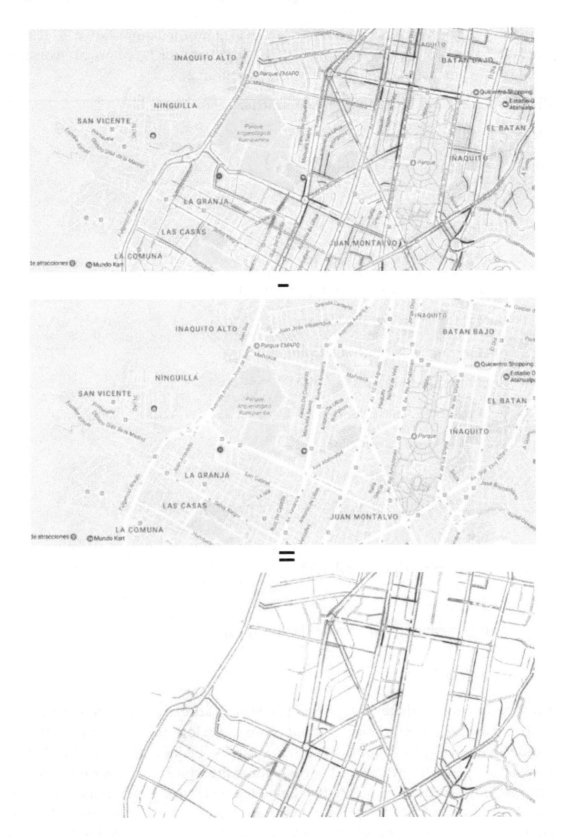

Figure 1. Description of the principle of background removal. The background image (b) is subtracted from the image that includes the traffic (a). The result is a picture with the traffic information only (c).

(lines 14 and 15 of Algorithm 2). On the contrary, if the brightness difference is higher than the threshold, the color of the pixel does not change (lines 16 and 17 of Algorithm 2). Thanks to this method, it is possible to extract only the color information of the traffic.

The calculation of the value of the difference is based on the computation of the distance between each color component of a pixel (RGB). In other words, colors are considered as points in a three-dimensional space (line 13 of Algorithm 2).

Algorithm 2. Generating the background subtraction.

```
1: for(int i = 0, i < allFrame, i++)
2:      for(int x = 0, x < width, x++)
3:          for(int y = 0, y < height, y++)
4:              int. pos = x + y * width
5:              color frameColor = frame[i].pixels[pos]
6:              color refColor = background.pixels[pos]
7:              float rFrame = red(frameColor)
8:              float gFrame = green(frameColor)
9:              float bFrame = blue(frameColor)
10:             float rRef = red(refColor)
11:             float gRef = green(refColor)
12:             float bRef = blue(refColor)
13:             float diff = dist(rFrame, gFrame, bFrame, rRef, gRef, bRef)
14:             if (diff <30)
15:                 image.pixels[pos] = color(255)
16:             else
17:                 image.pixels[pos] = frame[i].pixels[pos]
```

3.1.1.3. Pixel extraction

To identify traffic density, three categories of pixel colors are extracted: green, orange, and red (see Algorithm 3). The green, orange, and red pixels mean low, medium, and high amount of traffic, respectively. The pixel number of each category is obtained by getting the RGB component of the whole pixels in the image. After excluding the white pixels (line 6 of Algorithm 3), three rules are implemented to classify the remaining pixels in one or another category (lines 7 to 12 of Algorithm 3). Once the picture is entirely read, the percentage of each category is calculated by dividing the number of green, orange, and red pixels by the total number of colored pixels.

Algorithm 3. Generating the pixel color extraction.

```
1: for(int i = 0, i < allFrame, i++)
2:      float red = 0, orange = 0, green = 0
```

```
3:        image(frame[i], 0, 0)

4:        for(int x = 0, x < width, x++)

4:            for(int y = 0, y < height, y++)

5:                color c = get(x, y)

6:                if(red(c) < 200 || green(c) < 200 || blue(c) < 200)

7:                    if(red(c) > green(c) && abs(green(c)-blue(c)) < 20)

8:                        red++

9:                    else if(red(c) > green(c) && green(c) > blue(c))

10:                       orange++

11:                   else if(green(c) > red(c) && red(c) > blue(c))

12:                       green++
```

3.1.1.4. Hourly averaging

Since the machine-learning models are based on hourly data analysis, it is required to determinate for each hour the trend of the six 10 minute recording. To do so, the average of the six percentages per hour and for each color is calculated. Then, these values are added into the final dataset.

3.1.2. Data transformation

A last data preparation is necessary before running the machine-learning algorithms. The polar coordinates of time (think of time as an analog clock of 24 × 60 minutes, in which minute hand describes an angle) are transformed into Cartesian coordinates (Eqs. (6) and (7)). This mathematical transformation permits a more accurate feature representation of the data with respect to the traffic density at night. Otherwise, it would be impossible to find a correlation between time and traffic around midnight, since a similar traffic would correspond to a completely different number of minutes (before midnight ≈ 1440 minute, and after midnight ≈ 0 minute). This transformation is particularly relevant for machine-learning algorithms based on linear regression, because it relies on a continuous relationship between parameters [13].

$$Xminutes = cos\left(\frac{minutes \cdot \pi}{720}\right) \tag{6}$$

$$Yminutes = sin\left(\frac{minutes \cdot \pi}{720}\right) \tag{7}$$

Thus, the final dataset is composed of a number of five features, which are: Xminutes, Yminutes, %orange, %red, and $PM_{2.5}$ (= feature to predict). The %green can be discarded, because it provides a redundant data with the information brought by %orange and %red.

3.2. Single models

Two possible approaches can be considered to predict the level of $PM_{2.5}$ from other attributes. The first one is to build a single model for the whole day. Another approach is to consider several successive models, since the human activity and the atmospheric conditions change during the day. This section presents the former method.

A machine-learning algorithm based on a linear regression, as described in Section 2.1, is applied on the dataset. The models are trained and tested according to a 10-fold cross-validation technique. Then, the performance of the models is assessed by two metrics: the correlation coefficient and the root-mean-squared error (RMSE). The correlation coefficient (r) measures the strength of the linear relationship between two or more variables. The advantage of r over the other metrics is to be based on a scale with a maximum (±1) and a minimum (0) to quantify the strength of the relationship. The closer to 1 is the absolute value of r, the better is the correlation. The root-mean-squared error (RMSE) is the square root of the averaged squared error per prediction (MSE). RMSE is an intuitive evaluation metric that is frequently used, because it provides a performance in the same unit as the predicted attribute itself. The lower is the value of RMSE, the more accurate is the model prediction.

3.2.1. Time only

Since the transportation is the main source of pollution in Quito, and this human activity is relatively stereotypic all day long, the simplest approach is to build a predictive model of $PM_{2.5}$ based on time parameters, only. In this case, the number of features is limited to three, which are Xminutes, Yminutes, and $PM_{2.5}$.

The linear regression model obtained after running the algorithm is as follows:

$$PM_{2.5} \quad =$$

$$-2.2242 \quad * \quad \textbf{Xminutes} \quad +$$

$$-1.7366 \quad * \quad \textbf{Yminutes} \quad +$$

$$13.8294$$

The prediction accuracy of the model is evaluated as

$$r \quad = 0.21$$

$$RMSE = 8.76$$

In the present model, the coefficients attributed to both features are negative. It means that the higher are the two temporal attributes, the lower are the concentrations of fine particulate matter. However, the performance of this first model is quite low ($r \approx 0.2$). This is confirmed by the value of the RMSE, which is around nine out of an average level of $PM_{2.5} = 13.8$ $\mu g/m^3$ for the studied period.

3.2.2. Time and traffic

The result of the previous model suggests that it is necessary to consider additional information, such as traffic data, to improve the prediction accuracy of the regression model. To do so, the present analysis takes into account the traffic information provided by Google Maps and processed as described in Section 3.1.1. Thus, the used dataset is composed of five parameters, which are Xminutes, Yminutes, %red, %orange, and $PM_{2.5}$.

The linear regression model obtained after running the algorithm is as follows:

$$PM_{2.5} =$$

$$1.2093 \quad * \quad \text{Xminutes} \quad +$$

$$2.0369 \quad * \quad \text{Yminutes} \quad +$$

$$-23.3875 \quad * \quad \text{\%red} \quad +$$

$$40.6166 \quad * \quad \text{\%orange} \quad +$$

$$7.0578$$

The prediction accuracy of the model is evaluated as

$$r \quad = 0.32$$

$$RMSE = 8.48$$

The model shows that the parameters with the highest weight is %orange. It means that the quantification of the medium amount of traffic is an important feature to estimate the level of $PM_{2.5}$. It is to note that this model, which includes data regarding human activity (i.e., transportation), provides a higher prediction accuracy than a model based on temporal information, only.

3.2.3. Traffic only

One of the main objectives of a machine-learning approach is to produce the most accurate prediction with a model as simple as possible. Since the temporal features seem to have a lower weight than the traffic features, we propose to build a model based on traffic only and assessing its reliability. Here, the number of attributes is three: %orange, %red, and $PM_{2.5}$.

The linear regression model obtained after running the algorithm is as follows:

$$PM_{2.5} =$$

$$-18.8914 \quad * \quad \text{\%red} \quad +$$

$$28.618 \quad * \quad \text{\%orange} \quad +$$

$$9.2185$$

The prediction accuracy of the model is evaluated as

$$R \quad = 0.31$$

$$RMSE = 8.51$$

Again, the model shows that the weight of the %orange parameter is the largest. The higher is the medium amount of traffic, the higher is the level of $PM_{2.5}$. In terms of performance, this model based on two predictive features has an accuracy similar as the previous model with four features ($r \approx 0.3$ in both cases).

3.2.4. Simple regression model

Since the %orange parameter is the attribute with the highest weight, it would be possible to build a predictive model of $PM_{2.5}$ based on a simple regression. The advantage of such a model is its simplicity and the fact that it is visually interpretable from a bidimensional graph (see **Figure 2**). Thus, the used dataset for this analysis has two features, only: %orange and concentrations of $PM_{2.5}$.

The linear regression model obtained after running the algorithm is as follows:

$$PM_{2.5} \quad = $$

$$20.1012 \quad * \quad \%orange \quad +$$

$$9.6609$$

The prediction accuracy of the model is evaluated as

$$r \quad = 0.31$$

$$RMSE = 8.53$$

The simple regression model and **Figure 2** show a growing trend of the level of $PM_{2.5}$ when the %orange parameter increases. This very elementary model (a single predictive feature) allows for a prediction performance quite comparable with the two preceding models ($r \approx 0.3$), which are more complex (four and two predictive features, respectively).

3.2.5. Interpretation of the results

The performance accuracy of the models evaluated by a metric in terms of correlation coefficient and RMSE between traffic and $PM_{2.5}$ is slightly above 0.3 and around 8.5, respectively. The models that consider traffic monitoring provide a higher accuracy than a model based on time only. This result means that traffic is more reliable than time to predict air quality. This difference could be reduced if the weekends (air pollution levels usually low) are excluded, since the traffic is quite stereotypic during the workdays. Also, the accuracy of a model based on traffic monitoring is not significantly improved by adding the time of day, because this information is mostly redundant with the traffic data.

Overall, it seems that Google Maps Traffic can provide a fair information to predict the level of $PM_{2.5}$. From this data source, the number of orange pixels (medium amount of traffic) would be the most relevant feature. It could be explained by the fact that the medium traffic has the largest amplitude of variation all day long, and thus, this is the category that best represents the traffic density in the city. Nevertheless, the accuracy of the model could be improved if we consider an air pollution modeling based on several daily models, defined by the variation of air pollution levels all day long (two peaks a day), instead of a single one.

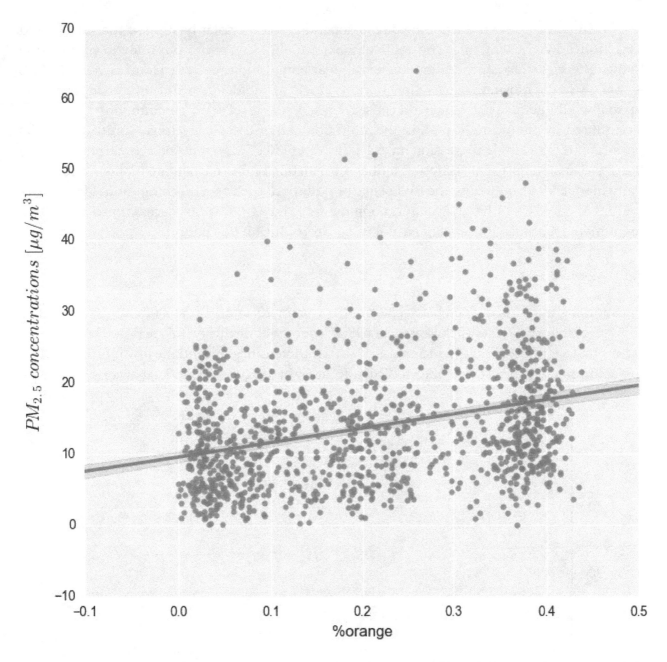

Figure 2. Representation of the value of PM$_{2.5}$ against the ratio of medium traffic (each dot is an observation) and the respective simple linear regression between these two features (line). The higher is the medium amount of traffic (%orange), the larger is the concentration of fine particulate matter (PM$_{2.5}$).

3.3. Multiple models

In the city of Quito as in most of the cities worldwide, there are two peaks of PM$_{2.5}$ pollution during the day. The first peak is in the morning (around 10 am) and the second is in the evening (around 7 pm). **Figure 3** is a graphical representation of the two daily peaks of fine particulate contamination averaged over the last 10 years (2007–2016) for the district of Belisario (These peaks occur approximately at the same time in any district of Quito.) During the morning hours, the rush hour actually lasts longer than the visible PM$_{2.5}$ concentration peak, but a sudden decline can be observed due to the deepening of the planetary boundary layer (PBL). PBL growth during the day is dependent on the solar heating of the surface and thus induced vertical mixing. The depth of maximum PBL can vary from 1 day to another due to the difference in solar radiation intensity, solar angle, and especially cloud cover [14]. PBL is shallow in the morning (up to a few hundred meters) and deepens during the day reaching up to few kilometers [15]. This has a consequence on the level of air contaminants, which are less diluted in the morning than in the afternoon. All of these variations would reduce the performance of a single regression model a day to predict $PM_{2.5}$ from the vehicle emissions in the city. Thus, the present section describes a prediction of fine particulate matters from three daily models determined by the two peaks of pollution, such as a morning model [6–10 h], a midday model [10–14 h], and an afternoon model [14–19 h]. It is not necessary to consider a night model, because the level of air pollution drops during this period.

3.3.1. Morning model

The morning model is defined between 6 am (360th minute) and 10 am (600th minute). **Figure 3** shows that there is a constant increase in the $PM_{2.5}$ concentration during this period. The two main factors that should explain this increase are the traffic intensification and the low morning PBL. If this assumption is correct, then the predictive accuracy of a regression model that considers traffic

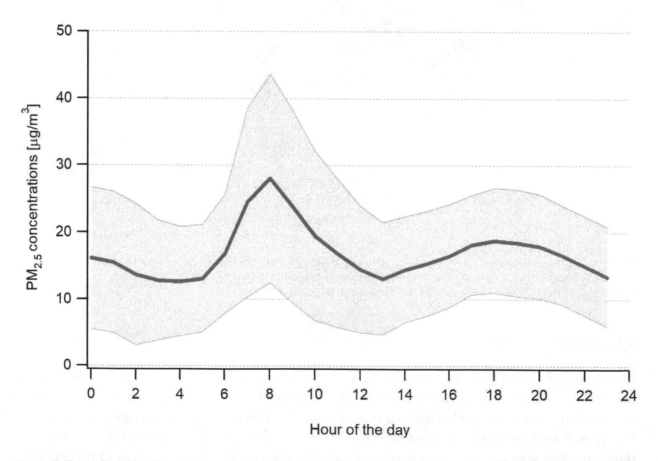

Figure 3. Typical profile of the $PM_{2.5}$ concentrations during the day in the Belisario district of Quito (2007–2016 data). Although, a slight reduction in the level of pollution was observed throughout the years, the air contamination peaks are always located at the same time of day (around 10 am and 7 pm).

data as features should be improved in comparison with the single models. The characteristic of the used dataset is as follows: 110 instances and 4 features (minutes, %red, %orange, and $PM_{2.5}$).

The linear regression model obtained after running the algorithm is as follows:

$PM_{2.5}$ =

0.0444 * minutes +

−123.0175 * %red +

89.1856 * %orange +

−15.4187

The prediction accuracy of the model is evaluated as

r = 0.49

RMSE = 10.13

As observed in the single model approach, the weights of the traffic attributes are significantly larger than the coefficient of time. The most representative feature, which is %orange, shows that the higher is the medium amount of traffic, the higher is the value of $PM_{2.5}$. In terms of performance, the prediction accuracy is around 0.5, for the correlation coefficient, and around 10 out of an average value of $PM_{2.5}$ = 17.4 µg/m³, for the RMSE. As hypothesized, this limited analysis on a morning window provides a regression model more accurate than the models based on the full day.

3.3.2. Midday model

The midday model is defined between 10 am (600th minute) and 2 pm (840th minute). **Figure 3** shows that there is a constant decrease in the $PM_{2.5}$ concentration during this period. The two main factors that should explain this drop are the traffic diminution and the elevation of the PBL that increases the dilution of air contaminants. In such a situation, the correlation between traffic and $PM_{2.5}$ should decrease. Here, the regression algorithm is applied on a dataset composed of 116 instances and 4 features (minutes, %red, %orange, and $PM_{2.5}$).

The linear regression model obtained after running the algorithm is as follows:

$PM_{2.5}$ =

−0.0354 * minutes +

−68.1378 * %red +

55.4262 * %orange +

35.2107

The prediction accuracy of the model is evaluated as

r = 0.29

RMSE = 10.36

The coefficients of the resulting model are lower than in the morning model, for all the features. It suggests that the weight of the traffic data to predict $PM_{2.5}$ is less important at midday than in the morning, as hypothesized. It is confirmed by the performance evaluation of the model, which is similar as the accuracy obtained from the single models ($r \approx 0.3$).

3.3.3. Afternoon model

The afternoon model is defined between 2 pm (840th minute) and 7 pm (1140th minute). **Figure 3** shows that there is a constant increase in the $PM_{2.5}$ concentration, although the evening peak is lower than the morning peak due to the fact that the PBL has reached its peak and is not changing at this time of day, until a nocturnal boundary layer starts forming due to the absence of surface heating. Besides the elevated PBL, the air pollution increases because of the traffic growth at the end of the day. Again, the important dilution of pollutants in the atmosphere should reduce the correlation between traffic and $PM_{2.5}$ concentrations. The used dataset to build the model is as follows: 145 instances and 4 features (minutes, %red, %orange, and $PM_{2.5}$).

The linear regression model obtained after running the algorithm is as follows:

$PM_{2.5}$ =

0.0242 * minutes +

20.7938 * %orange +

−14.6845

The prediction accuracy of the model is evaluated as

r = 0.28

RMSE = 7.65

The feature with the maximum weight in the afternoon model is still %orange, although its value continues to decrease. The time coefficient is extremely low, and %red is filtered by the M5 attribute selection method. As expected, the model accuracy assessed by the correlation coefficient is relatively low ($r \approx 0.3$). It means that the traffic input is not a good predictor to estimate the level of $PM_{2.5}$ in the afternoon. The important dilution of the air contaminants in the atmosphere would explain this result. Surprisingly, the RMSE (<8) is lower than in the two previous models (>10). This reduced error of prediction can be explained by the lower standard deviation (SD) of the $PM_{2.5}$ values in the afternoon (SD = 8) than in the morning (SD = 11.6) and midday (SD = 10.8). In other words, the better power of prediction is not due to the reliability of the model per se (essentially based on the traffic), but due to the limited variation in the $PM_{2.5}$ concentrations in the afternoon.

3.3.4. Interpretation of the results

There is a significant improvement in the prediction of $PM_{2.5}$ in the morning ($r \approx 0.5$). The performance can be explained by the fact that the PBL is relatively low in the morning. Thus, the pollution dilution is reduced and consequently the level of $PM_{2.5}$ becomes strongly correlated with the pollution produced by the vehicles. The higher is the traffic activity, the higher is the concentration of fine particulate matter (see the high weight of the %orange parameter).

For the two other models, the accuracy is around the same value as a global model ($r \approx 0.3$). Their predictive performance seems reduced, because the depth of the PBL increases with the augmentation of the solar radiation (maximal around noon). The poor power of prediction of these two models would be caused by the reduction of the influence of the traffic on the level of $PM_{2.5}$, since the weight of the %orange parameter drops at midday and afternoon.

Nevertheless, the average performance of an approach based on three models per day provides an accuracy slightly better than the single model (see Eq. (8)). It suggests that the best prediction of $PM_{2.5}$ from the traffic monitoring is obtained by analyzing the typical daily fluctuation of $PM_{2.5}$ concentration and applying a specific model according to the occurrence of the pollution peaks, especially in the morning.

$$\bar{r} = \frac{0.49 + 0.29 + 0.28}{3} = 0.35 \tag{8}$$

This performance could be further improved by analyzing a reduced image of the traffic map that closely matches the footprint of $PM_{2.5}$ concentrations measured by the monitoring station. In this study, the used picture represents an area of 22.4 km^2 and the footprint area for Belisario station (monitoring station height 10 m) would be around 3 km^2, only [16]. However, we chose a bigger traffic map area to have a more representative traffic situation of the city.

4. Adding meteorological factors

The ambient air pollution levels are mainly modulated by meteorological conditions [9, 17]. Consequently, considering these parameters in a model should improve the prediction of the concentration of fine particulate matter. Since the required equipment to proceed with the recording of these data is significantly cheaper than the air quality sensors, we present models that can predict the level of $PM_{2.5}$ from the selected meteorological features as follows: solar radiation (SR), temperature (T), pressure (P), precipitation (rain), relative humidity (RH), wind speed (WS), and wind direction (WD).

4.1. Dataset

4.1.1. Data acquisition

Seven meteorological parameters (wind speed and direction, temperature, relative humidity, atmospheric pressure, precipitation, and solar radiation) were measured using Vaisala WXT536 instrumentation, with an exception of Kipp&Zonnen netradiometer to measure solar radiation. To get the hourly value of SR, T, P, rain, RH, and WS, we simply have to calculate the average value from the six records per hour of the used dataset (one record each 10 minutes).

However, the calculation of the WD is a bit more complex. It is not possible to compute the mean direction per hour, because it can provide a completely wrong result. For instance, if the wind angle is four times around the east (90°) and the two other times is around the west (270°), the mean WD will be the south-southeast (150°), even if the wind never originated in that direction. To tackle this issue, the calculation of the most representative WD for each hour is carried out through the process as follows:

- Sampling of the WD to transform continuous values into discrete values.

- Fit a normal distribution to the data.

- Take the mean of the Gaussian as the hourly WD.

Figure 4 represents an example regarding the approach the WD is obtained.

4.1.2. Data transformation

Another data preparation is required before running the machine-learning algorithms. The polar coordinates of the WD (0–360°) are transformed into Cartesian coordinates, by consider-

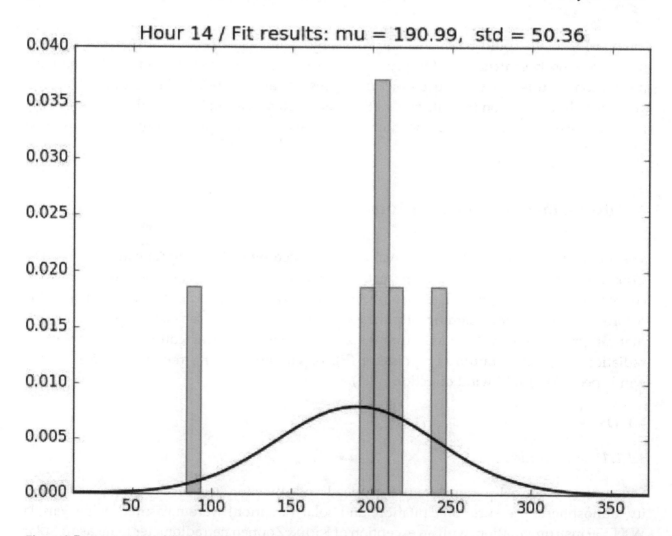

Figure 4. Representation of the calculation of the WD for a specific hour. The graphic indicates the WD angles, in degrees (x-axis), and their respective ratio of occurrences (y-axis). The black curve represents the normal distribution that fits the data. Here, the value of the hourly WD is mu ≈ 191°.

ing both WD and WS in a same formula (see Eqs. (9) and (10)). This mathematical transformation permits a more accurate feature representation of the data with respect to the WD around the north axis. Otherwise, it would be impossible to find a correlation between WD and PM$_{2.5}$, since some similar WD pointing north could have completely different values (slightly higher than 0° or slightly lower than 360°) according to the polar coordinates. This transformation is particularly relevant for machine-learning algorithms based on linear regression, because this modeling relies on a continuous relationship between parameters [9].

$$Xwind = \cos\left(\frac{WD \cdot \pi}{180°}\right) \cdot WS \qquad (9)$$

$$Ywind = \sin\left(\frac{WD \cdot \pi}{180°}\right) \cdot WS \qquad (10)$$

Thus, the final dataset is composed of 13 features, which are Xminutes, Yminutes, %orange, %red, SR, T, P, rain, RH, WS, Xwind, Ywind, and PM$_{2.5}$ (= feature to predict).

4.2. Single models

Two models are proposed. The first one is based on a multiple regression algorithm as described in Section 2.1. The second one implements a model tree that allows for a larger flexibility (but also complexity) than a linear regression for modeling the data.

4.2.1. Multiple regression model

The linear regression model obtained after running the algorithm is as follows:

PM$_{2.5}$ =

2.199	*	Yminutes	+
−18.0966	*	%red	+
39.7399	*	%orange	+
0.2636	*	RH	+
1.0088	*	pressure	+
0.8186	*	temperature	+
1.3403	*	Xwind	+
−753.8078			

The prediction accuracy of the model is evaluated as

r   = 0.58

RMSE = 7.32

The result shows that the regression model considers all the three classes of parameters (time, traffic, and weather) to predict the value of PM$_{2.5}$. Nevertheless, in terms of meteorological

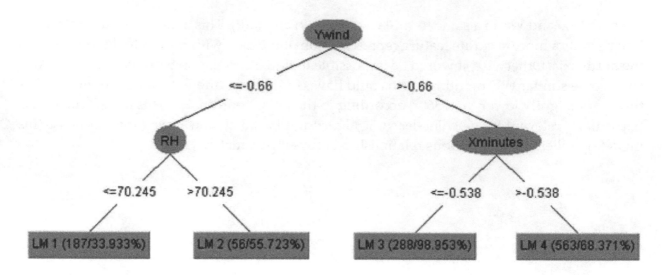

Figure 5. Graphical representation of the model tree and its respective decision rules to invoke the best regression models (LM 1–4) to predict the value of $PM_{2.5}$.

factors, the solar radiation and the precipitation are filtered by the M5 method (see Section 2.1 for more details). The rain attribute is certainly removed, since it occurs only 71 times, which represents 6.4% of the total instances. The SR is also excluded from the model, because it is an attribute mostly redundant with some of the other meteorological factors, and the filtering method is essentially based on an elimination of the redundant information. As hypothesized, including the weather conditions in the model allows for a significant improvement of the prediction accuracy. The value of correlation coefficient is almost twice higher than a model that does not consider meteorological data.

4.2.2. Regression model tree

A model tree is a more complex and flexible modeling of the data, since it is composed of several rules and each of these rules are associated with a regression model [18]. In other words, in such a tree representation, there is a different linear regression model at the leaves to predict the response of the instances that reach the leaf. In the present modeling, we use a pruned tree, in which the minimum number of instances allowed at a leaf node is nine.

Figure 5 represents the resulting model tree. It is composed of four rules as follows:

1: if Ywind ≤ −0.66 and RH ≤ 70.245

      model = LM 1

2: else if Ywind ≤ −0.66 and RH > 70.245

      model = LM 2

3: else if Ywind > −0.66 and Xminutes ≤ −0.538

      model = LM 3

4: else if Ywind > −0.66 and Xminutes > −0.538

      model = LM 4

The linear regression models associated to each rule are:

- LM 1

    $PM_{2.5}$ =

3.3209	*	Xminutes	+
0.1278	*	Yminutes	+
−1.0521	*	%red	+
22.0077	*	%orange	+
0.1359	*	RH	+
0.0587	*	pressure	+
0.0101	*	SR	+
−0.3479	*	temperature	+
0.8434	*	Xwind	+
−41.7637			

- LM 2

    $PM_{2.5}$ =

0.5269	*	Xminutes	+
0.1278	*	Yminutes	+
−1.0521	*	%red	+
6.595	*	%orange	+
0.3362	*	RH	+
0.0587	*	pressure	+
−0.0346	*	SR	+
1.5505	*	temperature	+
0.2383	*	Xwind	+
−72.0163			

- LM 3

    $PM_{2.5}$ =

−0.0904	*	Xminutes	+
10.1893	*	Yminutes	+

$$
\begin{array}{rcll}
-41.9183 & * & \%red & + \\
51.2883 & * & \%orange & + \\
0.3139 & * & RH & + \\
1.6439 & * & pressure & + \\
-0.0056 & * & SR & + \\
1.7683 & * & temperature & + \\
2.2056 & * & WS & + \\
3.1792 & * & Xwind & + \\
-0.0401 & * & Ywind & + \\
-1233.2713 & & &
\end{array}
$$

- LM 4

$$PM_{2.5} =$$

$$
\begin{array}{rcll}
-0.0474 & * & Xminutes & + \\
-2.2031 & * & Yminutes & + \\
8.5034 & * & \%red & + \\
14.6847 & * & \%orange & + \\
0.2603 & * & RH & + \\
-0.9338 & * & pressure & + \\
-0.0001 & * & SR & + \\
0.048 & * & temperature & + \\
0.6414 & * & WS & + \\
0.3914 & * & Xwind & + \\
-1.3052 & * & Ywind & + \\
669.5642 & & &
\end{array}
$$

The prediction accuracy of the model is evaluated as

$$r \quad = 0.63$$

$$RMSE = 6.95$$

The root node of the tree is Ywind. It means that wind direction and wind speed are the fundamental factors to proceed with the selection of one or another regression model. Then, the second level of discrimination is based on two other important parameters, which are relative humidity and Xminutes. The regression models that depend on the RH threshold (nine features) are slightly simpler than the models that depend on the Xminutes threshold (11 features). To note that when the tree algorithm is applied, the SR is included in the model, even though its weight is quite low. As expected, the model tree (four rules and an average of 10 features per rule) is more complex than the linear regression model (seven features). Nevertheless, the model tree is still easy to interpret and provides a prediction performance slightly better than the linear regression (+0.05 for the correlation coefficient of the tree).

4.2.3. Interpretation of the results

This analysis shows that including meteorological factors as model inputs improves the prediction accuracy of $PM_{2.5}$ concentrations (r = 0.58). The performance is slightly improved by applying a model tree, which is composed of four linear regressions (r = 0.63).

Thus, the results suggest that the use of a quite affordable meteorological station enables us to significantly improve the prediction of the concentration of fine particulate matter (The correlation coefficient is twice higher than with the traffic monitoring only.) All the meteorological factors are relevant for the prediction, except the precipitation accumulation. Rain seems to be excluded from the model, because it is a very rare event.

Next, it is studied if a multiple model approach, based on three models a day, could improve the prediction accuracy.

4.3. Multiple models

The same division of the dataset into three periods as in Section 3.3 is carried out. Since the day is analyzed into three independent parts, the dataset can be reduced to 12 features: minutes, %orange, %red, SR, T, P, rain, RH, WS, Xwind, Ywind, and $PM_{2.5}$ (= feature to predict). The three datasets are composed of 110, 116, and 145 instances for the morning, midday, and afternoon models, respectively.

4.3.1. Morning model

The linear regression model obtained after running the algorithm is as follows:

$$PM_{2.5} =$$

$$0.0513 \quad * \quad minutes +$$

$$41.7958 \quad * \quad \%orange \quad +$$

$$-0.23 \quad * \quad RH \quad +$$

$$-2.8397 \quad * \quad temperature \quad +$$

$$2.5325 \quad * \quad Xwind \quad +$$

$$8.5432 \quad * \quad \text{Ywind} \quad +$$

$$38.6386$$

The prediction accuracy of the model is evaluated as

$$r \quad = 0.58$$

$$\text{RMSE} = 9.56$$

The model presents six features, only. It means that many attributes are filtered, especially in terms of meteorological factors (SR, pressure, rain, and WS are removed). It can be explained by the fact that the prediction of the level of $PM_{2.5}$ in the morning would be mainly correlated with the density of the traffic (see Section 3.3). However, the morning model does not seem to be significantly different than the single multiple regression neither in terms of features (five identical attributes) nor in terms of performance (r = 0.58 in both cases).

4.3.2. Midday model

The linear regression model obtained after running the algorithm is as follows:

$$PM_{2.5} \quad =$$

$$-0.0636 \quad * \quad \text{minutes} +$$

$$28.7942 \quad * \quad \%\text{orange} \quad +$$

$$0.4791 \quad * \quad \text{RH} \quad +$$

$$-10.0519 \quad * \quad \text{rain} \quad +$$

$$-0.0141 \quad * \quad \text{SR} \quad +$$

$$2.5065 \quad * \quad \text{temperature} \quad +$$

$$3.8358 \quad * \quad \text{Xwind} \quad +$$

$$-2.4909$$

The prediction accuracy of the model is evaluated as

$$r \quad = 0.56$$

$$\text{RMSE} = 9.13$$

The model is still composed of the same nucleus of features: minutes, %orange, RH, temperature, and wind. The only new parameter that appears as predictive feature is the precipitations. It can be explained by the fact that the rain events usually occur in Quito at midday. This factor has a negative coefficient, because the precipitation has a cleaning effect on the concentration of fine particulate matter [19]. The performance of the model is maintained at a constant accuracy (r = 0.56).

4.3.3. Afternoon model

The linear regression model obtained after running the algorithm is as follows:

$PM_{2.5}$ =

−0.02	*	minutes	+
28.0895	*	%red	+
0.4498	*	RH	+
−2.7491	*	pressure	+

−2002.1108

The prediction accuracy of the model is evaluated as

r   = 0.56

RMSE = 6.61

This model is simpler (only four features) and does not consider exactly the same attributes than the two previous models (Pressure is used, and %red is preferred to %orange.) In Section 3.3.3, differences were already noted in the afternoon model with respect to the morning and midday. The explanation seemed to be related to the difficulty to get a reliable predictive model of $PM_{2.5}$ when the particulates are strongly diluted in the atmosphere. In such a situation, the fair performance of the model (r = 0.56; RMSE = 6.61) would be more caused by the reduced fluctuation of the $PM_{2.5}$ values (**Figure 3** shows a maximum peak at around 20 µg/m³, against 30 µg/m³ in the morning) than the reliability of the prediction per se.

4.3.4. Interpretation of the results

Eq. (11) presents the average prediction accuracy by modeling the air pollution through the three daily models.

$$\bar{r} = \frac{0.58 + 0.56 + 0.56}{3} = 0.57 \tag{11}$$

Although the morning model is slightly more accurate than the two other ones, the mean value of the regression coefficient is not better than the regression coefficient of the single model, especially if this model is obtained by a model tree algorithm.

Thus, when meteorological factors are taken into account, it does not seem to be advantageous to consider three regression models per day. It can be explained by the fact that the weather conditions have a very strong effect on the levels of $PM_{2.5}$ (e.g., rain and wind tend to clean the atmosphere). Thus, including these factors as model features reduces the mere influence of the traffic on the value of $PM_{2.5}$. And since the impact of this human activity is more significant in the morning than in the rest of the day, because of the low dilution of the vehicle emissions in the atmosphere, adding meteorological parameters in the model decreases the performance differences between the three daily models.

5. Adding trace gas concentrations

This part intends to verify the prediction accuracy of the methods as described in the previous sections. To do so, the precision of the prediction based on low-cost data collection is compared with a pollution monitoring that makes use of costlier technologies (i.e., EPA-approved chemical sensors). Then, a hybrid model is proposed from a selection of the most relevant features to minimize the prediction error.

5.1. Prediction from chemical monitoring

The concentrations of $PM_{2.5}$ are commonly correlated with other air pollutants, such as SO_2, NO_2, CO, etc. [20]. However, the monitoring of these substances involves a more specialized equipment than traffic or weather monitoring. The performance of the models built in this section is used as referential to assess the quality of the previous models and investigates if a selection of the most affordable chemical records can significantly improve the overall prediction accuracy. Four additional criteria pollutants were measured (CO, NO_2, SO_2, and O_3). For SO_2 concentrations, ThermoFisher Scientific 43i high-level SO_2 analyzer was used based on ultraviolet florescence (EPA No. EQSA-0486-060). For O_3 concentration data collection, ThermoFisher Scientific 49i ozone analyzer was used based on ultraviolet absorption (EPA No. EQOA-0880-047). For NOx concentration data collection, ThermoFisher Scientific 42i NOx analyzer was used based on chemiluminescence method (EPA No. RFNA-1289-074). Finally, for CO concentration data collection, ThermoFisher Scientific 48i was used based on infrared absorption (EPA No. RFCA-0981-054). The used dataset is composed of 1118 observations and 5 features: CO, NO_2, O_3, SO_2, and $PM_{2.5}$ (= feature to predict).

The prediction accuracy of the model is evaluated as

$$r = 0.75$$

$$RMSE = 5.89$$

The evaluation of this model demonstrates that only the chemical factors are very high predictors of the level of fine particulate matter. A model built with these parameters provides a significantly lower RMSE and higher r than the traffic and meteorology based models. This outcome was expected as the levels of anthropogenic $PM_{2.5}$ that are directly related to the emission of other air pollutants, such as a number of different contaminants that come from the same sources. It can be concluded from this analysis that selecting some low-cost chemical recordings should improve the prediction accuracy of the affordable models.

5.2. Prediction from full data sources

This section explores the possibility to get a better prediction of air pollution if we build a hybrid model that uses a combination of the whole data sources mentioned previously. The objective is to define the best predictive model to estimate the concentration of $PM_{2.5}$ from all the available types of data.

5.2.1. Single model

The full dataset is used for this analysis. There is a total number of 17 features, which are Xminutes, Yminutes, %red, %orange, relative humidity, precipitation, pressure, solar radiation, temperature, wind Speed, Xwind, Ywind, CO, NO_2, O_3, SO_2, $PM_{2.5}$ (= feature to predict).

The linear regression model obtained after running the algorithm is as follows:

$PM_{2.5}$ =

1.4412	*	Yminutes	+
0.2212	*	RH	+
−0.0035	*	SR	+
0.9367	*	temperature	+
1.2377	*	WS	+
0.7501	*	Xwind	+
0.3971	*	Ywind	+
0.2691	*	NO_2	+
0.1878	*	O_3	+
1.0463	*	SO_2	+
8.3473	*	CO	+
−30.8553			

The prediction accuracy of the model is evaluated as

r = 0.81

RMSE = 5.31

The results show that the regressive model considers three classes of parameters (time, meteorology, and criteria pollutants) out of four to predict the value of $PM_{2.5}$. Traffic information is filtered, certainly because of its redundancy with time. After attribute selection (M5 method), the final model is composed of 11 features out of 16. As hypothesized, a model based on a hybrid data source allows for a significant improvement of the prediction accuracy. The values of the correlation coefficient and the RMSE are better for the hybrid than the chemical model.

5.2.2. Multiple models

5.2.2.1. Morning model

The linear regression model obtained after running the algorithm is as follows:

$PM_{2.5}$ =

0.0379	*	minutes	+
0.3438	*	RH	+
−1.7248	*	pressure	+
−0.6846	*	temperature	+
4.5902	*	CO	+
0.4294	*	NO_2	+
2.0133	*	SO_2	+
0.6343	*	O_3	+
1209.4494			

The prediction accuracy of the model is evaluated as

r   = 0.85

RMSE = 6.04

5.2.2.2. Midday model

The linear regression model obtained after running the algorithm is as follows:

$PM_{2.5}$ =

−0.0362	*	minutes	+
−1.1911	*	pressure	+
−0.0122	*	SR	+
2.3857	*	temperature	+
1.4346	*	Ywind	+
0.2274	*	RH	+
14.8788	*	CO	+

0.3632	*	NO_2	+
0.796	*	SO_2	+
0.2348	*	O_3	+
835.1936			

The prediction accuracy of the model is evaluated as

$$r = 0.87$$

$$RMSE = 5.33$$

5.2.2.3. Afternoon model

The linear regression model obtained after running the algorithm is as follows:

$$PM_{2.5} =$$

21.026	*	%red	+
−14.9417	*	%orange	+
0.3291	*	RH	+
0.8285	*	temperature	+
1.2914	*	WS	+
−1.1325	*	pressure	+
−0.0109	*	SR	+
0.3909	*	NO_2	+
0.6993	*	SO_2	+
0.2503	*	O_3	+
790.3383			

The prediction accuracy of the model is evaluated as

$$r = 0.66$$

$$RMSE = 6.29$$

5.2.2.4. Interpretation of the results

The results of the Eq. (12) shows that the average prediction accuracy (evaluated by the regression coefficient metrics) by modeling the air pollution through three models is

$$\bar{r} = \frac{0.85 + 0.87 + 0.66}{3} = 0.79 \tag{12}$$

Thus, it seems that using several models with all the available features for the prediction of fine particulate matter is only justified to predict the level of $PM_{2.5}$ from 6 am to 2 pm ($r \approx 0.86$). After this period, the model gets more complex and less reliable. This result confirms the previous analyses that tend to demonstrate that the model accuracy to estimate $PM_{2.5}$ concentrations from traffic, meteorology, and air pollutants is stronger when the gases and particulates are less diluted in the atmosphere.

6. Simplification and recommendations

6.1. The simplest best model

Since the full feature model (Section 5.2) is quite complex, the present stage consists of removing insignificant and/or redundant features in order to optimize the modeling. The goal is to find a simple model that is still able to provide a reliable estimation of $PM_{2.5}$ concentrations. The simplest best model is defined as a model that maintains a high accuracy ($r \geq 0.8$) with a maximum number of features equal to eight. The method used to get this model is the ranker search method. This technique sorts the attributes according to their evaluation and allows for a specification of the number of attributes to retain.

The linear regression model obtained after running the algorithm is as follows:

$$PM_{2.5} =$$

0.2032	*	RH	+
0.6507	*	temperature	+
−0.0021	*	SR	+
0.4549	*	Xwind	+
0.225	*	NO_2	+
0.2159	*	O_3	+
1.0707	*	SO_2	+
8.8163	*	CO	+

−23.9476

The prediction accuracy of the model is evaluated as

$r = 0.8$

$RMSE = 5.34$

Table 1 represents the ranked attributes, in which the features are sorted in the descending order of their individual performance to predict the output value.

Ranking	Performance	Feature
1	0.0311	SO_2
2	0.0256	CO
3	0.0193	Relative humidity
4	0.0172	NO_2
5	0.0133	O_3
6	0.0125	Solar radiation
7	0.0109	Xwind
8	0.0065	Temperature

Table 1. Ranked attributes.

The simplest best model is composed of the whole chemical parameters and a selection of meteorological factors (RH, SR, Xwind, and T). As suggested by the previous analyses, the individual performance to accurately estimate the values of $PM_{2.5}$ is globally higher for the chemical (first, second, fourth, and fifth positions) than the meteorological features (third, sixth, seventh, and eighth positions). In other words, $PM_{2.5}$ are firstly correlated with the emission of chemical substances (especially SO_2 and CO) and secondly with the weather conditions (especially relative humidity and solar radiation). It is to note the negative correlation between the value of SR and the concentration of $PM_{2.5}$. This result can be explained by the fact that the larger is the SR, the deeper is PBL, and consequently, the bigger is the dilution of fine particulate matter in the boundary layer. The other factors are positively correlated with $PM_{2.5}$. Besides its simplicity (eight features only), the model is able to predict the level of fine particulate matter with the same accuracy than a model using all the features ($r = 0.8$ and RMSE = 5.3, in both cases).

6.2. Recommendations based on model performances

The final objective of this study is to find the best predictive model that uses the less costly data recording of relevant features. As previously mentioned, the accurate measurement of trace gases requires expensive equipment. Thus, the best affordable model can be defined as the model that gets the best performance with no more than two trace gases. The model performances with the whole affordable attributes and only one or two trace gases are presented in **Table 2**. The model accuracy is assessed according to the value of r. The main diagonal represents the performance by considering a single trace gas, whereas the other cells take into account two gases.

The results show that it is still possible to build a model with high prediction accuracy with two trace gases, only. The best performance is obtained by considering SO_2 and NO_2 ($r = 0.78$). It can be explained by the fact that these two trace gases are strongly correlated with the values of $PM_{2.5}$ (see **Table 1**). In the case that only one trace gas sensor is affordable, it has to be a device that measures the levels of CO or NO_2 ($r = 0.73$). It is to note that O_3 is a gas that can

	SO_2	CO	NO_2	O_3
SO_2	0.7			
CO	0.77	0.73		
NO_2	0.78	0.76	0.73	
O_3	0.7	0.75	0.73	0.58

Table 2. Model performance (r value) with all the affordable attributes (e.g., time, traffic, and meteorology) and only one (main diagonal) or two (other cells) trace gases.

be automatically discarded, since its power of prediction is the lowest (Section 4 shows that models without O_3 get a better r). This finding could be expected as there is no direct relationship between the level of O_3 (a secondary pollutant) and the concentrations of $PM_{2.5}$.

7. Conclusions and perspectives

This study demonstrates that the $PM_{2.5}$ prediction performance depends on the available input information. The first finding shows that it is possible to get a reasonable prediction of $PM_{2.5}$ concentrations only using public access traffic data. Ambient $PM_{2.5}$ pollution prediction based on traffic can be significantly improved by using three models a day instead of a single one, especially for the morning hours. During the morning rush hour, planetary boundary layer is shallow, resulting in a continuous traffic emission buildup showing a cumulative growth of $PM_{2.5}$ concentrations. The latter start decreasing with the dilution effect of the PBL deepening, due to surface heating, increase in temperatures and ventilating wind effect. Thus, using an affordable meteorological station data further improves the prediction accuracy. In this case, a regression model tree gives a better prediction than a linear regression model. As expected, the best model is obtained by including a hybrid data sources as features (time, traffic, meteorological, and the concentrations of atmospheric criteria pollutants). The complexity of the resulting model can be reduced from seventeen to eight most relevant features without reducing the performance (r ≈ 0.8, and RMSE ≈ 5.3). These eight selected attributes are composed of criteria pollutants (CO, NO_2, O_3, SO_2) and meteorological factors (humidity, solar radiation, temperature, wind speed, and direction). Thus, our results suggest to proceed with a selection of chemical sensors based on the best ratio prediction/cost. For example, if only one trace gas sensor is affordable, the best performance can be reached with CO or NO_2 concentrations, while the use of two trace gases (SO_2 and NO_2) are sufficient to get very close to the best possible accuracy. In contrast, O_3 is a secondary pollutant that can be excluded from the models with no significant consequences on the prediction of $PM_{2.5}$, suggesting a low impact of photochemical component in $PM_{2.5}$ formation.

The proposed approach is easily generalizable to other cities worldwide. A storage and regression analysis of 2-month data were sufficient to build models that are able to predict fine particulate matter with high accuracy. The main limitation of the present method is to predict $PM_{2.5}$ when the PBL is deep. Nevertheless, it is often less of an issue in terms of air quality since an elevated PBL enhances dilution and, consequently, reduces the concentration of atmospheric contaminants. Further work will focus on improving the model performance at evening rush hours. More refined models are expected to be obtained by including additional observations and features into the dataset. For example, some additional studies are anticipated to investigate the impact of PBL depth on the dilution of the $PM_{2.5}$ pollution.

Furthermore, it is motivating to investigate the current model performance with the data acquired by the lower tier equipment. In this study, the air pollution and meteorology were measured with USEPA-approved equipment, not affordable to a large fraction of cities in the developing countries, thus limiting air pollution studies and awareness to the main cities. It has been shown, however, that small cities are often more polluted than the big agglomerations, presenting the necessity for a wide set of options to promote the consciousness of the air quality [21].

Author details

Yves Rybarczyk[1,2]* and Rasa Zalakeviciute[1]

*Address all correspondence to: y.rybarczyk@fct.unl.pt

1 Intelligent & Interactive Systems Lab (SI^2 Lab), Universidad de Las Américas, Quito, Ecuador

2 Department of Electrical Engineering – CTS/UNINOVA, Nova University of Lisbon, Monte de Caparica, Portugal

References

[1] United Nations, Department of Economic and Social Affairs, Population Division. World Population Prospects: The 2015 Revision, Key Findings and Advance Tables. 2015. Working Paper No. ESA/P/WP.241. Retrieved from: https://esa.un.org/unpd/wpp/publications/files/key_findings_wpp_2015.pdf

[2] World Health Organization, Media Centre. Air pollution levels rising in many of the world's poorest cities [Internet]. 2016. Available from: http://www.who.int/mediacentre/news/releases/2016/air-pollution-rising/

[3] UNEP. Status of Fuel Quality and Vehicle Emission Standards Latin America [Internet]. 2016. Available from: http://www.unep.org/urban_environment/Issues/urban_air. [Accessed: 22 October 2016]

[4] Lelieveld J, Evans JS, Fnais M, Giannadaki D, Pozzer A. The contribution of outdoor air pollution sources to premature mortality on a global scale. Nature. 2015;**525**(7569): 367-371

[5] Karagulian F, Belis CA, Dora CFC, Prüss-Ustün AM, Bonjour S, Adair-Rohani H, Amann M. Contributions to cities' ambient particulate matter (PM): A systematic review of local source contributions at global level. Atmospheric Environment. 2015;**120**:475-483

[6] Castell N, Dauge FR, Schneider P, Vogt M, Lerner U, Fishbain B, Broday D, Bartonova A. Can commercial low-cost sensor platforms contribute to air quality monitoring and exposure estimates? Environment International. 2017;**99**:293-302

[7] Borrego C, Costa AM, Ginja J, Amorim M, Coutinho M, Karatzas K, Sioumis T, Katsifarakis N, Konstantinidis K, De Vito S, Esposito E, Smith P, André N, Gérard P, Francis LA, Castell N, Schneider P, Viana M, Minguillón MC, Reimringer W, Otjes RP, von Sicard O, Pohle R, Elen B, Suriano D, Pfister V, Prato M, Dipinto S, Penza M Assessment of air quality microsensors versus reference methods: The EuNetAir joint exercise. Atmospheric Environment. 2016;**147**:246-263.

[8] USEPA. Evaluation of emerging air pollution sensor performance. 2017. Available from: https://www.epa.gov/air-sensor-toolbox/evaluation-emerging-air-pollution-sensor-performance. [Accessed: 28 August 2017]

[9] Kleine Deters J, Zalakeviciute R, Gonzalez M, Rybarczyk Y. Modeling PM2.5 urban-pollution using machine learning and selected meteorological parameters. Journal of Electrical and Computer Engineering. 2017. 14 pages. Article ID 5106045. DOI: 10.1155/2017/5106045

[10] Brokamp C, Jandarov R, Rao MB, LeMasters G, Ryan P. Exposure assessment models for elemental components of particulate matter in an urban environment: A comparison of regression and random forest approaches. Atmospheric Environment. 2017;**151**:1-11

[11] Quinlan RJ. Learning with continuous classes. In: Proceedings of the 5th Australian Joint Conference on Artificial Intelligence. Singapore; 1992. pp.343-348. Retrieved from: http://citeseerx.ist.psu.edu/viewdoc/download?doi=10.1.1.34.885&rep=rep1&type=pdf

[12] Rybarczyk Y. 3D markerless motion capture: A low-cost approach. In: Rocha A, Correia AM, Adeli H, Reis LP, Teixeira MM, editors. New Advanced in Information Systems and Technologies; Recife, Brazil. Switzerland: Springer; 2016. pp. 731-738. DOI: 10.1007/978-3-319-31232-3

[13] Mierswa I, Wurst M, Klinkenberg R, Scholz M, T. Yale E. Rapid prototyping for complex data mining tasks. In: Proceedings of the 12th ACM SIGKDD International Conference on Knowledge Discovery and Data Mining. Philadelphia: USA; 2006; pp. 935-940. Retrieved from: https://pdfs.semanticscholar.org/5722/e63d03edba571262ba258fe5aaffed4147c9.pdf

[14] Stull RB. An Introduction to Boundary Layer Meteorology. Boston, Massachusetts: 13Kluwer Academic Publishers; 1988.

[15] Cazorla M. Air quality over a populated Andean region: Insights from measurements of ozone, NO, and boundary layer depths. Atmospheric Pollution Research. 2016;**7**:66-74

[16] Hsieh CI, Katul G, Chi TW. An approximate analytical model for footprint estimation of scalar fluxes in thermally stratified atmospheric flows. Advances in Water Resources. 2000;**23**:765-772

[17] Rybarczyk Y, Zalakeviciute R. Machine learning approach to forecasting urban pollution: A case study of Quito, Ecuador. In: Ecuador Technical Chapters Meeting (ETCM). Guayaquil, Ecuador: IEEE; 12-14 Oct. 2016, 2016. DOI: 10.1109/ETCM.2016.7750810

[18] Wang Y, Witten I H. Induction of model trees for predicting continuous classes. In: van Someren M, Widmer G, editors. Proceedings of the 9th European Conference on Machine Learning; April 1997. Prague, Czech Republic. Springer; 1997

[19] Li Y, Chen Q, Zhao H, Wang L, Tao R. Variations in PM10, PM2.5 and PM1.0 in an urban area of the Sichuan basin and their relation to meteorological factors. Atmosphere. 2015;**6**:150-163

[20] Ni X, Huang H, Du W. Relevance analysis and short-term prediction of PM2.5 concentrations in Beijing based on multi-source data. Atmospheric Environment. 2017;**150**:146-161

[21] Zalakeviciute R, Rybarczyk Y, López-Villada J, Diaz Suarez M. Quantifying decade-long effects of fuel and traffic regulations on urban ambient PM 2.5 pollution in a mid-size south American city. Atmospheric Pollution Research. 2017. DOI: 10.1016/j.apr.2017.07.001

7

Multiple Kernel-Based Multimedia Fusion for Automated Event Detection from Tweets

Suhuai Luo, Samar M. Alqhtani and Jiaming Li

Abstract

A method for detecting hot events such as wildfires is proposed. It uses visual and textual information to improve detection. Starting with picking up tweets having texts and images, it preprocesses the data to eliminate unwanted data, transforms unstructured data into structured data, then extracts features. Text features include term frequency-inverse document frequency. Image features include histogram of oriented gradients, gray-level co-occurrence matrix, color histogram, and scale-invariant feature transform. Next, it inputs the features to the multiple kernel learning (MKL) for fusion to automatically combine both feature types to achieve the best performance. Finally, it does event detection. The method was tested on Brisbane hailstorm 2014 and California wildfires 2017. It was compared with methods that used text only or images only. With the Brisbane hailstorm data, the proposed method achieved the best performance, with a fusion accuracy of 0.93, comparing to 0.89 with text only, and 0.85 with images only. With the California wildfires data, a similar performance was recorded. It has demonstrated that event detection in Twitter is enhanced and improved by combination of multiple features. It has delivered an accurate and effective event detection method for spreading awareness and organizing responses, leading to better disaster management.

Keywords: data fusion, data mining, event detection, kernel method, multiple kernel learning, text features, image features

1. Introduction

Social media platforms such as Facebook, Twitter, and Instagram allow their users to easily connect and share information. The unprecedented data generated by millions of users from all around the world make social media ideal places of finding what is happening in the wider world beyond direct personal experience. As a microblog site, Twitter enables its users to post instantly what is happening in their location in 140-character messages, or tweets. Twitter is an information system that provides a real-time reflection of its users. As a consequence, Twitter serves as a rich source for exploring what is attracting users' attention and what is happening around the world. For example, for news and communications in time of a disaster, social media users use Twitter to tweet and post text, images, and video through their smartphones and tablets. As a result, Twitter becomes a good source for detection of events such as disasters [1].

An event is the basis on which people form and recall memories. Events are a natural way to refer to any observable occurrence that groups persons, places, times, and activities together. They are useful because they help us make sense of the world around us, helping to recollect real-world experiences, explaining phenomena that we observe, or assisting us in predicting future events. Social events are the events that are attended by people and are represented by multimedia content shared online. Instances of such events are concerts, disasters, sports events, public celebrations, or protests. Twitter platform forms a rich site for news, events, and information mining. It allows the posting of images and videos to accompany tweets produced by users of the site. As a result, the site contains multimedia content which can be mined using complicated algorithms. However, due to the huge burst in information, event detection in Twitter is a complicated task that requires a lot of skill and expertise in data mining. Here, an event detection is a data mining task aiming to identify the event in a media collection. To enhance the process of event detection, an automatic algorithm needs be developed to mine multimedia information.

Many approaches have been proposed for event detection [2–4]. For event detection using Twitter data, there are different ways to detect event, including using part of speech technique [5], hidden Markov model (HMM) [6], and term frequency and inverse document frequency (TF-IDF), and part-of-speech (POS) tagging and parsing. Alqhtani et al. [7] introduced a data fusion approach in multimedia data for earthquake detection in Twitter by using kernel fusion. It had achieved a high detection accuracy of 0.94, comparing to accuracy of 0.89 with texts only, and accuracy of 0.83 with images only. Sakaki et al. [8] showed that mining of relevant tweets can be used to detect earthquake events and predict the earthquake center in real time by using TF-IDF. In the process of event detection, the method utilized TF-IDF to eliminate redundant information or keywords. It provided a way of real-time interaction for earthquakes in Twitter. It developed a classifier based on several features including keywords, the number of words and the context, location and time of the words. It used a probabilistic spatiotemporal model to detect the location of the earthquake happened in Japan. Yardi and Boyd [9] used keyword search to present the role of stream news in spreading local information from Twitter for two accidents including a shooting and a building collapse. Ozdikis et al. [10] discussed an event detection method for various topics in Twitter using semantic similarities between hashtags based on clustering. Zhang et al. [11] proposed an event detection from online microblogging stream. It combined the normalized term frequency and user's social relation to weight words. Although many approaches have been proposed for event detection using Twitter data, most of them used no images but only textual analysis of tweet texts. With the cases of using images, restrictions had been applied. For example, Nguyen et al. [12] used textual features and image features for event detection. However, they focused on the principle that no one user could be in multiple events at the given time, demanding that the image was separated by user at the beginning.

This chapter introduces a novel algorithm to detect a major event such as a wildfire through mining social media Twitter. In developing an efficient event detection algorithm, our considerations are: For Twitter users, it is much easier than ever before to post about natural disaster like wildfire, by posting different kinds of multimedia like pictures, rather than just typing a message. Using both image and text can improve disaster management than using image only or text only. Furthermore, Twitter has been used as a source for obtaining information about wildfires, specifically when landlines and mobile phone lines are damaged. Therefore, we propose to use visual information as well as textual information to improve the performance of automatic even detection. The algorithm starts with monitoring a Twitter stream to pick up tweets having texts and images. Secondly, it preprocesses the Twitter data to eliminate unwanted data and transform unstructured data into structured data. Thirdly, it extracts features from the text and image. Fourthly, a multiple kernel learning is applied to the features to fuse the multimedia data. Finally, a decision on event detection is made.

The chapter is organized as follows. After this section, Section 2 describes the proposed event detection method, which consists of Twitter data collection, data preprocessing, feature extraction, multiple kernel learning fusion, and event classification. Section 3 gives experiment design, results, and discussion. Section 4 presents conclusion.

2. The proposed algorithm

The proposed automatic event detection method includes five steps, including Twitter data collection, data preprocessing, features extraction, multimedia data fusion, and final event detection. The block diagram of the proposed method is shown in **Figure 1**. The following subsections explain the details of these five steps of the proposed algorithm.

2.1. Twitter data collection

Data about specific events have been obtained through the use of a Twitter application program or through Twitter partner sites. This study characterizes public responses on Twitter for different kinds of events such as storm, earthquake, wildfire, terror attacks, and other events. Two recent extreme events which happened in the last 4 years were used as case studies, including Brisbane hailstorm and California wildfire.

Figure 1. The block diagram of the proposed method of event detection from Twitter.

2.1.1. Brisbane hailstorm 2014

The Brisbane hailstorm occurred in Brisbane, Australia on November 27, 2014. It was the worst hailstorm in a decade, causing injury to about 40 people and costing around 1.1 billion Australian dollars. The data about this hailstorm were collected between November 27, 2014 and November 28, 2014 and contained both texts and images. The dataset contained 280,000 tweets. **Figure 2** presents an example of the twitters (left column) and the word cloud for the data (right column). A word cloud is an image consisting of the words used in the data, where the size of each word indicates its occurrent frequency.

2.1.2. California wildfires 2017

The 2017 wildfire season in California started in April and extended to December. 1,381,405 acres were burned and the economic cost was over 13.028 billion American dollars. The data for this event were collected for 5 days in July 2017. It contained 600,000 tweets with some tweets consisting of both text and images.

2.2. Data preprocessing

The goal of data preprocessing is to discover important features from collected raw data. Preprocessing is a set of techniques used prior to analysis to remove imperfection, inconsistency, and redundancy. In this study, there was a high need to preprocess text data, because many tweets were not properly formatted or contained spelling errors. As a result, using a filter, cleaning is done before the text data are further handled. For image data in Twitter, we extracted the image's hyperlink and removed a tweet if its hyperlink was empty or did not work, since in this study, the tweet must contain both image and text. After preprocessing, the data will be ready for feature extraction.

Figure 2. An example of tweets on Brisbane hailstorm (left) and the word cloud for the event (right).

2.3. Feature extraction

In event detection, a set of features is required. A feature vector is a set of features used to reduce the dimensionality of the data, especially in the case of large volume data. Feature extraction involves reducing the amount of resources required to describe a large set of data accurately. Two approaches to feature extraction were employed for different data sets: content-based and description-based. Content-based feature extraction is based on the content of an object, whereas description-based extraction relies on metadata such as keywords. In this study, content-based features were used for images, and description-based features were used for texts.

2.3.1. Textual features

In extracting textual features, two major processes are executed, including filtering and feature calculation. The filtering will derive the key information out of tweets. The feature calculation will represent the significance of a word within a given document using a measurement named term frequency-inverse document frequency (TF-IDF) [13].

The filtering consists of five major steps including: filtering tweets in such way that they are in English only; converting all words to lowercase; converting the string to a list of tokens based on whitespace; removing punctuation marks from the text; eliminating common words that do not tell anything about the dataset (such as the, and, for, etc.); and reducing each word to its stem by removing any prefixes or suffixes.

After the filtering, TF-IDF is calculated, which is a statistical measure that details the significance of a word within tweets based on how often the word occurs in an individual tweet compared with how often it occurs in other tweets [14]. The advantage of using the TF-IDF algorithm technique is that it allows the retrieval of information since the TF-IDF values increase proportionally with the number of times a certain keyword appears in a document, being offset by the frequency of the word in the database. The TF-IDF algorithm utilizes a combination of term frequency and inverse document frequency.

Suppose there is a vocabulary of k words, then each document is represented by a k-vector $V_d = (t_1, \ldots, t_i, \ldots, t_k)^T$ of weighted word frequencies with components t_i. TF-IDF is computed as follows:

$$t_i = \frac{n_{id}}{n_d} \log \frac{N}{n_i} t_i = \frac{n_{id}}{n_d} \log \frac{N}{n_i} \ t_i = \frac{n_{id}}{n_d} \log \frac{N}{n_i} \tag{1}$$

where n_{id} is the number of occurrences of word i in document d, n_d is the total number of words in document d, n_i is the number of occurrences of term i in the database, and N is the total number of documents in the database. It can be seen that TF-IDF is a product of the word frequency $\left(\frac{n_{id}}{n_d}\right)$ and the inverse document frequency $\left(\log\frac{N}{n_i}\right)$. For a word i, the more it occurs in document d (i.e., the higher the n_{id} is), the bigger the t_i is, meaning the word i is more significant. Note here, the significance of the word i in document d is offset by the frequency of the word in the whole database. This offsetting will result in different t_i for word i that are unevenly distributed among the documents.

2.3.2. Visual features

In calculating visual features, each image is represented with a visual-word vector consisting of visual words. A visual word is a cluster in an image that represents a specific pattern shared by keypoints in that cluster. A keypoint in an image is a section of the image that is highly distinctive, allowing its correct match in a large database of features to be found. A keypoint is detected based on various image features. In this study, four types of features are used to detect a keypoint, including histogram of oriented gradients (HOG) [15], gray-level co-occurrence matrix (GLCM) [16], color histogram (CH) [17], and scale-invariant feature transform (SIFT) [14].

HOG is a feature descriptor that is calculated by counting occurrences of gradient orientation in localized portions of an image. Operating on local cells, HOG is invariant to geometric and photometric transformations, but for object orientation.

GLCM is got by calculating how often pairs of pixel with specific values and in a specified spatial relationship occur in an image. It is used to describe texture such as a land surface. It can provide useful information about the texture of an object but not information about the shape or size.

CH is defined as the distribution of colors in an image. It represents the actual number of pixels of a certain color in each of a fixed list of color ranges. A major drawback of a color histogram is that it does not take into account the size and shape of object.

SIFT is an algorithm to detect and describe local features in images. It produces an image descriptor for image-based matching and recognition. It mainly detects interest points from a gray image, at which statistics of local gradient directions of image intensities are accumulated to give a summarizing description of the local image structures around each interest point. The descriptor is used for matching corresponding interest points between different images.

In calculating visual word, the four types of features are firstly calculated for an image. Then, keypoints are derived based on these features. Thirdly, K-means clustering algorithm is used to cluster the keypoints into a large number of clusters. Each cluster is then considered as a visual word that represents a specific pattern. In this way, the clustering process generates a visual-word vocabulary describing different patterns in the images. The number of clusters determines the size of the vocabulary.

2.4. Multimedia data fusion

Starting from an introduction of multimedia data fusion, this section discusses the principle of kernel-based data fusion, then presents the details of the proposed multiple kernel learning for data fusion, and finally gives the details of final event detection.

2.4.1. About multimedia data fusion

Multimedia data fusion is the process in which different features of multimedia are brought together for the purpose of analyzing specific media data. Some common multimedia analyses that enable understanding of multimodal data include event detection, human tracking, audio-visual speaker detection, and semantic concept detection. The purpose of data fusion is to ensure that the algorithm of a process is improved. Through the use of a fusion strategy, the multimedia analysis can improve the accuracy of the output, resulting in more reliable decision-making.

There are many fusion methods such as linear fusion, linear weighted fusion, nonlinear fusion, and nonlinear weighted fusion. This study relates to a fusion strategy of combining both textual and visual modalities in the context of event detection. A new method of multimedia fusion has been proposed. It is based on multiple kernel learning (MKL). It has the advantage of incorporating with classifier learning and handling a big volume of data.

2.4.2. Kernel-based data fusion

Kernel methods are based on a kernel function, which is a similarity function that finds similarities over pairs of data points. The kernel function enables the kernel method to operate in a high-dimensional space by simply applying an inner product. The kernel method introduces nonlinearity into the decision parameters by simply mapping the original features of the original sources onto a higher dimensional space. For kernel function $\kappa(x, y)$ and mapping function $\phi : \mathcal{X} \to \mathcal{F}$, the model built by the kernel method can be expressed as an inner product in the following equation:

$$\kappa(x,y) = \langle \phi(x) \cdot \phi(y) \rangle \tag{2}$$

where $\kappa(x, y)$ is positive semidefinite and $\phi : \mathcal{X} \to \mathcal{F}$ maps each instance x, y into feature space $\mathcal{F}$, which is a Hilbert space. With the kernel method, a simple mining technique such as classification can be applied further to analyze the data.

Kernel methods can be described as a class of algorithms for pattern analysis, whose best member is the support vector machine [18]. There are many kernel methods including polynomial, fisher, radial basis functions (RBF), string, and graph kernels. Several commonly used kernel functions are:

$$\text{Linear function} : \kappa(x_i, x) = x_i \cdot x \tag{3}$$

$$\text{Polynomial function} : \kappa(x_i, x) = [(x_i \cdot x) + 1]^p \tag{4}$$

$$\text{Radial basis function (RBF)} : \kappa(x_i, x) = e^{-\|x_i - x\|^2 / 2\sigma^2} \tag{5}$$

where x_i and x are two samples represented as feature vectors, $\|x - x'\|$ is the distance between the two feature vectors, σ is a free parameter, and p is a constant.

Studies show that nonlinear kernels, for example, string kernel or RBF, have a significantly higher level of accuracy for multimedia data compared to linear classification models [19]. Kernel-based data fusion, denoted as kernel fusion, has been pioneered by Lanckriet et al. [20] as a statistical learning framework for genomic data fusion and has been applied widely in various applications. In particular, kernel representation resolves the heterogeneities of data sources by transforming different data structures into kernel matrices.

2.4.3. Multiple kernel learning for fusion

When dealing with multimedia input, Kernel-based data fusion can be applied so that it merges all the features from different sources into a concatenated vector before achieving classification. However, it is hard to combine features into one representation without facing the problem of dimensionality [21]. Multiple kernel learning (MKL) is one of the most popular fusion technologies (Lan et al.), which allows us to combine possibly heterogeneous data sources, making use of the reduction of heterogeneous data to the common framework of kernel matrices. The reduction of heterogeneous data is achieved by using a kernel for each type of feature rather than using one kernel for all the features. For a set of base kernels κ_l, the optimal kernel combination is calculated as:

$$\kappa_{optimal} = \sum_l \beta_l \kappa_l \tag{6}$$

where β_l is the weight for each base kernel κ_l.

Multiple kernel learning is flexible for multimodal data, since each set of data features is assigned a different notion of similarity, i.e., a different kernel. Instead of building a specialized kernel for the applications with multimodal data, it is possible to define a kernel for each of these data and linearly combine these kernels [22]. Multiple kernel learning presents the solution of the optimal combination of the kernels. In this study, semi-infinite programming [23] is used to achieve robustly and automatically optimizing the kernel weights. It solves the MKL in two steps: the first step is the initialization of the problem with a small number of linear constraints and the second step is to solve the parameters.

In event detection, the MKL framework defines a new kernel function as a linear combination of l base kernels:

$$\kappa(x_i, x) = \sum_l \beta_l \kappa_l(x_i, x) \tag{7}$$

where each base kernel κ_l is selected for one specific feature, the nonnegative coefficient β_l represents the weight of the lth base kernel in the combination, and $\sum_{l=1} \beta_l = 1$.

A kernel is utilized for each of the features followed by a combination of multiple features as indicated in Eq. (7). To select the spread parameter σ for each kernel, a cross-validation is performed with grid search for the range 0.001–0.01. Such selection is suitable for our data, resulting in the best classification accuracy without need for long time processing. The cross-validation is a model evaluation method that is applied during the training phase to find unknown parameters. To find the best kernel for image features and text features, cross-validation is applied. The best kernel means the best σ of the RBF kernel. The final kernel is the weighted sum of each feature kernel, with each feature kernel having its optimal σ.

MKL is coupled with classifier learning, such as support vector machine (SVM) [24] in our method, enhancing mutually interpretability of results. Support vector machine is formalized as solving an optimization problem. In the process, it finds the best hyperplane separating relevant and irrelevant vectors by maximizing the size of the margin between the two sets. By using a kernel, it can find the maximum-margin hyperplane in a transformed space.

For a given set of n training examples, $\left\{ \left(x_i, y_j \right)_{i=1}^{n}, x_i \in \mathbb{R}^d \text{ and } y_i \in \{+1, -1\} \right\}$, where x_i is a training example and y_i is the corresponding class label. The nonlinear support vector machine maps a training example x_i in the input space to a higher dimensional space $\phi(x_i)$ using a nonlinear mapping function ϕ. It constructs an optimal hyperplane, defined by Eq. (8), to separate the two classes.

$$w^T \phi(x) + b = 0 \tag{8}$$

where $b \in R$, w is a normal vector. The hyperplane constructed in kernel feature space is a maximum-margin hyperplane, one which maximizes the margin between the two datasets. This is achieved by solving the primal SVM problem:

$$\min \left(\frac{1}{2} \|w\|^2 + C \sum_i \xi_i^2 \right) \quad \text{subject to}$$
$$y_i \left(w^T \phi(x_i) + b \right) \geq 1 - \xi_i, \quad i = 1, 2, \ldots, n \tag{9}$$
$$\xi_i \geq 0 \quad i = 1, 2, \ldots, n$$

where ξ_i are nonnegative slack variables and C is a regularization parameter that determines the trade-off between the margin and the error in training data. The minimizing operation is against parameters w, b, and ξ_i. The corresponding SVM dual problem for the primal problem described in Eq. (9) is its Lagrangian defined as:

$$\max \left(\sum_{i=1}^{n} \alpha_i - \frac{1}{2} \sum_{i=1}^{n} \sum_{j=1}^{n} \alpha_i \alpha_j y_i y_j \left(k(x_i, x_j) + \frac{1}{C} \boxtimes_{ij} \right) \right) \quad \text{subject to}$$
$$\sum_{i=1}^{n} y_i \alpha_i = 0 \tag{10}$$
$$0 \leq \alpha_i \leq C, \quad i = 1, 2, \ldots, n$$

where δ_{ij} is the Kronecker δ defined to be 1 if $i = j$ and 0.

The dual problem is a keypoint for deriving SVM algorithms and studying their convergence properties. The function $k(x_i, x_j) = \phi(x_i)^T \phi(x_j)$ is the kernel function and α_j are the Lagrange coefficients. The Karush-Kuhn-Tucker (KKT) conditions are necessary conditions for the solution to the optimal parameters when there are one or more inequality constraints. Here, the KKT conditions for Eq. (10) are also sufficient for optimality since Eq. (10) meets the following three conditions: the object function is concave, the inequality constraint is a continuously differentiable convex function, and the equality constraint is an affine function. According to the KKT conditions, the optimal parameters α^*, w^*, and b^* must satisfy:

$$\alpha_i^* \left[y_i \left(\sum_{j=1}^{n} \alpha_j^* y_j k\left(x_i, x_j\right) + b^* \right) - 1 + \xi_i \right] = 0, \quad i = 1, 2, ..., n \tag{11}$$

In classification, only a small subset of the Lagrange multipliers α_i^* tend to be nonzero usually. The training examples with nonzero α_i^* are defined as support vectors. They construct the optimal separating hyperplane as:

$$\mathbf{w}^{*T} \phi(x) + b^* = \sum_{j=1}^{n} \alpha_j^* y_j k\left(x, x_j\right) + b^* = 0 \tag{12}$$

In SVM framework, the task of multiple kernel learning is considered as a way of optimizing the kernel weights at the same time of training SVM. For multiple kernels, Eq. (12) can be converted into the following equation to derive the dual form for MKL.

$$\max \left(\sum_{i=1}^{n} \alpha_i - \frac{1}{2} \sum_{i=1}^{n} \sum_{j=1}^{n} \alpha_i \alpha_j y_i y_j \sum_{l=1}^{m} \beta_l k_l \left(x_i, x_j\right) \right) \text{ subject to}$$

$$\sum_{i=1}^{n} y_i \alpha_i = 0 \tag{13}$$

$$0 \leq \alpha_i \leq C, \quad i = 1, 2, ..., n$$

$$\beta_l \geq 0, \quad \sum_{l=1}^{m} \beta_l = 1, \quad l = 1, 2, ..., m$$

In Eq. (13), both the base kernel weights β_l and the Lagrange coefficients α_j need to be optimized. A two-step procedure is considered to decompose the problem into two optimization problems.

In the first step, through grid search and cross-validation, the best weights β_l are derived by minimizing the 2-norm soft margin error function using linear programming. The weights for text features and image features are changed according to the type of data. For example, for wildfire data, the weight for text features was chosen as 0.70, and the weight for image features was chosen as 0.30. In the second step, the Lagrange coefficients α_j are obtained by maximizing Eq. (13) using quadratic programming. The interior point method is used to solve quadratic programming in the proposed method, which achieves optimization by traversing the convex interior of the feasible region.

2.5. Final event detection

As described above, the training process of multimedia data fusion builds the system by deriving parameters α_j, b, x_i, β_l, and k_l. For a test input x, the decision function for MKL, i.e., the event detection function $F(x)$, is a convex combination of basis kernels, computed as:

$$F(x) = \text{sign}\left(\sum_i \sum_l \beta_l (k_l(x_i, x).\alpha_i + b)\right) \tag{14}$$

where x_i are support vectors, α_i denote Lagrange multipliers corresponding to support vectors, and b is a bias which intercepts the hyperplane that separates the two groups in the normalized data space.

Depending on the sign of Eq. (14), the Twitter data are divided into two groups. The first group contains twitters of a positive class, meaning the event has happened. The second group contains twitters of a negative class, meaning the event has not happened. Both classes are based on image and text features which are extracted from the same tweet.

3. Experiment design, result, and discussion

3.1. Experiment design

Experiments have been done to build the event detection method and test its performance on real twitters. The algorithm is implemented in Matlab. In the experiments, the tweets that contain both text and image are collected from the Twitter streams. The data collection is for two events: Brisbane hailstorm and California wildfire.

The data are separated into two sets, including training and testing. Training data are divided into two groups: the event has happened or the event has not happened, which are manually labeled. Each group has the same number of tweets. The same process is applied to the testing data. The numbers of samples for the two sets are the same. The reasons to have the same number of samples are: the greater the size of the training set and testing sets, the better the algorithm is trained and tested, and the total number of samples is big enough to split the data into two equal sets. For each tweet set to be used for detecting whether an event has happened or not, its features are extracted for fusing operation.

In order to validate the performance of the proposed MKL event detection using both text and image, two other methods are also built and tested. Both the other two methods are based on single kernel learning, with one method taking text only as input and the other taking image only as input.

3.2. Performance evaluation parameters

In order to measure the performance of the proposed method and those of other comparing methods more objectively and comprehensively, four performance parameters are used, including accuracy (A), precision, recall, and F-score [25]. They are defined below.

The accuracy for the event detection method is defined as

$$A = \frac{TP + TN}{TP + TN + FP + FN} \tag{15}$$

where *TP*, *TN*, *FP*, and *FN* represent true positive, true negative, false positive, and false negative, respectively. In classifying an event such as a wildfire, a true positive (*TP*) is considered to be when a wildfire happened and a tweet from the wildfire data is classified as wildfire. If a tweet from the wildfire data is classified as not wildfire, this is a false negative (*FN*). In contrast, when a tweet from the data about a nonwildfire event is classified as wildfire, that is a false positive (*FP*). If a tweet from the data about a nonwildfire event is classified as not wildfire, that is a true negative (*TN*). For other events such as hailstorm, the classification is applied in the same way.

Precision is a term that refers to the fraction of correctly retrieved tweets. It is a function of true positives and false positives. It is defined as:

$$precision = \frac{TP}{TP + FP} \tag{16}$$

The term recall refers to the fraction of relevant tweets that were retrieved. It is a function of correctly classified examples, i.e., true positives, and the false negatives true positive rate. It is defined as:

$$recall = \frac{TP}{TP + FN} \tag{17}$$

F-score is introduced as the harmonic mean of precision and recall, in this way combining and balancing precision and recall. It is defined as:

$$F - score = 2* \frac{precision*recall}{precision + recall} \tag{18}$$

F-score measures how well a learning algorithm applies to a class. It is based on the weighted average of precision and recall.

3.3. Result and discussion

In order to validate the performance of the proposed event detection based on multiple kernel learning, two other single kernel-based methods are also built and tested. Both of the other two methods take single media as input, i.e., text or image. The performance metrics of the proposed method and that of the other two methods for two events are given in **Table 1**.

From the table, it can be seen that for both the Brisbane hailstorm event and California wildfire event, the proposed method consistently achieved a better performance in all the four metrics than the methods using text only or image only. For example, the proposed method achieved an accuracy of 0.93 for Brisbane hailstorm, whereas the method of using text only achieved 0.89 and the method of using image only achieved 0.85. For California wildfire, the accuracy of the proposed method is 0.92, better than that of 0.90 and 0.86 of the other two methods. Comparing to the other two single kernel-based methods, it can also be seen that the proposed method has improved about 5%, 6%, 5%, and 6%, respectively, in accuracy, precision, recall,

Event	Data	Accuracy	Precision	Recall	F-score
Brisbane hailstorm	Text only	0.89463	0.90662	0.90171	0.90416
	Image only	0.85981	0.82759	0.90566	0.86486
	The proposed method	0.93434	0.93578	0.94444	0.94009
California wildfire	Text only	0.90981	0.91533	0.91116	0.91324
	Image only	0.86406	0.88971	0.84912	0.86894
	The proposed method	0.92736	0.9311	0.93721	0.93414

Table 1. Event detection performance of the proposed method in comparison with the performance of two methods that use text only or image only.

and *F*-score. The experiment results have proven that event detection from multimedia data in Twitter is enhanced and improved by using a combination of multiple features for both images and text.

4. Conclusion

In this chapter, a method for detecting hot events, in particular disasters such as hailstorm and wildfires, is proposed. The approach uses visual information as well as textual information to improve the performance of detection. It starts with monitoring a Twitter stream to pick up tweets having texts and images, and storing them in a database. After that, Twitter data is preprocessed to eliminate unwanted data and transform unstructured data into structured data. Then, features in both texts and images are extracted for event detection. For feature extraction from the text, the term frequency-inverse document frequency technique is used. For images, the features extracted are: histogram of oriented gradients descriptors for object detection, gray-level co-occurrence matrix for texture description, color histogram, and scale-invariant features transform. In the next step, text features and image features are input to the multiple kernel learning (MKL) for fusion. MKL can automatically combine both feature types in order to achieve the best performance. The proposed method was tested on two datasets from two events, including Brisbane hailstorm 2014 and California wildfires 2017. The method is compared with a method that used text only and another method that used images only. With the Brisbane hailstorm data, the proposed method achieved the best performance, with a fusion accuracy of 0.93, compared to 0.89 with text only, and 0.85 with images only. With the California wildfires data, the proposed method achieved the best performance, with a fusion accuracy of 0.92, compared to 0.90 with text only, and 0.86 with images only. It has demonstrated that event detection from multimedia data in Twitter is enhanced and improved by our approach of using a combination of multiple features for both images and text. The proposed method also improves computational efficiency when handling big volumes of data, and gives better performance than other fusion approaches. It has delivered an accurate and effective detection method for detecting events, which can be used for spreading awareness and organizing responses.

The research presents a breakthrough in terms of risk management strategies, one that can improve public health preparedness and lead to better disaster management actions.

Author details

Suhuai Luo[1]*, Samar M. Alqhtani[2] and Jiaming Li[3]

*Address all correspondence to: suhuai.luo@newcastle.edu.au

1 School of Electrical Engineering and Computing, The University of Newcastle, Callaghan NSW, Australia

2 College of Computer Science and Information Systems, Najran University, Najran, Saudi Arabia

3 Quantitative Imaging Research Team, CSIRO Data61, NSW, Australia

References

[1] Computing Community Consortium. Computing for Disasters: A Report from the Community Workshop, Visioning Workshop on Computing Disaster Management, Washington, DC; 2012

[2] Scherp A, Jain R, Kankanhalli M, Mezaris V. Modeling, detecting, and processing events in multimedia. In: Proceedings of the 18th ACM International Conference on Multimedia; 2010. pp. 1739-1740

[3] Petkos G, Papadopoulos S, Mezaris V, Troncy R, Cimiano P, Reuter T, et al. Social event detection at MediaEval: A three-year retrospect of tasks and results. In: Proceedings of the ICMR 2014 Workshop on Social Events in Web Multimedia (SEWM); 2014. pp. 27-34

[4] Xu Z, Liu Y, Yen N, Mei L, Luo X, Wei X, et al. Crowdsourcing based description of urban emergency events using social media big data. IEEE Transactions on Cloud Computing; 2016;**99**:1-1, DOI: 10.1109/TCC.2016.2517638

[5] Kirsch S. Sustainable mining. Dialectical Anthropology. 2010;**34**:87-93

[6] Ting IH. Social Network Mining, Analysis, and Research Trends: A Phenomenal Analysis. Boston, MA: Cengage Learning; 2012

[7] Alqhtani S, Luo S, Regan B. A multiple kernel learning based fusion for earthquake detection from multimedia Twitter data. In: Multimedia Tools and Applications - An International Journal. June 16, 2017. ISSN: 1380-7501 (Print) 1573-7721 (Online), DOI: 10.1007/s11042-017-4901-9

[8] Sakaki T, Okazaki M, Matsuo Y. Earthquake shakes Twitter users: Real-time event detection by social sensors. In: Proceedings of the 19th International Conference on World Wide Web; 2010; pp. 851-860

[9] Yardi S, Boyd D. Tweeting from the Town Square: Measuring geographic local networks. In: Proceedings of the ICWSM; 2010. pp. 194-201

[10] Ozdikis O, Senkul P, Oguztuzun H. Semantic expansion of hashtags for enhanced event detection in Twitter. In: Proceedings of the 1st International Workshop on Online Social Systems; 2012

[11] Zhang X, Chen X, Chen Y, Wang S, Li Z, Xia J. Event detection and popularity prediction in microblogging. Neurocomputing. 2015;**149**:1469-1480

[12] Nguyen T V, DaoMS, Mattivi R, Sansone E, De Natale F G, Boato G. Event Clustering and Classification from Social Media:Watershed-Based and Kernel Methods. Editors: M. Larson, et al. Proceedings of the MediaEval 2013 Multimedia Benchmark Workshop, Barcelona, Spain, October 18-19, 2013, volume 1043 of CEUR Workshop Proceedings; 2013

[13] Wu H, Luk R, Wong K, Kwok K. Interpreting TF-IDF term weights as making relevance decisions. ACM Transactions on Information Systems. 2008;**26**(3):13-49

[14] Wang Z, Shawe-Taylor J. A kernel regression framework for SMT. Machine Translation. 2010;**24**(2):87-102

[15] Dalal N, Triggs B. Histograms of oriented gradients for human detection. In: Proceedings of Computer Vision and Pattern Recognition; 2005

[16] Mohanaiah P et al. Image texture feature extraction using GLCM approach. International Journal of Scientific and Research Publications. 2013;**3**(5):1-5. ISSN 2250-3153

[17] Zhang D, Islam MM, Lu G. A review on automatic image annotation techniques. Pattern Recognition. 2012;**45**(1):346-362

[18] Pelillo M. Similarity-Based Pattern Analysis and Recognition. Berlin, Germany: Springer Science & Business Media; 2013

[19] Borra S, Rocci R, Vichi M, Schader M. Advances in Classification and Data Analysis. Berlin, Germany: Springer Science & Business Media; 2012

[20] Lanckriet GR, Cristianini N, Bartlett P, Ghaoui LE, Jordan MI. Learning the kernel matrix with semidefinite programming. Journal of Machine Learning Research. 2004;**5**:27-72

[21] Snoek CG, Worring M, Smeulders AW. Early versus late fusion in semantic video analysis. In: Proceedings of the 13th Annual ACM International Conference on Multimedia, ACM; 2005. pp. 399-402

[22] Lan Z, Bao L, Yu S, Liu W, Hauptmann AG. Multimedia classification and event detection using double fusion. Multimedia Tools and Applications. 2014;**71**(1):333-347

[23] Sonnenburg S, Rätsch G, Schäfer C, Schölkopf B. Large scale multiple kernel learning. Journal of Machine Learning Research. 2006;7:1531-1565

[24] Cristianini N, Shawer-Tatlor J. An Introduction to Support Vector Machines and Other Kernel-Based Learning Methods. Cambridge, United Kingdom: Cambridge University Press; 2005. ISBN 0521780195

[25] Sokolova M, Lapalme G. A systematic analysis of performance measures for classification tasks. Information Processing and Management. 2009;45(4):427-437

8

A Multilevel Evolutionary Algorithm Applied to the Maximum Satisfiability Problems

Noureddine Bouhmala, Kjell Ivar Øvergård and
Karina Hjelmervik

Abstract

The maximum satisfiability problem that is known to be nondeterministic polynomial (NP) complete plays a central role problem in many applications in the fields of very large-scale integration (VLSI) computer-aided design, computing theory, artificial intelligence, and defense. Given a set of m clauses and n Boolean variables, the maximum satisfiability problem refers to the task of finding an assignment of values to the variables that maximizes the number of satisfied clauses (or minimizes the number of unsatisfied clauses) In this chapter, a multilevel evolutionary algorithm is proposed for the maximum satisfiability problem. The multilevel process works by grouping the variables defining the problem to form clusters, uses the clusters to define a new problem, and is repeated until the problem size falls below some threshold. The coarsest problem is then given an initial assignment of values to variables and the assignment is successively refined on all the problems starting with the coarsest and ending with the original.

Keywords: maximum satisfiability problem, genetic algorithm, multilevel paradigm, discrete optimization, effect size

1. Introduction

Combinatorial optimization is a lively field of applied mathematics, combining techniques from combinatorics, linear programming, and the theory of algorithms, to solve optimization problems over discrete structures. Utilizing classical methods of operations research often fails due to the exponentially growing computational effort. It is commonly accepted that these methods might be heavily penalized by the nondeterministic polynomial (NP)-hard nature of the problems and consequently will then be unable to solve large-size instances of a problem.

Therefore, in practice meta-heuristics are commonly used even if they are unable to guarantee an optimal solution. The driving force behind the high performance of meta-heuristics is their ability to find an appropriate balance between intensively exploiting areas with high-quality solutions (the neighborhood of elite solutions) and moving to unexplored areas when necessary. The evolution of meta-heuristics has taken an explosive upturn. The recent trends in computational optimization move away from the traditional methods to contemporary nature-inspired meta-heuristic algorithms though traditional methods can still be an important part of the solution techniques for small-size problems. As many real-world optimization problems become increasingly complex and hard to solve, better optimization algorithms are always needed. Nature-inspired algorithms such as genetic algorithms (GAs) are regarded as highly successful methods when applied to a broad range of discrete as well as continuous optimization problems. This chapter introduces the multilevel paradigm combined with genetic algorithm for solving the maximum satisfiability problem. Over the past few years, an increasing interest has arisen in solving hard optimization problems using genetic algorithms. These techniques offer the advantage of being flexible. They can be applied to any problem (discrete or continuous) whenever there is a possibility for encoding a candidate solution to the problem, and a mean of computing the quality of any candidate solution through the so-called objective function. Nevertheless, GAs may still suffer from premature convergence. The performance of GAs deteriorates very rapidly mostly due to two reasons. First, the complexity of the problem usually increases with its size, and second, the solution space of the problem increases exponentially with the problem size. Because of these two issues, optimization search techniques tend to spend most of the time exploring a restricted area of the search space preventing the search to visit more promising areas, and thus leading to solutions of poor quality. Designing efficient optimization search techniques requires a tactical interplay between diversification and intensification [1, 2]. The former refers to the ability to explore many different regions of the search space, whereas the latter refers to the ability to obtain high-quality solutions within those regions.

In this chapter, a genetic algorithm is used in a multilevel context as a means to improve its performance. This chapter is organized as follows. Section 2 describes the maximum satisfiability problem. Section 3 explains the hierarchical evolutionary algorithm. In Section 4, we report the experimental results. Finally, Section 5 discusses the main conclusions and provides some guidelines for future work.

2. The maximum satisfiability problem

Given a set of n Boolean variables and a conjunctive normal form (CNF) of a set of m disjunctive clauses of literals, where each literal is a variable or its negation which takes one of the two values *True* or *False*, the task is to determine whether there exists an assignment of truth values of the variables that satisfy the maximum number k of clauses. Multilevel approaches are special techniques which aim at producing smaller and smaller problems that are easier to solve than the original one. These techniques were applied to different combinatorial optimization problems. Examples include graph-partitioning problem [3–7], the traveling salesman problem [8, 9], graph coloring and graph drawing [10, 11], feature selection problem in biomedical data [12], and maximum satisfiability problem [13–16]. A recent survey over multilevel techniques can be found in [1, 17, 18].

3. The multilevel evolutionary algorithm

3.1. Main idea

The multilevel paradigm works by merging the variables defining the problem to form clusters, uses the clusters to define a new problem, and the process is repeated until the problem size reaches some threshold. A random initial assignment is injected to the coarsest problem and the assignment is successively refined on all the problems starting with the coarsest and ending with the original. The multilevel evolutionary algorithm is described in Algorithm 1.

Algorithm 1. The multilevel evolutionary algorithm

---

    input : Problem P_0

    output: Solution $S_{final}(P_0)$

1 begin

2   level := 0 ;

3   **while** *Not reached the desired number of levels* **do**

4 $P_{level+1}$:=Reduce (P_{level}) ;

5   level := level + 1 ;

6   /* Proceed with Memetic algorithm */ ;

7 $S_{start}(P_{level})$ = Initial-Assignment (P_{level}) ;

8 $S_{final}(P_{level})$ = Refinement (P_{level}) ;

9   **while** $(level > 0)$ **do**

10 $S_{start}(P_{level-1})$:=Project $\left(S_{final}(P_{level})\right)$;

11 $S_{final}(P_{level-1})$:=Refinement $(S_{start}(P_{level-1}))$;

12   level := level − 1

13 end

3.2. Reduction phase

This process (lines 3–5 of Algorithm 1) is graphically illustrated in **Figure 1** using an example with 10 variables. The coarsening phase uses two levels to coarsen the problem down to three

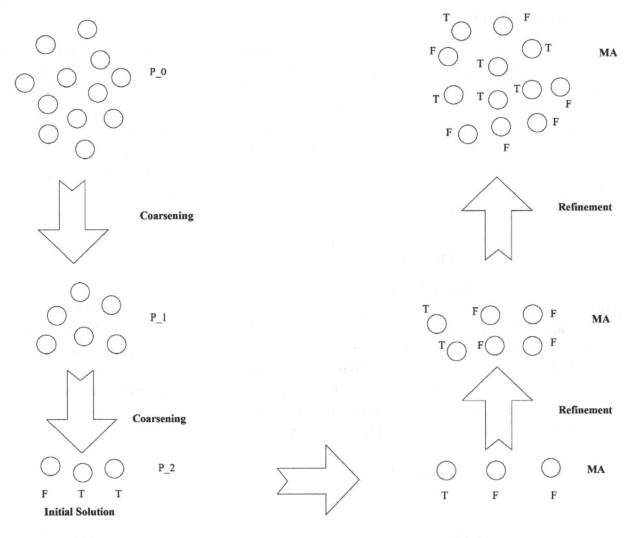

Figure 1. The various phases of the multilevel evolutionary algorithm.

clusters. P_0 corresponds to the original problem. The random-coarsening procedure is used to randomly merge the literals in pairs leading to a coarser problem (level) with five clusters. This process is repeated leading to the coarsest problem (P_3) with three clusters. An initial population is generated where the clusters are randomly assigned the value of true or false. The figure shows an initial solution where one cluster is assigned the value of true and the remaining two clusters are assigned the value false. Thereafter, the computed initial solution is then improved with the evolutionary algorithm referred to as MA. As soon as the convergence criteria are reached at P_2, the uncoarsening phase takes the whole population from that level and then extends it so that it serves as an initial population for the parent level P_1 and then proceeds with a new round of MA. This iteration process ends when MA reaches the stop criteria that is met at P_0.

3.3. Initial solution

The coarsening phase stops when the problem size reaches a threshold. A random procedure is used to generate an initial solution at the coarsest level. The clusters of every individual in the population are assigned the value of true or false in a random manner (line 7 of Algorithm 1).

3.4. Projection and refinement phases

The projection phase is the opposite process followed during the coarsening phase. The assignment reached at $level_{m+1}$ is now to be extended on is parent $level_m$. The extension algorithm is simple; if a cluster which belongs to $level_{m+1}$ is assigned the value of true, then the grouped pair of clusters that it represents, which belong to $level_m$, are also assigned the true value (line 10 of Algorithm 1). The evolutionary algorithm explained in the next section is used to improve the assignment during each level. The population reached at $level_{m+1}$ will serve as the initial population for $level_m$. The projected population already contains individuals with high fitness value leading MA to converge quicker within a few generations to a better assignment (lines 8 and 11 of Algorithm 1).

3.5. Evolutionary algorithm (MA)

The evolutionary algorithm proposed in this chapter and described in Algorithm 2 combines a genetic algorithms and local search. The algorithm maintains a population of solutions for the problem at hand (i.e., a pool having several solutions simultaneously). Each of these solutions is called an individual. Each generation consists of updating a population of individuals, hopefully leading to better solutions. The individuals from the set of solutions, which is called population, will evolve from generation to generation by repeated application of genetic operators and a local search scheme. Over many generations, the population becomes uniform and converges to optimal or near-optimal solutions.

Algorithm 2. Evolutionary algorithm

---

begin

    Generate initial population ;

    Evaluate the fitness of each individual in the population ;

    while *(Not Convergence reached)* **do**

        Select individuals according to a scheme to reproduce ;

        Breed if necessary each selected pairs of individuals through crossover;

        Apply mutation if necessary to each offspring ;

        Apply local search to each chromosome ;

        Evaluate the fitness of the intermediate population ;

        Replace the parent population with a new generation

end

- **Fitness function:** it is a numerical value that expresses the performance of an individual (solution) so that different individuals can be compared. The fitness function is defined as the number of unsatisfied clauses.

- **Initial population:** the initial population consists of individuals generated randomly in which each gene's allele is assigned randomly the value 0 (false) or 1 (true).

- **Crossover:** new solutions are produced by matching pairs of individuals in the population and then applying a crossover operator to each chosen pair. An unmatched individual i_k is matched randomly with an unmatched individual i_l. Thereafter, the two-point crossover operator is applied using a crossover probability to each matched pair of individuals. The two-point crossover draws two random points within a chromosome and then interchanges the two parent chromosomes between these points to produce two new offspring. The work presented in [19] shows that the results produced by the two-point crossover are excellent especially when the problem is hard to solve.

- **Mutation:** let $C = c_1, c_2, ..., c_m$ be a chromosome represented by a binary chain where each of whose gene c_i is either 0 or 1. Each gene c_i is mutated through flipping this gene's allele from 0 to 1 or from 1 to 0 if the probability test is passed. The mutation probability guarantees that, theoretically, every part of the region of the search space is explored. The mutation operator adds diversity to the population while increasing the likelihood of generating individuals with better fitness values.

- **Selection:** based on each individual quality, the roulette method is used to determine the next population. The selection is stochastic and biased toward the best individuals. The first step is to calculate the cumulative fitness of the whole population through the sum of the fitness of all individuals. After that, the probability of selection is calculated for each individual as being $P_{Selection_i} = f_i / \sum_1^N f_i$.

- **Local search:** the last part of the algorithm is the use of a local search. A fast and simple heuristic is applied for each offspring during which it seeks for the new variable-value assignment which best decreases the number of unsatisfied clauses being identified.

4. Experimental results

4.1. Benchmark instances

We evaluated the performance of the multilevel evolutionary algorithm (MLVMA) against its single variant (MA) using a set of instances taken from SATLIB. (http://www.informatik.tu-darmstadt.de/AI/SATLIB). **Table 1** shows the instances used in the experiment. IBM SPSS Statistics version 19 was used for statistical analysis. Due to the randomization nature of the algorithms, each problem instance was run 100 times with a cutoff parameter (max time) set to 15 min. The 100 runs were adopted because pilot runs had shown the size of the difference to be so large that 100 runs were enough for an acceptable statistical power (*power* $>$ .95); this is in accordance with the suggestions given in a recent report on statistical testing of randomized algorithms [20].

The tests were carried out on a DELL machine with 800 MHz CPU and 2 GB of memory. The code was written in C and compiled with the GNU C compiler version 4.6. The list of parameters used in the experiments are as follows:

Instance	Number of variables	Number of clauses
2bitadd$_{10}$.cnf	590	1422
2bitadd$_{11}$.cnf	649	1562
2bitadd$_{12}$.cnf	708	1702
2bitcomp$_5$.cnf	125	310
2bitmax$_6$.cnf	252	766
2bitadd$_{31}$.cnf	8432	31,310
2bitadd$_{32}$.cnf	8704	32,316
3block.cnf	283	9690
4blocks.cnf	758	47,820
4blocksb.cnf	410	24,758
e0ddr2-10-by-5-1.cnf	19,500	103,887
e0ddr2-10-by-5-4.cnf	1728	104,527
enddr2-10-by-5-1.cnf	20,700	111,567
enddr2-10-by-5-8.cnf	21,000	113,729
ewddr2-10-by-5-1.cnf	21,800	118,607
ewddr2-10-by-5-8.cnf	22,500	123,329

Table 1. Benchmark set of the SAT competition Beijing.

- Crossover probability = 0.85

- Mutation probability = 0.1

- Population size = 50

- Stopping criteria for the coarsening phase: the coarsening stops as soon as the size of the smallest problem reaches 100 variables (clusters). At this level, MA generates an initial population.

- Convergence: if the fitness of the best individual does not improve during 10 consecutive generations, MA is assumed to have reached convergence and moves to a higher level.

5. Results

5.1. Observed trends

The time development of the multilevel evolutionary algorithm against its single variant in solving the instances is shown in **Figures 2–8**. The plots show the 100 runs of both algorithms with a cutoff at 15 min as well as the mean of these runs. The search occurs in two phases. In the first phase, the best solution improves rapidly at first, and then flattens off as the search reaches the plateau region, marking the start of the second phase. The plateau region corresponds to a region in the search space where moves does not alter the best assignment, and

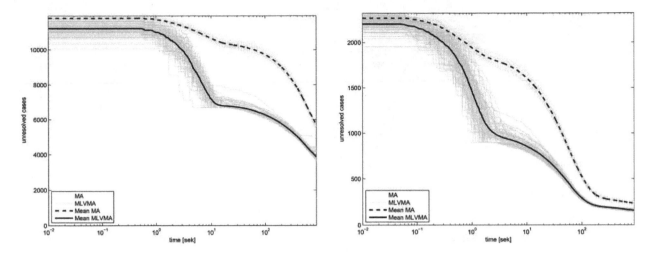

Figure 2. MLVMA versus MA: (left) 2bitadd_{10}.cnf, (right) 2bitadd_{11}.cnf—time development for 100 runs in 15 min.

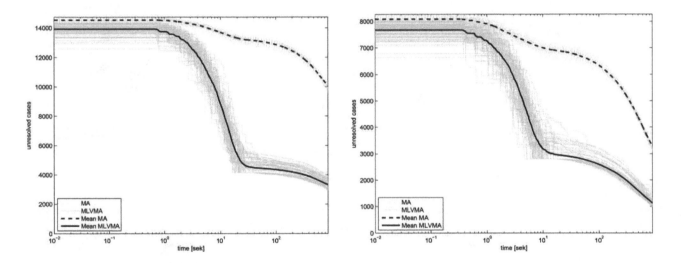

Figure 3. MLVMA versus MA: (left) 2bitadd_{12}.cnf, (right) 2bitcomp_{5}.cnf—time development for 100 runs in 15 min.

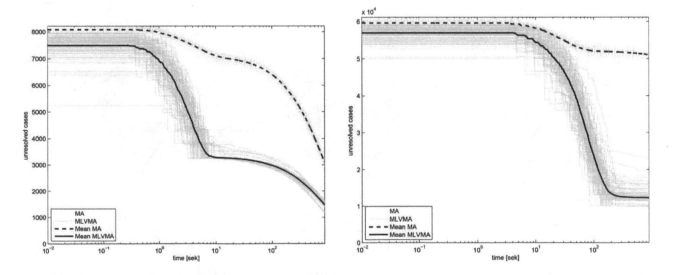

Figure 4. MLVMA versus MA: (left) 2bitmax_{6}.cnf, (right) 3bitadd_{31}.cnf—time development for 100 runs in 15 min.

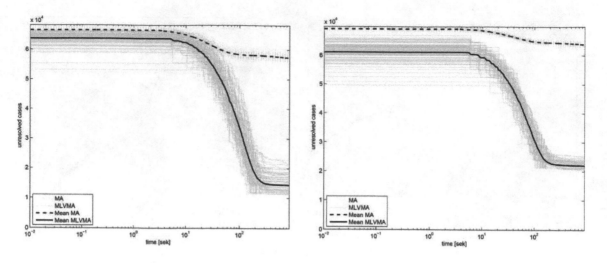

Figure 5. MLVMA versus MA: (left) 3bitadd$_{32}$.cnf, (right) 3block.cnf—time development for 100 runs in 15 min.

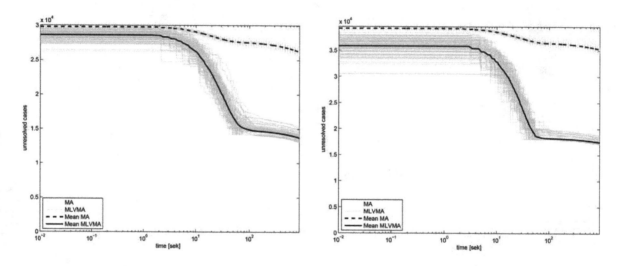

Figure 6. MLVMA versus MA: (left) 4blocks.cnf, (right) 4blocksb.cnf—time development for 100 runs in 15 min.

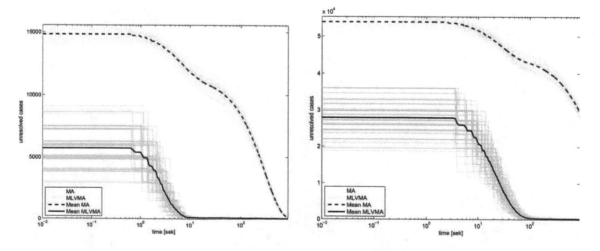

Figure 7. MLVMA versus MA: (left) e0ddr2-10-by-5-1.cnf, (right) e0ddr2-10-by-5-4.cnf—time development for 100 runs in 15 min.

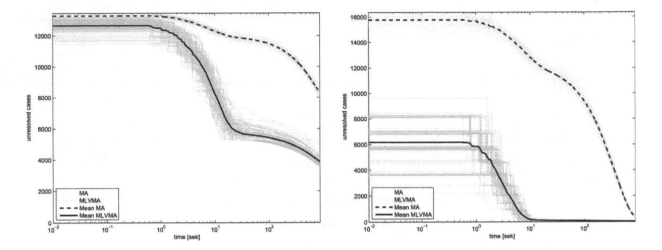

Figure 8. MLVMA versus MA: (left) enddr2-10-by-5-1.cnf, (right) enddr2-10-by-5-8.cnf—time development for 100 runs in 15 min.

occurs more specifically once the refinement reaches the finest level. The plots show that MLVMA offers a better asymptotic convergence compared to MA especially for large instances. The test cases where both algorithms reach approximately the same solution quality (with MLVMA being marginally better), the multilevel paradigm offers a cost-effective solution strategy considering the amount of time required (**Figure 9**).

This multilevel paradigm has two main advantages which enables the evolutionary algorithm to become much efficient. The coarsening process offers a better mechanism for performing diversification (i.e., searching different parts of the search space) and intensification (i.e., reaching better solutions within those regions). The coarsening allows the gene of each individual to represent a cluster of variables, leading the search to become guided and restricted to only those solutions in the solution space in which the variables grouped within a cluster are assigned the same value. As the size of the clusters varies from one level to another, the crossover and mutation operators are able to explore different regions in the search space

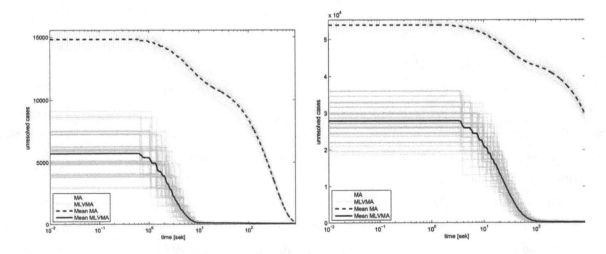

Figure 9. MLVMA versus MA: (left) ewddr2-10-by-5-1.cnf, (right) ewddr2-10-by-5-8.cnf—time development for 100 runs in 15 min.

while intensifying the search by exploiting the solutions from previous levels in order to reach better solutions.

5.2. Statistical analysis

Tables 2 and **3** summarize the results. M and SD represent the mean standard deviation of unsolved clauses for the MLVMA and MA algorithms. The range of solutions from each algorithm is also shown in order to analyze the overlap between solution spaces for any given instance. Statistical inferential analysis was done with an independent samples t-test which compares the difference in means between the two groups. Comparison using the non-parametric Mann-Whitney U-test gave identical results. The non-parametric effect size measure $\widehat{A}_{12}$ [21] was used to evaluate the relative dominance of one algorithm over the other. The $\widehat{A}_{12}$ effect size measure is calculated using the rank sum which is a common component in any non-parametric analysis such as the Mann-Whitney U-test [20]. Calculating $\widehat{A}_{12}$ is done according to the following formula:

$$\widehat{A}_{12} = (R_1/m - (m+1)/2)/n. \tag{1}$$

where R_1 is the rank sum of algorithm MLVMA, m is the number of observations in the first

#Case	MLVMA		MA	
	M (SD)	Range	*M* (SD)	Range
2bitadd$_{10}$.cnf	2.0 (.7)	[1–3]	16.3 (2.3)	[11–25]
2bitadd$_{11}$.cnf	1.7 (.7)	[1–4]	16.3 (3.2)	[8–24]
2bitadd$_{12}$.cnf	1.5 (.7)	[1–3]	1.6 (.7)	[1–4]
2bitcomp$_5$.cnf	1.0 (0)	[1–2]	1.0 (0.1)	[1–2]
2bitmax$_6$.cnf	1.0 (.2)	[1–2]	1.0 (0.1)	[1–2]
2bitadd$_{31}$.cnf	132.6 (10.9)	[122–216]	1106.2 (142.1)	[923–2620]
3bitadd$_{32}$.cnf	135.7 (11.9)	[123–186]	1366.9 (179.1)	[1125–1974]
3blocks	4.0 (1.8)	[2–9]	7.2 (1.0)	[4–9]
3blocks	8.2 (3.1)	[2–14]	13.0 (1.0)	[11–18]
4blocksb	5.2 (1.8)	[2–8]	7.3 (0.7)	[5–8]
e0ddr2-10-by-5-1	343.4 (119.0)	[261–697]	10871.1 (324.5)	[9895–11,527]
e0ddr2-10-by-5-4	320.6 (80.8)	[271–718]	10969.1 (360.1)	[10,190–11,784]
enddr2-10-by-5-1	371.9 (144.0)	[281–1021]	12042.9 (378.1)	[111,64–12,897]
enddr2-10-by-5-8	358.9 (136.1)	[278–967]	12241.3 (400.0)	[11,169–13,446]
ewddr2-10-by-5-1	399.8 (166.9)	[289–1124]	12939.7 (407.9)	[11,960–13,835]
ewddr2-10-by-5-8	354 (107.0)	[293–710]	13537.5 (423.8)	[12,393–14,736]

Table 2. Statistical comparisons.

#Case	Difference		Estimates of effect size	
	M diff. [95% CI of M diff.]	p	Obs. $\widehat{A}_{12}$	$\widehat{A}_{12}$[95% CI of $\widehat{A}_{12}$]
2bitadd$_{10}$.cnf	14.4 [13.8,14.9]	***	1	c
2bitadd$_{11}$.cnf	14.5 [13.9,15.2]	***	1	c
2bitadd$_{12}$.cnf	0.1 [−0.1,0.3]	.247	.548	.547 [.476,.622]
2bitcomp$_5$			.5	
2bitmax$_6$	0.0 [−0.1,0.3]	.653	.459	.459 [.475,.515]
2bitadd$_{31}$	973.6 [945.5,1001.7]	***	1	c
3bitadd$_{32}$	1231.1 [1195.8,1266.6]	***	1	c
3bloks	3.2 [2.8,3.6]	***	.918	.920 [.877,.958]
4blocks	4.8 [4.1,5.4]	***	.916	.917 [.878,.953]
4blocksb	2.1 [1.7,2.4]	***	1	c
e0ddr2-1-by-5-1	10527.7 [10459.5,10595.8]	***	1	c
e0ddr2-1-by-5-4	10648.5 [10575.8,10721.3]	***	1	c
enddr2-10-by-5-1	10671.0 [11591.2,11750.8]	***	1	c
enddr2-10-by-5-8	11882.4 [11799.1,11965.7]	***	1	c
ewddr2-10-by-5-1	12539 [12453.0,112626.8]	***	1	c
ewddr2-10-by-5-8	13182.9 [13096.7,13269.1]	***	1	c

*** means $p < 0.0001$.

Table 3. Comparing effect sizes.

data sample, and n is the number of observations in the second data sample. Calculating $\widehat{A}_{12}$ results in a number between 0 and 1 which represent the probability that MLVMA will yield a better solution than MA. If the two algorithms are equivalent, then $\widehat{A}_{12} = .5$, while a complete dominance of algorithm MLVMA over MA would entail $\widehat{A}_{12} = 1$.

$\widehat{A}_{12}$ is more easily interpreted than the more common parametric Cohen's d [22] which represents the mean difference between two groups in standard deviations for several reasons. First, Cohen's d assumes that the observed samples are normally distributed [20]. Second, when dealing with solutions to optimization problems, a researcher or a practitioner would only be interested in the single best solution given a sample of different solutions from one or more algorithms. Hence, using an effect size measure that indicates the probability that one algorithm would lead to a better solution than another (given the same amount of time) would be more informative and more easily interpretable for an optimization practitioner. The 95% confidence intervals of $\widehat{A}_{12}$ shown in **Table 3** (where applicable) are calculated using a bootstrapping procedure [23] which is used to estimate the 95% confidence interval of $\widehat{A}_{12}$. The procedure uses a computer-intensive step-by-step process that consists of the following three steps:

1. Random resampling with replacement from the original observations to create new data sets.

2. Calculation of the rank sum of MLVMA for each new data set.

3. Using the rank sum to calculate $\widehat{A}_{12}$ with Eq. (1). The three steps are then repeated 1000 times and the resulting statistic $\widehat{A}_{12}$ is saved to create a sampling distribution of the statistic $\widehat{hat}_{12}$.

The results show how MLVMA outperforms MA in 10 out of the 16 instances. MLVMA dominates MA in three instances (the 3blocks, 4blocks, and 4blocksb-instances, $\widehat{A}_{12}$, is .918, .916, and .847, respectively). For the remaining three problems ($2bitadd_{10}$, $2bitadd_{11}$, and $2bitadd_{12}$), there is no statistically identifiable difference between the two algorithms. However, when inspecting the time series for these instances it is clear that MLVMA reaches a solution much faster than MA. To test possible causes for the difference in solution quality, the relationship between the number of clauses and the quality of solutions provided by the two algorithms was analyzed. The relationship between the mean percentage of unsolved clauses and the number of clauses in each instance was estimated using a linear regression. The relationship between the mean percentage of unsolved clauses and the number of clauses for the MLVMA was much lower ($t(15) = 3.059$, = 2.041–8, 95% CI [1.163–8, 2.714–8], $p = .008$, $r = .633$) than for the MA ($t(15) = 10.067$, = 9.341–7, 95% CI [8.232–7, 1.04–6], $p < .001$, $r = .937$) indicating that the hierarchical paradigm is less affected by the size of the problem than the standard single-level evolutionary algorithm.

6. Conclusion

In this chapter, a multilevel evolutionary algorithm for solving the maximum satisfiability problem is presented. During the coarsening phase, a sequence of smaller problems, each with fewer variables, is constructed. Each child level is constructed from its parent level by collapsing pairs of variables. The new formed variables are used to define a new and smaller problem and recursively iterate the coarsening process until the size of the problem reaches some desired threshold. An evolutionary algorithm is applied through several optimization levels, where the converged population at a child level will serve as the starting population for a parent level. A set of instances were used to compare the performance of the new approach. The results obtained assert the superiority of the evolutionary algorithm when combined with the multilevel paradigm and always return a better solution for the equivalent run-time compared to MA.

Author details

Noureddine Bouhmala*, Kjell Ivar Øvergård and Karina Hjelmervik

*Address all correspondence to: noureddine.bouhmaa@usn.no

Department of Maritime Technology and Innovation, SouthEast University, Norway

References

[1] Blum C, Puchinger J, Raidl GR, Roli A. Hybrid metaheuristics in combinatorial optimization: A survey. Applied Soft Computing. 2011;**11**:4135-4151

[2] Blum C, Roli A. Metaheuristics in combinatorial optimization: Overview and conceptual comparison. ACM Computing Surveys. September 2003;**35**(3):268–308

[3] Barnard ST, Simon HD. A fast multilevel implementation of recursive spectral bisection for partitioning unstructured problems. Concurrency: Practice and Experience. 1994;**6**(2): 101-117

[4] Hadany R, Harel D. A multi-scale algorithm for drawing graphs nicely. Discrete Applied Mathematics. 2001;**113**(1):3-21

[5] Karypis G, Kumar V. A fast and high quality multilevel scheme for partitioning irregular graphs. SIAM Journal on Scientific Computing. 1998;**20**(1):359-392

[6] Karypis G, Kumar V. Multilevel k-way partitioning scheme for irregular graphs. Journal of Parallel and Distributed Computing. 1998;**48**(1):96-129

[7] Walshaw C, Cross M. Mesh partitioning: A multilevel balancing and refinement algorithm. SIAM Journal of Scientific Computing. USA. 2000;**22**(1):63-80

[8] Walshaw C. A multilevel approach to the traveling salesman problem. Operational Research. 2002;**50**(5):862-877

[9] Walshaw C. A multilevel Lin-Kernighan-Helsgaun algorithm for the travelling salesman problem. Technical Report 01/IM/80, Mathematics and Computing Science. London, UK: University of Greenwich; 2001

[10] Rodney D, Soper A, Walshaw C. The application of multilevel refinement to the vehicle routing problem. In: Fogel D. et al., editors. Proceedings of the CISChed 2007. Piscataway, NJ: IEEE Symposium on Computational Intelligence in Scheduling; 2007. pp. 212-219

[11] Walshaw C. A multilevel algorithm for forced-directed graph-drawing. Journal of Graph Algorithms and Applications. 2003;**7**(3):253-285

[12] Oduntan IO, Toulouse M, Baumgartner R, Bowman C, Somorjai R, Crainic TG. A multilevel tabu search algorithm for the feature selection problem in biomedical data. Computers & Mathematics with Applications. 2008;**55**(5):1019-1033

[13] Bouhmala N. A multilevel genetic algorithm for the clustering problem. International Journal of Information and Communication Technology. 2016;**9**(1):101-116

[14] Bouhmala N. A multilevel learning automata for MAX-SAT. International Journal of machine Learning Cybernetics. Berlin Heidelberg: Springer-Verlag. 2015;**6**(6):911-921. DOI: 10.1007/s13042-015-0355-4

[15] Bouhmala N, Hjelmervik K, Kjell Ivar O. Single vs hierarchical population-based evolutionary algorithm for SAT-encoded industrial problems: A statistical comparison. International Journal of Artificial Intelligence Applications. 2012;**3**(6):57-73

[16] Bouhmala N, Granmo OC. GSAT enhanced with learning automata and multilevel paradigm. International Journal of Computer Science Issues. 2011;**8**(3)

[17] Pirkwieser S, Raidl GR. Multilevel variable neighborhood search for periodic routing problems. In: Cowling PI, Merz P, editors. Proceedings of EvoCOP 2010 10th European Conference on Evolutionary Computation in Combinatorial Optimization. Vol. 6022 of Lecture Notes in Computer Science. Berlin, Germany: Springer-Verlag; 2010. pp. 226-238

[18] Walshaw C. Multilevel refinement for combinatorial optimization: Boosting metaheuristic performance. In: Blum C. et al., editors. Heidelberg, Berlin, Germany: Springer; 2008. pp. 261-289

[19] Spears W. Adapting crossover in evolutionary algorithms. In: Proceedings of the Fourth Annual Conference on Evolutionary Programming. MIT Press; 1995. pp. 367-384

[20] Arcuri A, Briand L. A Hitchhiker's guide to statistical tests for assessing randomized algorithms in software engineering. Technical report, simula research laboratory, number 13/2011

[21] Bouhmala N. A multilevel evolutionary algorithm for large SAT-encoded problems. Evolutionary Computation. 2012;**20**(4):641-664

[22] Cohen J. Statistical Power Analysis for the Behavioral Sciences. 2nd ed. New York University: Lawrence Erlbaum; 1998

[23] Mooney CZ, Duval RD. Bootstrapping—A Nonparametric Approach to Statistical Inference. Sage University Press; 1993

9

Overcoming Challenges in Predictive Modeling of Laser-Plasma Interaction Scenarios: The Sinuous Route from Advanced Machine Learning to Deep Learning

Andreea Mihailescu

Abstract

The interaction of ultrashort and intense laser pulses with solid targets and dense plasmas is a rapidly developing area of physics, this being mostly due to the significant advancements in laser technology. There is, thus, a growing interest in diagnosing as accurately as possible the numerous phenomena related to the absorption and reflection of laser radiation. At the same time, envisaged experiments are in high demand of increased accuracy simulation software. As laser-plasma interaction modelings are experiencing a transition from computationally-intensive to data-intensive problems, traditional codes employed so far are starting to show their limitations. It is in this context that predictive modelings of laser-plasma interaction experiments are bound to reshape the definition of simulation software. This chapter focuses an entire class of predictive systems incorporating big data, advanced machine learning algorithms and deep learning, with improved accuracy and speed. Making use of terabytes of already available information (literature as well as simulation and experimental data) these systems enable the discovery and understanding of various physical phenomena occurring during interaction, hence allowing researchers to set up controlled experiments at optimal parameters. A comparative discussion in terms of challenges, advantages, bottlenecks, performances and suitability of laser-plasma interaction predictive systems is ultimately provided.

Keywords: predictive modeling, machine learning, deep learning, big data, cloud computing, laser-plasma interaction modeling

1. Introduction to laser-plasma interaction simulations

Numerous significant technological advancements mark the nearly six decades that have elapsed since the invention of the laser. We are nowadays facing a dramatic increase in terms of attainable laser powers and intensities concomitantly with a drastic shortening of pulses duration. Super-intense lasers such as HERCULES [1], TPL [2], Vulcan [3] and Astra Gemini [4] or PHELIX [5] constitute a notable achievement in terms of chirped pulses intensity: an increase by six orders of magnitude within less than 10 years. Next generation 10-PW laser systems are currently under consideration in various laboratories around the world. To resume to just one example, the 10-PW ILE APOLLON [6] is envisaged to deliver an energy of 150 J in 15 fs at the last stage of amplification after the front end, with a repetition rate of one shot per minute, its intensity being expected to reach 10^{24} W·cm^{-2}. Such elevated intensities are the foregoers of the so called ultrarelativistic regime applications, a regime in which not only the electrons but also the ions become relativistic within one laser period. As matter under extreme conditions can now be relatively easily generated and investigated, we are witnessing a worldwide advent of laboratory research in totally "new physics", from ultrarelativistic laser plasmas to high-energy particle acceleration and generation of high-frequency radiation in the extreme-ultraviolet (XUV) and soft-X-ray regions. X-ray production by means of high intensity laser-plasma interaction experiments is of particular interest for the scientific community since this is a way of attaining increased brightness X-rays, with good coherence and consequently high quality sources of radiation. Among the variety of laser-based mechanisms deployed for this purpose, the most notable are betatron generation from laser wakefield acceleration [7] and high-order harmonics generation (HHG) [8].

In spite of the multitude of opportunities, there are still technological issues to be addressed and there are still numerous phenomena occurring during the interaction that are not yet fully understood. Some of these may be potentially damaging to experiments (e.g. hydrodynamic or parametric instabilities, hot electrons), hence their mitigation is vital. Ultimately, optimizing interaction conditions requires state-of-the-art theoretical and computational investigations.

In terms of simulation software, traditional approaches entail either hydrodynamic (fluid) or kinetic codes, in accordance with the laser-plasma interaction regime. Often, choosing between the two implies an inevitable dismissal of certain phenomena within reasonable accuracy limits. Modeling processes like particles' acceleration, plasma heating, parametric instabilities that occur during the interaction of ultrashort (pulse duration of sub-picoseconds down to tens of femtoseconds) and intense (intensity higher than 10^{17} W·cm^{-2}) laser pulses with plasma requires mainly a kinetic treatment and this is normally achieved through the Particle-In-Cell method (PIC) [9], the most reputed among the numerical tools employed in plasma physics and in laser-plasma interaction investigations. Albeit being recognized as a suitable approach for analyzing the highly transient physical processes in the non-linear regime associated with ultrafast laser energy coupling to matter, PIC based codes are subject to nonphysical behaviors such as statistical noise, non-physical instabilities, non-conservation, and numerical heating. Secondly, they require considerable computational resources, being far more demanding than the fluid ones that are normally deployed to study phenomena on a nanosecond scale with "coarser" accuracy. For instance, running a 1D PIC with a reasonable number of particles per cell, a fine grid and a small time resolution can claim up to more than 20 CPU hours on a single-processor PC for simulating what happens during a few femtoseconds of interaction. The distribution function at any given time, in a 3D3V PIC code is six dimensional in nature. Should 100 grid points be allocated for each dimension and representing each grid point in eight byte double precision, then, the system would require as far as 7 TB alone, just to store this data structure. In spite of the recent advent of computing technologies, running high accuracy 3D or even 2D kinetic simulations is still a challenging task even if we are talking about a full migration towards the GPUs.

Various simplified codes have been hitherto been built and successfully used with reasonable compromises between accuracy on one hand and storage requirements and speed on the other. The LPIC++ [10, 11], XOOPIC [12] and PIConGPU [13] are some good examples in this sense. Restraining the number of dimensions, in conjunction either with object oriented programming, either with code parallelization, makes it possible to gain increased resolution (but over fewer dimensions) with less fancy hardware. Among the state-of-the-art PICs employed for simulating a variety of laser-plasma problems are the well-established EPOCH [14], VSim [15], OSIRIS [16–18], and QuickPIC [19, 20]. Fully relativistic, parallelized and multidimensional, they all incorporate additional features accounting for phenomena normally disregarded by traditional PIC methods, therefore moving the simulations closer to the real world. For example, EPOCH includes multiphoton, tunneling and collisional ionisations. The latter two can also be found in OSIRIS. VSim is a hybrid code (combining kinetic and hydrodynamic treatments), while OSHUN [21, 22] permits the user to introduce multiple ion species. At the same time, system resources can be spared by either reducing the number of dimensions (user option encountered in EPOCH) or by separating out the time scale of the evolution of the driver from the plasma evolution, thus transforming a fully 3D electromagnetic field solve and particle push into a sequence of 2D solves and pushes (QuickPIC's algorithm). Highly optimized to run even on a single CPU, these codes are scalable over a large number of cores, featuring the dynamic load balancing of the processors. Parallelization approaches include not only the MPI and Open MP but SIMD Vectorization, with most of these above mentioned simulation environments having CUDA enabled versions as well. Running a PIC code on top of the line GeForce or on Tesla can lead to significant improvements in terms of speed [23–32] while maintaining a fairly large number of particles per cell. Breakthroughs have been reported especially with the particle push [33–35] and particle weighing [36–38] algorithms but also with the parallelization during the current deposition phase [39, 40]. Successful attempts of integrating these schemes while trying to mitigate some of the factors known to limit GPU performance—communication overhead between GPU and CPU, memory latency versus bandwidth, the relatively low level of multitasking or I/O efficient management when reading and writing to files—count in Jasmine [41, 42] or FBPIC [43, 44].

As cloud, big data and AI based technologies are nowadays becoming pervasive in all the fields of the economy, predictive modeling should become just as ubiquitous in every research area, being a comfortable and reliable alternative for designing optimized experiments or for estimating potential results.

This chapter is presenting an overview of an entire class of predictive systems for laser-plasma interaction built at the National Institute for Lasers, Plasma and Radiation Physics—blending in big data, advanced machine learning algorithms and deep learning—with improved accuracy and speed. Making use of terabytes of already available information (literature as well as simulation and experimental data) such systems have the potential of revealing various physical phenomena occurring in certain situations, hence enabling researchers to set up controlled experiments at optimal parameters. Whilst the most obvious advantage of deploying predictive and/or prescriptive modeling is the considerably diminished running time in comparison to classic simulation codes, the motivation goes further than this, to having a readily compiled report containing the most favorable interaction conditions or warnings on the imminent presence of destructive phenomena. However, efficiently extracting, interpreting, and learning from very large and heterogeneous datasets requires new generation scalable algorithms as well as new data management technologies and cloud computing. In this sense, a big step forward was the deployment of Hadoop [45], together with its MapReduce [46] algorithm and the Mahout library [47, 48]. Several other libraries were jointly used for deep learning purposes, namely Theano [49], TensorFlow [50], Keras [51] and Caffe [52]. Promising results—correctly predicted high order harmonics in HHG experiments along with the occurrence of hot electrons in certain interaction scenarios—have been obtained by combining deep neural networks (DNNs) and convolutional neural networks (CNNs) [53] with ensemble learning [54–56]. The DNNs and CNNs were built by grid search [57, 58], in conjunction with dropout [59–62] and constructive learning [63–67], with the CNNs exhibiting somewhat better performances in terms of speed and comparable accuracy in estimations. The chapter offers a comparative discussion of these alternate predictive modeling solutions, highlighting the performance improvement gained by deploying each combination of advanced machine learning and deep learning algorithms. Moreover, a significant part of this analysis is devoted to the challenges, advantages, caveats, accuracy, easiness of usage and suitability to the actual interaction scenario of these systems.

The last section proceeds to arguing the implications of big data and AI based predictive modeling for the scientific community, its potential, not only in joining together experimental observations, theory and simulation data, but also the potential and future prospects in deriving meaningful analysis and recommendations out of the already available information.

2. Big data and deep learning based predictive modeling for laser-plasma interaction

2.1. Opportunities and challenges for predictive modeling systems

The emergence of cloud computing and of open source big data designated platforms like Hadoop, Spark [68] and the framework ROOT [69, 70], along with the rise of deep learning [71–74] have rendered data processing and analysis trivially inexpensive. Massive amounts of a wide variety of information can today be interpreted at an unprecedented rate of speed. The consequence is particularly important for science because of various reasons. Firstly, migrating from expensive in-house computing systems to infrastructure as a service (IaaS) significantly cuts costs with capital investment. Secondly, the increased storage capacity and computer power make the cloud ideal for scientific big data applications development [75], specifically for statistics, analytics and recommender systems. Furthermore, workload optimization strategies can easily be incorporated in order to use the resources to maximum capacity. For applications that are both computational and data intensive the processing models combine different techniques like in-memory big data [76] or combined CPU—GPU processing.

Predictive modeling in a continuously evolving field like laser-plasma interaction is challenging from several points of view, mainly because this is an area previously unexplored with machine learning techniques and smart agents. Simulations serving this purpose have to this day relied almost exclusively on codes that calculate according to various theories and approximations, hence on programmed software not on software that adapts and learns from experience and common knowledge. ROOT remains the only physics designated package that took some efforts in this new direction. Although it is mainly oriented towards signal treatment techniques and statistics, ROOT also incorporates machine learning algorithms to a lower extent.

Designing an intelligent predictive or recommender system for laser-plasma interaction should take into consideration quite many aspects. The start point and, at the same time, a central decisive factor in the design is actually the available interaction data, its amount and its structure. Specifically, interaction data for a particular kind of experiment is mostly heterogeneous in the sense that it can comprise experimental findings along with simulation yields and literature references, a situation bound to pose potential problems in terms of hardware, software environments and applicable machine learning paradigms. Storing and converting the available information in the same file format—especially if we are talking about terabytes or petabytes—is a time consuming operation. This caveat may be conveniently mitigated by using the NoSQL databases, a notable feature of big data platforms such as Hadoop or Spark. Furthermore, the NoSQL is schema-free, therefore facilitating structure modifications of data in applications. Through the management layer, data integration and validation can be easily attained. A second aspect of interaction data concerns features like inconsistency, incompleteness, redundancy or intrinsic noisiness. For a particular kind of experiment (e.g. a certain type of laser interacting with a specific target, in a predefined interaction configuration) there might be multiple results due to the fact that the same experiment was performed in different laboratories across the world. Consequently, the above mentioned data characteristics can be explained through the differences in diagnostic equipment or in its placement, through slight variations in the interaction configurations, in target compositions or the type of optical components. Simulations performed with different codes or theoretical estimations might also exist in the literature. Two other possible situations concern unavailable data and divergent or conflictual reports. Such variety entails various signal processing techniques like reduction, cleaning, filtering, integration, transforms and interpolations in order to remove noise, correct the inconsistencies and improve the decision-making process. However, these operations can be important consumers of resources, so they should be performed via distributed computing in conjunction with fast analytics purpose tools such as Apache Impala [77] and Apache Kudu [78].

Further applying machine learning algorithms [79] on this type of extended sets complicates things even more, firstly because we are talking about large volumes of data (at least 1 TB and easily up to several hundreds of TBs), and secondly because training even classical multilayer perceptrons (MLP) [80–83], self-organizing maps (SOM) [84, 85] and especially support vector machines (SVM) [86, 87] on conventional computers renders the process extremely difficult. Practically, this is a striking argument in favor of the custom-made clouds that provide not only computing power but also modularity, scalability and resilience. Beyond Hadoop's substantial parallelization, jobs dispatching and resource allocation capabilities, considerable speedup may be achieved within the Spark environment, owing to its graph technology. Built-in Mahout and MLib [88] machine learning libraries integrate a lot of the commonly deployed algorithms allowing the user to modify or add any new self-written modules. Within these frameworks, a common MLP can easily evolve towards deep learning due to the fact that multiple hidden layers (or cascaded MLPs) are no longer an impediment to fast training and rapid convergence. The grid search algorithm permits testing multiple MLP topologies for the best performance on training and test sets, subsequently returning the best one. When stating multiple, an order of a few tens is perfectly feasible. Another useful tool, the dropout methods, randomly exclude various neurons along with their incoming and outgoing connections in order to achieve performance improvements and to avoid overfitting [89–91]. Some versions do not drop out units but just omit another portion of training data in each of the training cases, ultimately "averaging" over all the yielded MLPs (structures with the same topology but different weights, a consequence of the variation in the training set). This approach mitigates both, overfitting and potential falloffs or stagnations in the learning rate, effects associated primarily with sets featuring high percentages of redundant data. Other algorithms apply the "averaging" over networks with dropped out units or over many networks with different weights instead of merely considering the best configuration. Regardless of what is actually averaged, these solutions act similarly to ensemble learning and can be also combined with unsupervised techniques [92–94]. Inversely, constructive learning allows the user to add units or connections to the network during training, an approach known to be highly effective in escaping local minima of the objective function. All of the above classes of algorithms can be deployed for both CNNs and DNNs and, with slight modifications, even for 3D topologies of SOMs. Considerable boosts in terms of speed may be attainable through MapReduce acceleration [95] or GPU accelerated computing.

Practically, the choice of algorithms is of crucial importance when designing a predictive modeling system as they influence its overall performance both in terms of speed as well as in terms of accuracy and robustness. A high degree of modularity and scalability of the system is also desirable since it is fundamental to be able to add new algorithms and tools, or to replace others, as easily as possible without major reconfiguration and training issues. As new interaction data becomes available on a regular basis, retraining the system and its subsequent functionality are not supposed to be problematic. At the same time, hardware modifications within the cloud should only improve performances and not increase the risk of system crashes. Good predictions should be prevalent even when facing undesired events like hardware failures, software bugs and data corruption and from this point of view, the combination cloud-Hadoop-deep learning is ideal, mainly since Hadoop offers most of all resilience.

2.2. Engineering aspects of big data and deep learning based predictive systems

The development of intelligent systems with direct application in optimizing laser-plasma interaction experiments is a highly demanding task. Since it requires above all, enough hardware resources, the underlying infrastructure supporting the construction and deployment of the predictive systems was chosen to be a private cloud. Interaction with users is achieved via internet, hence, by extension one can consider this a "client–server" system, schematically displayed in **Figure 1**.

The "server-side" offers various functionalities in five areas. Firstly, it ensures the communication with users and handles the requests queues. Concerning the data management, the "server" is also responsible for the data storage, data manipulation and related processing operations. Thirdly, it stores and facilitates the incorporation of new software libraries. It provides computing power for establishing the optimal structure of the intelligent systems,

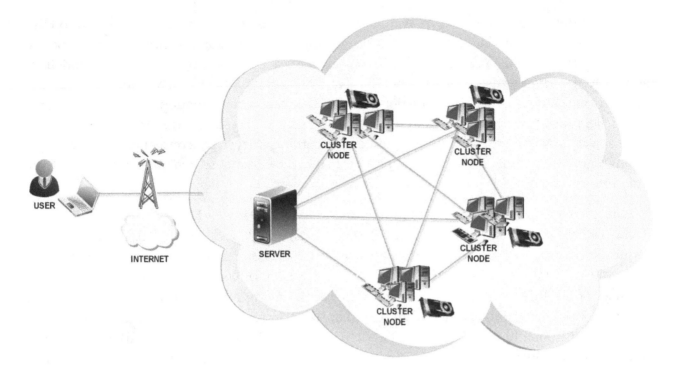

Figure 1. Client–server model of the supporting infrastructure. The server side is the private cloud on top of which resides Hadoop. It handles all tasks, from communications with the users to data storage, heavy computational tasks and ultimately, the deployment mode.

for training and validation. Last but not least, it supports the deployment mode of the validated predictive systems. At this stage, the users introduce the input parameters and obtain the predictions and/or recommendations. Among the advantages offered by a private cloud platform built using Hadoop are the rapid access to information, rapid processing and rapid transmission of results to the end user. But beyond processing and querying vast amounts of heterogeneous data over many nodes of commodity hardware, another significant advantage of the Hadoop streaming utility is the fact that it allows Java as well as non-Java programmed MapReduce jobs to be executed over the Hadoop cluster, in a reliable, fault-tolerant manner. The combination HDFS, HBase [96], Hive [97] and MapReduce is robust. Not only HDFS ensures data replication with redundancy across the cluster but every "map" and "reduce" job is independent of all other ongoing "maps" and "reduces" in the system. However, HDFS based data lakes lack what is a fundamental capability for complex applications that make use of the stored big data, and that is the random reads and writes capability. There is no point in trying to speed up data processing by developing new algorithms if accessing it translates into brute-force readings of an entire file system.

In this sense HBase was deployed on top of the HDFS data lake since it allows the fast random reads and writes that cannot be handled otherwise. As a NoSQL database, it is primarily useful because it can store data in any format. Additionally, HBase can also handle a variety of information that is growing exponentially, something which relational databases cannot. In other words, it supports the real-time updating and querying of the dataset which Hive does not and this is highly suitable for applying dropout and constructive learning on datasets. In contrast, Hive provides structured data warehousing facilities on top of the Hadoop cluster together with a SQL like interface that facilitates the creation of tables and subsequently, the storage of structured data within these tables. Although, existing HBase structures can be mapped to Hive and operated on easily due to the efficient management of large datasets, inconveniently enough for certain cases, the data can be further used only in batch operations. The predictive modelings subject to this chapter use alternatively HBase and Hive as suitable to each of the combinations of algorithms. For a particular interaction scenario, the relevant information is extracted from the data lake, processed for cleaning and then stored into either HBase or Hive. As these sets of data are subject to MapReduce jobs and to machine learning, they may consequently suffer alterations, hence the modified versions are also written to the warehouse. Database dumps to HDFS are performed after each successful prediction experiment.

Within the cloud, the server is running Ubuntu Server 16.04 with MyEclipse 2015 Stable 2.0, Tomcat 8.5.5, JDK 8, release 1.8.0_102, Hadoop 2.7.3, HBase 2.7.3, Hive 2.0.0 installed. User requests are handled via JDBC (with Phoenix for HBase accessing) while the communication with the user is done via servlet developed in MyEclipse. Each of the four cluster nodes consists of six PCs, connected to a switch and each having a QuadCore CPU, a hard drive (1 TB, 6 Gbps, 7200 rpm, 32 MB cache), 16 GB of RAM and a 1000 Mbps full duplex connectivity card. Additionally, four GeForce GTX Titan with 2688 CUDA cores and 6 GB memory were attached to the cluster, one by node, their intended purpose being to facilitate the deployment of the deep learning algorithms. GPU computing is reputed for being well suited to the throughput-oriented workload problems that are characteristic to large-scale data processing. However, integrating GPUs within a Hadoop cluster is not obvious. While, parallel data processing can easily be handled by using several GPUs together or by GPU clustering [98], implementing MapReduce on GPUs has enough limitations [99] and requires a lot of finagling. For example GPUs communicate with difficulty over a network, hence being recommended to function with an Infiniband connection. Moreover GPUs cannot handle virtualization of resources. Their system architecture is therefore not entirely suitable for MapReduce without excessive modifications [98] and, up to recently, GPU and Hadoop were not even compatible. Therefore, to keep things as uncomplicated as possible, MapReduce tasks were entirely handled by the CPU nodes at all times.

After multiple machine learning experiments performed on earlier versions of this cloud [100, 101], observed performances have triggered—apart from hardware upgrades—several other tunings towards its overall optimization and in preparation for applying deep learning on the interaction data sets. These modifications address issues related to increasing the speed of processing raw data along with the speed of MapReduce tasks, decreasing the associated latencies by using fast analytics designated tools and an efficient management of workflows and finally, the containerization of tools and applications. In the design phase of a big data based complex application, special attention is to be given to the way jobs are planned and executed as this contributes to a large extent to the software's performances. For this purpose, workflow engines are a very useful tool as they schedule jobs in the data pipelines ensuring that they are ordered by dependencies. A workflow engine tracks each of the individual jobs and monitors the overall pipeline state. Built-in kill/suspend/restart/resume capabilities bring-in considerable improvements by helping diminish the potential bottlenecks caused by failed and downstreamed jobs. There are quite a few workflow engines available but for integration with Hadoop, the most stable and flexible are Oozie [102], Azkaban [103], Luigi [104], Airflow [105] and Kepler [106]. Criteria for choosing between these take into account the way workflows are defined (configuration-based or code-based), the available support for various job types and its extensibility, the extent to which the state of a workflow may be tracked and most importantly, the manner in which the engine handles failures.

For the sake of simplicity and easiest integration, Oozie 4.2.0 was incorporated leading to a significant increase in the efficiency of all extract-transform-load (ETL) type of jobs as well as of the MapReduce ones. In spite of the lengthy and uneasy XML definition of workflows (configuration-based) and of individual jobs, Oozie is the only one that has built-in Hadoop actions, therefore enjoying the best compatibility with the Hadoop environment and the highest number of supported job types. Additionally, customized job support may be further integrated via available plugins. Within Oozie, workflow jobs are directed acyclic graphs (DAG) specifying a sequence of actions to be executed at certain time intervals, with a certain frequency and according to data availability. Recurrent and interdependent workflow jobs that form a data application pipeline are defined and executed through the Coordinator system. For a more efficient management, supplementary preventive or mitigating actions were coded in the coordinator application in order to cope with situations occurring due to partial, late, delayed or reprocessing of submitted data. A customized Java client that connects to the Oozie server was developed in order to monitor within the user interface, first of all, the workflow DAGs together with the corresponding states and secondly, to view and restart the failed tasks as soon as a notification in this sense is received. Since Oozie does not provide automatic notifications of failed jobs, this feature had to be implemented.

System resources are allocated to the jobs by YARN [107] with included optimizations in terms of efficiency and speed. YARN provides extensive support for long-running state-less batch jobs and analytical processing workloads such as machine learning algorithms. The containerization approach enhances even more these features however it does not rise to the same level of performance as Docker [108], and in this sense, it would be helpful to be able to install and deploy some other containerization technology on Hadoop in order to package applications and dependencies inside the container, to have a consistent environment for execution and, at the same time, enjoy the isolation from other applications or software installed on the host. The combination workflow engine—containerization is attractive for several reasons. First of all, it provides increased control both in the development phase as well as over the big data deployments. Secondly, it reduces significantly the rate of failed or stalling jobs and it offers uniformity and efficiency in resource allocation and resource sharing between different applications by orchestrating and organizing containers across any number of physical and virtual nodes. A containers' orchestrator mitigates the effects caused by failing nodes, adding more nodes or removing nodes from the cluster and by moving the containers from one node to another to keep them available at all times. Unfortunately, associating Hadoop with other container technologies than YARN is cumbersome as this system is not easily able to delegate the clustering functions to an external tool such as a container orchestrator. For instance, the particular installed version of Hadoop together with Docker for YARN grant the YARN NodeManager the possibility to launch YARN containers into Docker containers according to users' specification. However, this feature has certain caveats in terms of software compatibilities. Furthermore, the Docker Container Executor runs only in non-secure mode of HDFS and YARN and it requires Docker daemon to be running on the NodeManagers and the Docker client installed and able to start Docker containers. To prevent timeouts while starting jobs the

Docker images that are to be used by a job should already be found in the NodeManagers. Therefore, a reasonable compromise was met by installing the Docker Engine Utility only on the GPU nodes—without the YARN compatibility mode—with containers incorporating the deep learning libraries, including cuDNN.

Additionally, optimizations in terms of speed and latency mitigation within MapReduce tasks and the raw data processing and analysis are mainly due to Apache Tez [109] installed and configured atop of HDFS. Within a complex system such as a Hadoop cluster, latencies are common, inevitable and may have a variety of causes like storage I/O operations, network communications, architectural design imperfections or running software. Some latency is also inherent when launching jobs. As we have seen above, these latencies can be partially diminished by efficient resource allocation combined with scheduling of jobs. For MapReduce, its startup time is known to be one of the main sources of latencies, further performance enhancements being achievable by improving the dataflow processing and transmission from one stage to another. In this sense, the objective is to completely decouple the execution of the "mapper" from that of the "reducer" and have a direct output transmission from "mapper" to "reducer", with all "mappers" and "reducers" working in parallel. This approach might alleviate latency in jobs completion by up to 25 percent but unfortunately it tends to impact on the fault tolerance. Basically, a global sorting is potentially time-consuming—even when using multiple "mappers"—but it should be avoided mainly as this approach triggers by default the deployment of only one "reducer" which is very inefficient for large data sets.

An alternative strategy implies spilling files with intermediate results from "mapper" to "reducer" in order to preserve a certain degree of fault tolerance. Known as adaptive load moving, this technique leverages on a buffer attached to the output of each "mapper". On filled buffers, a combining function is applied for sorting purposes and the data is "spilled" out to storage. The spilled files are next adaptively pipelined to the "reducers" according to an "avoid overloading" policy and to a spilled files merging perspective. Fault tolerance is hence improved by reducing the risk of "mapper failure" which in turn limits the reducer's ability to merge files and process the information. Adaptive load moving applied to every "mapper" and "reducer" within the Hadoop cluster is better used in conjunction with process pooling for both the master and the worker nodes resulting in a significant spare of memory. Apache Tez was therefore employed to implement this strategy and to further improve other MapReduce related issues. For example, working with Hive and MapReduce often turns into costly operations and latencies of order of at least minutes, especially when executing a join, with "sky-high" query execution time and resource consumption. The data is often sharded and distributed across the network, thus performing a join requires matching tuples to be moved from one machine to another and consequently causing a lot of network I/O overhead. Tez is the one that gives Hive the possibility of running in real time, the query performance improvement being on average 50%. The major advantages of using Tez relate firstly to the adjustable number of "mappers" and "reducers" and secondly to the possibility of using the built-in cost-based query plan optimizations. Prior to executing a query, Tez determines the optimal numbers of "mappers" and "reducers" and automatically adjusts these numbers on the way based on the amount of processed bytes. Using the "Compute statistics" statement, the number of "mappers" and "reducers" can be monitored along with their speed in completing the corresponding tasks. Hence, should a bottleneck appear, its point of origin can be easily identified.

The high volumes of data employed here trigger high query execution times. Tez implements query planning by building up multiple plans and choosing the best one out of the available computed versions. Query plan optimization is constructed in steps, starting from containerization and multi-tenancy provisioning, continuing with vectorization and ultimately with the cost-based planning, evaluation of plans and picking up the optimal one. Multi-tenancy permits the re-use of a container within a query by releasing all containers idling for more than 1 second. Vectorized query execution implies performing operations like scans, aggregations, filtering and joins in batches of 1024 rows at once instead of row by row. Finally, cost-based optimization of query execution plans significantly improves running times and the consumption of resources by evaluating the overall cost of every query as resulted from its associated plan. The evaluation reveals the viable types of operations, computes the cost of each combination and determines to which extent an increased degree of parallelism speeds up the execution time while lowering the amount of commissioned resources and making use of their reusability as much as possible.

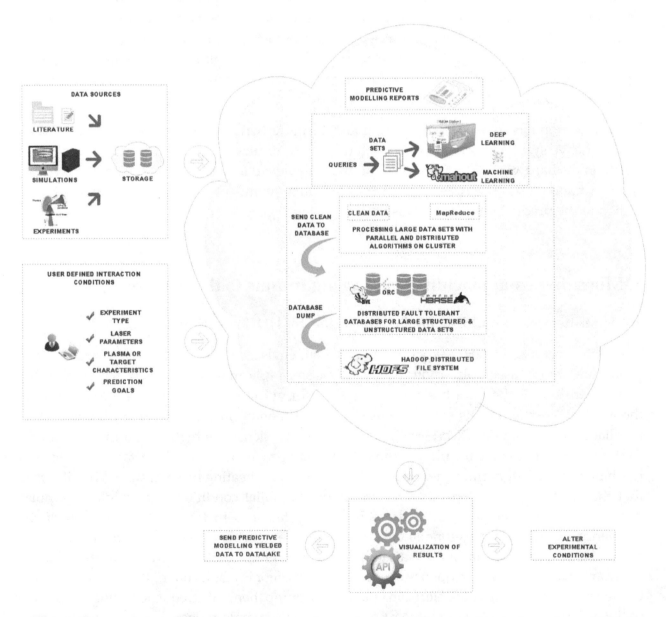

Figure 2. Conceptual design of an intelligent system that performs predictive modeling for laser-plasma interaction experiments.

Within a query, a MapReduce stage is followed by other stages. Tez checks the dependence between them and dispatches the independent ones to be executed in parallel. Another decision towards optimization concerns performing map joins instead of shuffle ones as the map joins minimize data movement and leverage on subsequent localized execution due to the fact that the hash map on every node is integrated into a global in-memory table and solely this table is being streamed, hence joins are made faster. A compromise has to be made, though, by provisioning larger Tez containers (much larger than the YARN ones) and by allocating one CPU and some GBs of memory per each of the containers. The performance of Hive queries can also be improved by enabling compression at the various stages, from table creation to intermediate data and final output. So, for these purposes a conversion to the ORC file format was done as these files result in 78% compression as compared to the initial text ones. Therefore, a search through 1 TB of data brings now only 5 seconds of latency.

Finally, to a reasonable extent, data intensive workloads also benefit from in-memory processing. Tez allows speculative executions to be attempted on faster nodes according to the Longest Approximate Time to End (LATE) strategy. These approaches were found to result in an overall speed performance improvement between one and one and a half orders of magnitude. In the case of iterative jobs, such as cost based function optimizations, an alleviation of up to 20 times in latency was obtained.

This subsection has so far been discussing just the underlying infrastructure used for building the predictive systems for laser-plasma interaction experiments optimizations, focusing not as much on the hardware but on the tools and tricks deployed for making the big data processing run faster and on less resources. However, some attention must be given also to the conceptual design of the predictive systems. This is displayed in **Figure 2**.

3. Migrating from machine learning algorithms to deep learning

3.1. First attempts in building predictive systems for HHG experiments

The particular cases of HHG experiments that were envisaged refer to the interaction of ultra-short and intense laser pulses with overdense plasmas (plasmas with density higher than the critical density). At the most basic level, this mechanism can be understood as the reflection of the incident laser and of its subsequently created harmonics on the oscillating plasma surface (oscillating mirror model OMM [110]). Since the plasma density is higher than the critical one, the laser cannot penetrate the plasma and thus it reflects on its surface. This surface is not flat and it exhibits an oscillatory movement due to the laser-induced heating mechanisms. While it is true that the yielded spectra depends a lot on the on the initial conditions—laser intensity, pulse duration, incidence angle, plasma density—the key factor is in fact the optimization of the resonance absorption as this fundamental process may account for up to 30% of the laser energy being absorbed by the plasma. Practically, the incident electromagnetic wave excites a plasma electron wave of the same frequency and the second harmonic results out of the mix between the plasma electron wave and the electromagnetic laser pump, hence its frequency being the double of the incident wave's. Although the second harmonic is mainly reflected, part of it can propagate inside the plasma and excite a wave of the same frequency, that in turn, by mixing with the incident laser pump yields the third order harmonic. Moreover, it was also demonstrated that there is a correlation between the nonlinear, ponderomotively driven plasma surface motion and the production of energetic electrons [111, 112]. A pronounced asymmetry of longitudinal oscillations in a steep density profile is known to lead to wave breaking which in turn causes fractions of electrons to be irreversibly accelerated into the target. This kinetic process results in further absorption of energy from the laser. Furthermore, the accelerated fast electrons can themselves drive Langmuir waves, in the overdense region as well as in the ramps that form in front of the target, eventually leading to the generation of harmonics. This mechanism, namely, coherent wave excitation (CWE) [113] is the main responsible for HHG at moderate intensities. Further increase in laser intensities improves the prospects for efficient surface high order harmonics generation and, in principle, with relativistic lasers, high harmonics intensities may even exceed the intensity of the focused pulse by several orders of magnitude.

The goal of developing and deploying predictive modeling for HHG experiments was to have an estimate of the maximum order of the highest observable harmonic, along with the intensity, duration, wavelength of the various high harmonics and their conversion efficiency, given a particular laser interacting with a particular kind of plasma. The available data set consisted mainly of simulation data obtained by running various PIC codes but also from experimental data collected from the published scientific literature. Initially the data set amounted to 2 TBs but with the passing of time it reached about 5 TBs so the last predictions using deep learning were performed taking full advantage of the 5 TBs.

The first attempts in performing predictive modeling for high order harmonics generation experiments [100, 101] involved, on one hand commodity hardware with lower performances than the cloud currently used, without any GPUs and, on the other, an earlier version of Hadoop, installed and configured without any of the optimizations introduced in the meantime. This combination implied, first of all, long running times –up to several hours—just for MapReduce and further ones for the machine learning algorithms implemented with Mahout. Each additional TB of data was yet another challenge for the system and its available resources. Supervised learning made an obvious choice, consequently the most popular of the universal functional approximators [114], the MLP, was chosen as a starting point due to its versatility. Using its famous backpropagation algorithm (BKP) [115, 116] for error minimization during training, the MLP solves problems stochastically being able to provide approximate solutions even for extremely complex tasks. The high degree of connectivity between the nodes and the increased nonlinearity of this neural network cause its generalization ability to be among the best, coping rather well even with noisy and missing data. However this comes at the expense of significant running times in the training phase. While increasing the number of hidden layers is likely to lead to the improvement of overall performances, potentially revealing key features embedded in the data, adding too many of them was beyond the old system's capabilities, thus bottlenecks were reached very quickly.

The training set's input values are the laser intensity, laser wavelength, pulse duration, polarization, incidence angle and the type of plasma (introduced as ionization degree and elemental Z number) and its initial density. The desired output values in the training set are the maximum order of the highest observable harmonic, intensity values for different harmonics (including the highest one), harmonics' wavelengths, durations as well as their conversion efficiencies. About 85% of the entire data formed the training set while the rest served as a test set and these percentages were hanged on to during the whole time up to the latest deep learning implementations. Multiple MLP topologies were tested, with different types and numbers of neurons, different numbers of hidden layers, batch or incremental training with various optimization algorithms. Deciding upon the number of neurons in the input layer depends mainly on the number of parameters that define a laser-plasma interaction scenario. The number of neurons in the output layer is generally a function of the yields that need to be classified or predicted. The number of hidden layers and the number of neurons within a layer were empirically determined. Hence, three of the investigated MLPs—henceforth labeled MLP1, MLP2 and MLP3, respectively—were found to exhibit satisfactory behavior in terms of accuracy. However the running hours were discouraging especially since, according to the results, it was obvious that an upgrade towards adding more hidden layers and more neural units was imminent. MLP1 has an input layer consisting of 8 Adaline neurons, two hidden layers, each with 12 sigmoidal neurons and an output layer of 5 sigmoidal units. It was trained with batch training, while the cost function was defined in terms of mean squared error (MSE) and optimized with Steepest Descent. MLP2 has three hidden layers, each with 10 sigmoidal neurons. The second difference from MLP1 is that its cost function was optimized with resilient backpropagation. Finally, MLP3 has two hidden layers, each with 11 sigmoidal units and it deploys the Levenberg-Marquardt algorithm for finding the global minimum of the cost function. For two HHG scenarios, **Table 1** displays the prediction results obtained with each of the three MLPs. Within the first scenario, laser's parameters are as follows: $I = 2 \cdot 10^{18}$ W/cm^2, $\lambda_0 = 800$ nm, polarization p, pulse duration $\tau_0 = 150$ fs, incidence angle $\alpha = 45°$, interacting with an aluminum overdense plasma of electronic density equal to $n_e = 4n_c = 6.875 \cdot 10^{21}$cm^{-3}. For the second scenario, the laser parameters are: $I = 10^{19}$W/cm^2, $\lambda_0 = 800$ nm, polarization p, pulse duration $\tau_0 = 100$ fs, incidence angle with the plasma surface $\alpha = 60°$, while the aluminum plasma has a density of $n_e = 8n_c = 1.375 \cdot 10^{22}$cm^{-3}. The obtained predictions were in good agreement with PIC simulations as well as the literature data. However, it is easy to notice that the predicted intensities of the highest observable harmonic are lower in comparison to both theory and PIC results. This is caused by several factors, one of them being the heterogeneity of the available interaction data and the fact that the sets were minimally processed for cleaning during the "machine learning stages". As the collected information originates from multiple sources, it is obvious that the errors affecting the recorded values have different distribution functions. Furthermore, for a particular interaction scenario, we may have several experimentally determined values for the intensity of the highest observable harmonic and several numerical results. This constitutes redundant data, its principal negative effect being the overfitting. For the MLP based predictive modeling, all the redundant data was kept as it was, without any merging or advanced filtering. Overfitting is known to produce unrealistic predictions in MLPs even with noise free data, let alone with redundancy or sparsity. On the other hand, for certain scenarios, there was no available reference. Hence, the problem of missing information was solved by running a modified version of LPIC++ and recording the corresponding yields. In spite of having applied sampling and some filtering in order to assemble equilibrated training sets, a certain degree of incipient overfitting was detected in case of MLP1 and MLP2, thus some relative underestimation or overestimation was to be expected.

		Highest observable harmonic			
	Max. Ord.	Intensity W/cm^2	Duration fs	Wavelength nm	Conv. efficiency
Scenario 1					
Lit. Data	50	$2 \cdot 10^{11}$	20	16	10^{-7}
PIC Data	58	$2.1 \cdot 10^{11}$	19	13.8	10^{-7}
MLP1	54	10^{11}	21	14.4	10^{-7}
MLP2	56	10^{11}	20	14.8	10^{-7}
MLP3	52	10^{11}	19	15.4	10^{-7}
DNN1	52	$2.18 \cdot 10^{11}$	21	16.3	10^{-7}
DNN2	51	$2.1 \cdot 10^{11}$	19	15	10^{-7}
EL1	50.6	$2.02 \cdot 10^{11}$	20	15.8	10^{-7}
EL2	50	$1.98 \cdot 10^{11}$	20	16	10^{-7}
CNN1	51	$2.12 \cdot 10^{11}$	20	16.2	10^{-7}
CNN2	50.2	$2.04 \cdot 10^{11}$	20	15.4	10^{-7}
CNN3	50	$2 \cdot 10^{11}$	20	16.06	10^{-7}
EL4	50	$2.06 \cdot 10^{11}$	20	16	10^{-7}
EL5	50.4	$1.96 \cdot 10^{11}$	20	16.02	10^{-7}
Scenario 2					
Lit. Data	72	$2 \cdot 10^{11}$	12	11	10^{-7}
PIC Data	76	$2.1 \cdot 10^{11}$	11	10.5	10^{-7}
MLP1	74	$1.5 \cdot 10^{11}$	12	10.8	10^{-7}
MLP2	76	10^{11}	11	10.5	10^{-7}
MLP3	72	$2 \cdot 10^{11}$	12	11	10^{-7}
DNN1	74	$2.16 \cdot 10^{11}$	13	11.5	10^{-7}
DNN2	73	$2.08 \cdot 10^{11}$	11	10	10^{-7}
EL1	72.4	$2 \cdot 10^{11}$	12	10.8	10^{-7}
EL2	72	$2 \cdot 10^{11}$	12	11	10^{-7}
CNN1	73	$2.06 \cdot 10^{11}$	11	12	10^{-7}
CNN2	72.08	$2 \cdot 10^{11}$	12	11	10^{-7}
CNN3	72	$2 \cdot 10^{11}$	12	11	10^{-7}
EL4	72	$2 \cdot 10^{11}$	12	11	10^{-7}
EL5	72.05	$2.08 \cdot 10^{11}$	13	10.6	10^{-7}

Comparative results.

Table 1. Predictive modeling of HHG Scenarios 1 and 2.

Another aspect to be noted is the fact that all the MLPs discussed in this chapter feature hidden and output layers of sigmoidal units and this is the most important factor responsible for underestimation. The sigmoid activation function has a non-zero mean being prone to cause non-zero values in the Hessian matrix of the objective function, hence modifying the global minimum of the latter. A high number of sigmoidal neurons in a network strongly influences the weights adjustment during training, specifically, the corresponding weights in the last layers tend to take very small values (close to zero) and this saturation can last a very long time. To a good extent, the effect was mitigated by using a random initialization of weights, not only in the very beginning but also during the training process. Respectively, after observing a persistent saturation situation for a number of epochs, I performed some adjustments by adding small random values to the stagnating weights. This was found to improve the MLP's estimations on one hand and to increase the predicted values on another. Perhaps this was also one of the causes in the overestimation of certain parameters. A slightly better and more stable behavior was observed in case of MLP3, having required far less additive procedures of random values to the weights. Comparatively with the other two, the errors during training were smaller, the convergence faster and the predicted values for the high order harmonics were, in general, closer to the literature data, owing to the Levenberg–Marquardt algorithm, an algorithm known to improve the overall convergence speed due to the combination between Newton's method and Steepest Descent.

As stated above, on the course of interaction, the laser heats the plasma through various mechanisms. Inherently, some of the electrons acquire a lot of energy and become "hot", having very high temperatures, much higher than the plasma temperature. The percentage of hot electrons is very low but, in spite of this, their effects are not always negligible and, for certain experiments, even damaging. For an HHG experiment, a high percentage of hot electrons can disturb the oscillations of the plasma surface, a situation that affects the reflection of the laser, the CWE mechanism and consequently the HHG. For instance, a strong Brunel effect [111] leads to more thermal electrons. Consequently, it is important to have an accurate estimation of electron temperatures within the plasma along with the corresponding fractions of particles. For this purpose, another MLP (MLP4) was designed since the previous three gave only modest evaluations. Input values in the training set incorporate apart from the previously stated ones, the plasma's initial electronic temperature. The desired output values are electron temperatures accompanied by the estimated percentages of electrons that have these temperatures and the corresponding time moments. The best performing topology was found to be an MLP with 9 Adaline neurons in the input layer, 2 hidden layers, each with 11 sigmoidal units and an output layer with 3 neurons, also sigmoidal. The training was performed incrementally and the cost function defined in terms of MSE and optimized with Levenberg-Marquardt. For the same interaction conditions discussed above plus two additional cases (for Scenario 1, the incidence angle was modified to $30°$ from the normal to the plasma surface, this constituting Scenario 3 while for the same parameters in Scenario 2, the incidence angle was changed to $45°$, this being labeled Scenario 4.) prediction results are shown in four graphs below. **Figures 3** and **4** display comparatively the percentage of electrons estimated to have a temperature above 10 keV at different time moments and above 100 keV, respectively. **Figure 3** refers to Scenarios 1 and 3, while **Figure 4** concerns the second and the fourth. The procedures of random initialization and adjustment (during training) of weights were also applied in an attempt of

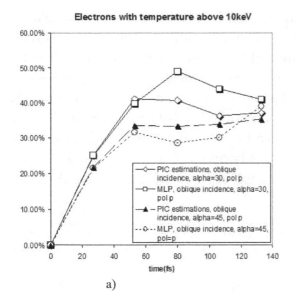

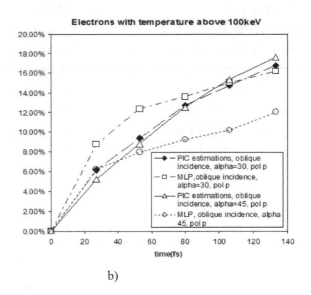

a)   b)

Figure 3. The variation in the percentage of electrons that exceed 10 and 100 keV, for interaction conditions consistent to Scenario 1 and Scenario 3. (a) Refers to the percentage of electrons that exceed 10 keV in temperature while. (b) Refers to those exceeding 100 keV.

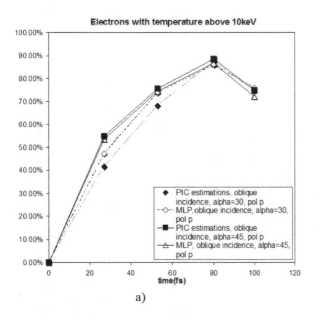

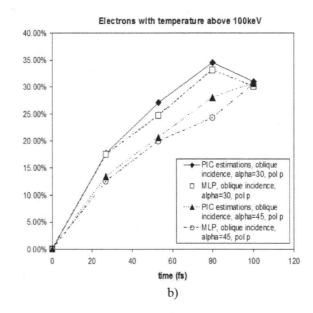

a)   b)

Figure 4. The variation in the percentage of electrons that exceed 10 and 100 keV, for interaction conditions consistent to Scenario 2 and Scenario 4. (a) Refers to the percentage of electrons that exceed 10 keV in temperature while. (b) Refers to those exceeding 100 keV.

improving MLP4's performance. However, it is the belief of this author that the combination between the network's topology, the sampling of available interaction data, the random additions and the incremental training, have led to some significant overestimations of the percentages of electrons (some 10%) in certain cases as values reported in the literature are smaller.

Prior to migrating towards deep learning, some trials were made with an unsupervised network, namely a SOM. The same training sets were used just that the data was differently organized, namely one entry in the training set consists of a 5 × 10 matrix. The matrix's columns stand for:

plasma (ionization degree, initial electronic temperature, initial plasma density, final plasma density, maximum plasma density), laser (intensity, wavelength, pulse duration, polarization, incidence angle) and 8 columns characterizing 8 different high order harmonics including the highest one (order, intensity, wavelength, duration, conversion efficiency). Several topologies were tested. However, just one of them yielded satisfactory results, namely a 2D network. The neurons' positions into the map were optimized based on Euclidian distance minimization and the competitive learning principle [117, 118]. SOM1 has a total of 16×21 nodes, disposed on a regular rectangular grid, with 16 nodes for mapping the harmonics' intensity and 21 for the orders of the harmonics. While a color code was employed for duration of pulses, the

Harmonic order	Harmonic's characteristics	PIC (calculated)	MLP1	MLP2	MLP3	SOM1
10	order	10	10	10	10	10
	intensity (W/cm^2)	$6 \cdot 10^{15}$	$4 \cdot 10^{15}$	$4 \cdot 10^{15}$	$6 \cdot 10^{15}$	$8 \cdot 10^{15}$
	duration (fs)	47	47	47	47	45
	wavelength (nm)	80	79.3	79.5	80.5	80
	conversion efficiency	10^{-3}	10^{-3}	10^{-3}	10^{-3}	10^{-3}
20	order	22	20	20	20	22
	intensity (W/cm^2)	$4 \cdot 10^{14}$	$3.5 \cdot 10^{14}$	$3.5 \cdot 10^{14}$	$4 \cdot 10^{14}$	$4 \cdot 10^{14}$
	duration (fs)	32	34	34	34	35
	wavelength (nm)	37	40	40	40	36.4
	conversion efficiency	10^{-4}	10^{-4}	10^{-4}	10^{-4}	10^{-4}
30	order	34	30	32	30	28
	intensity (W/cm^2)	$5 \cdot 10^{13}$	$4.5 \cdot 10^{13}$	$5 \cdot 10^{13}$	$4 \cdot 10^{13}$	$4.1 \cdot 10^{13}$
	duration (fs)	26	27	27	27	28
	wavelength (nm)	23.5	26.7	25	26.7	28.6
	conversion efficiency	10^{-5}	10^{-5}	10^{-5}	10^{-5}	10^{-5}
40	order	46	42	44	40	38
	intensity (W/cm^2)	$4.5 \cdot 10^{12}$	$4 \cdot 10^{12}$	$4.2 \cdot 10^{12}$	$4.2 \cdot 10^{12}$	$6 \cdot 10^{12}$
	duration (fs)	22	23	23	24	25
	wavelength (nm)	17.4	19	18.2	20	21
	conversion efficiency	10^{-6}	10^{-6}	10^{-6}	10^{-6}	10^{-6}
50	order	58	54	56	52	49
	intensity (W/cm^2)	$2.1 \cdot 10^{11}$	10^{11}	10^{11}	10^{11}	$4 \cdot 10^{11}$
	duration (fs)	19	21	20	19	21
	wavelength (nm)	13.8	14.4	14.8	15.4	14.4
	conversion efficiency	10^{-7}	10^{-7}	10^{-7}	10^{-7}	10^{-7}

Comparative results for harmonics of orders 10, 20, 30, 40 and 50.

Table 2. Predictive modeling of HHG Scenario 1 using a SOM.

wavelengths and conversion efficiencies were derived computationally and written in an additional text file accompanying the map. The large number of nodes in this network is the consequence of the need for a better visualization of the final results. However, this weighs considerably in terms of number of training epochs and computation time and it was found that the SOM required far more resources than the MLPs and it took longer to train. In principle, it would be ideal to add more units and some improvements in terms of algorithms, along with the elimination of the accompanying text file and the associated computationally derived values. This basically means a SOM with more than two dimensions which, at the time, it was nearly impossible to implement. Hence, I desisted to pursue the development of predictive modeling using unsupervised learning. For exemplification, MLP performances in predicting high order harmonics and their features—for the interaction conditions described in Scenario 1—are displayed in **Table 2**, together with the SOM's and the results obtained from PIC simulations. The agreement between the forecasts of the MLPs and the ones of SOM is quite good, the values being within the same range.

3.2. Deep learning: Towards improved predictive systems for HHG experiments

In the view of building better predictive systems and even recommender systems for optimized laser-plasma interaction experiments, hardware upgrades were firstly made. Apart from adding an extra cluster node, replacing the storage hard drives with increased capacity ones in all computers and adding extra 8GB of RAM to all of them, a total of four GeForce GTX Titan were attached to the cluster, one by node. At the most basic level, deep learning networks can be viewed as modified MLPs that contain a high number of units and layers and are algorithmically more complex than the classical MLPs. Hence, the GPUs provide support for heavy computations. The Docker engine was installed on the GPU nodes along with the necessary Nvidia drivers and the nvidia-docker. A Docker image containing Theano, TensorFlow, Keras, Caffe, cuDNN and of course CUDA 8.0 and Ubuntu 14.04 was downloaded from GitHub, built and deployed as a container on the GPUs. All the deep learning based predictive modeling systems described in this chapter were discovered (structurally), trained, built and tested using these libraries. The optimal ones were implemented and deployed on the Hadoop cluster. The containerization of GPU applications provides important benefits such as reproducible builds, ease of deployment, isolation of individual devices running across heterogeneous driver/toolkit environments, requiring only Nvidia drivers to be installed. The images are agnostic of the Nvidia driver, with the required character devices and driver files being mounted when starting the container on the target machine.

The designation of the deep learning based predictive modeling systems were, for start, the same HHG experiments. However, the data lake increasingly incorporates other related interaction data. It is expected that more available information on what happens during various experiments performed in similar conditions will help to better understand the physics of interaction and consequently, to foresee what phenomena might occur. Huge data sets needed for training - after having been subject to MapReduce—have to be transferred to the GPU nodes. While the GPU memory system provides a higher bandwidth as compared to the CPU memory system, transferring data between the main memory and GPU memory is very slow. Copying via DMA to and from the GPU over the PCIe bus involves expensive context switches that reduce the available bandwidth considerably. This is why directives such as "gmp shared" and "gmp private" have been added for identifying the data to be transferred between main memory and GPU memory. These directives are translated to relevant memory transfer calls, like cudaMalloc, cudaMemcpy, cudaFree within CUDA. Furthermore, potential redundant data transfers may slow down the GPU while running other jobs. These can be avoided through various dataflow and jobs workflow optimization techniques. For this reason, it was highly important to have the workflow engine and resource allocator configured and running on Hadoop. Additionally, the optimizations brought to MapReduce impact directly on the dataflow to GPUs.

The first deep learning networks that have been implemented were the DNNs. Since, basically, DNNs are MLPs with many hidden layers—commonly, a few tens—it was a relatively easy transition from machine learning to deep learning. In spite of this, things tend to get complicated when trying to guess out an optimal DNN configuration. This is a very tedious process. The solution comes from adopting a grid search algorithm combined with other two, namely constructive learning and dropout. This way, I was able to generate several hundreds of DNNs using constructive learning and dropout algorithms during the training phase and search for the optimal ones with grid search. Each of the tested configurations was cataloged and the best performance ones were prioritized for further usage. Both constructive learning and dropout can be performed in three ways, all of which have been tested. The first one involves adding more neurons to layers along with their corresponding connections to the others in the network (constructive learning) or simply removing ones (dropout) if performances are found to stagnate at an unsatisfactory level during the training phase. The training is continued and the evolution monitored. These actions, of adding and removing units may be performed several times during a training procedure. The second approach involves keeping the same network configuration while applying the algorithms on the data set instead of layers. Hence, instead of adding or removing units, one adds more data or removes portions of it from the training set. Last but not least, the third method is a combination of these, namely the construction and dropout procedures can be applied to both the network and the data. Although this is the most costly strategy, both in terms of resources as well as in terms of running times, it was by far the most effective one, yielding the best performances. This latter approach was also the one chosen for building the DNN based predictive systems.

Out of the huge pool of networks (nearly 500), two deep neural networks were found to perform better than all others. They will henceforth be labeled DNN1, respectively DNN2. DNN1 has an input layer consisting of 8 Adaline units, 20 hidden layers, containing only sigmoidal neurons. All layers have 12 units, except for the layers 3, 5, 6, 8 and 11. Layer 3 has 11 units, layer 5 has 15, layers 6 and 8 contain 12 each while layer 11 has just 7. The output layer features 5 sigmoidal neurons. DNN1 was trained with batch training and the cost function was optimized with Levenberg–Marquardt. DNN2 has an input layer consisting of 8 Adaline units, 36 hidden layers, containing only sigmoidal units. All layers are formed by 14 neurons, except for the layers 2, 6, 7, 9, 12, 16, 18, 23, 24, 25, 28, 30, 31, 32 and 35. Layer 2 has 15 units, layers 6, 9, 16, 25, 28 and 32 have 12, layers 7, 18 and 31 contain 13 each, layer 12 has 16, layer 23 has 15, layer 24 has 11, layer 30 contains 9 units while layer 35 has only 7. The output layer features 5 sigmoidal neurons. Training was performed also in batches and the cost function was optimized with Levenberg–Marquardt. For HHG Scenarios 1 and 2 discussed in the previous subsection, **Table 1** also includes the predictions obtained with DNN1 and DNN2. The following lines refer to predictions made with DNNs combined with ensemble learning and these are labeled EL1 and EL2, respectively. EL1 and EL2 were obtained by applying ensemble learning on the best 50 configurations of all tested DNNs—this being the case of EL1—and, respectively over all configurations (EL2). This means that the predictions offered either by the 50 DNNs, either by all of them, were averaged arithmetically and the result used as the prediction value. Although it might not seem appropriate to use averaging, this algorithm has its foundations in statistics and it is expected to offer better performances than a plain DNN. Using ensemble learning also mitigates the underestimation problem caused by the sigmoidal neurons although this problem tends to be less pregnant in the case of deep neural networks due to their increased numbers of layers and units. Consequently the effect on the cost function optimization is not as strong. As a general conclusion, the predictions furnished by the DNNs and the DNNs combined with ensemble learning are much closer to the ones reported in the scientific literature than the values offered by the MLPs.

For Scenarios 2 and 4 presented in Section 3.1, the temperatures of the electrons within the plasma along with the corresponding percentages were predicted using DNN3 and EL3. **Figure 5a** displays the evolution of the electrons having temperatures above 10 keV, in terms of percentages, for Scenario 2 while **Figure 5b** refers to the same evolution but for conditions consistent with Scenario 4. **Figure 6a, b** present the variation of electron percentages for electrons having temperatures higher than 100 keV for Scenarios 2 (**Figure 6a**) and 4 (**Figure 6b**), respectively.

In each of the graphs four curves can be noticed. This is because the two curves corresponding to DNN3 and to EL3 are accompanied by the predictions of the MLP4 presented in the previous subsection and also by the results of PIC simulations. DNN3 has an input layer consisting of 9 Adaline units, 43 hidden layers, containing only sigmoidal neurons. All layers are formed by 15 neurons, except for the layers 4, 6, 9, 13, 15, 19, 21, 27, 34, 35, 38, 40 and 41. Layer 4 has 16 units, layers 6, 9, 19, 34, 35 and 40 have 12, layers 13, 15 and 27 contain 11 each, layer 21 has 17, layer 38 has 14, and finally, layer 41 has 11. The output layer features 7 sigmoidal neurons. The training was performed also in batches and the cost function was optimized with Levenberg–Marquardt.

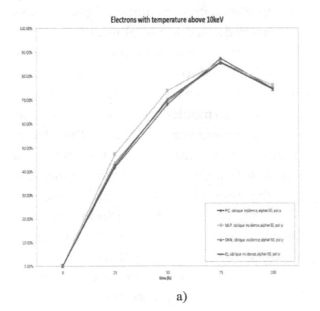

a)

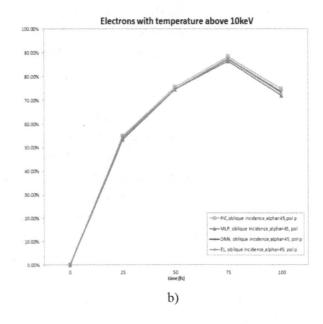

b)

Figure 5. The variation in the predictive percentage of electrons that exceed 10 keV, for interaction conditions consistent to Scenario 2 and Scenario 4. (a) Refers to Scenario 2 while (b) refers to Scenario 4.

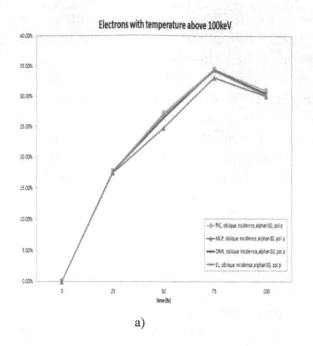

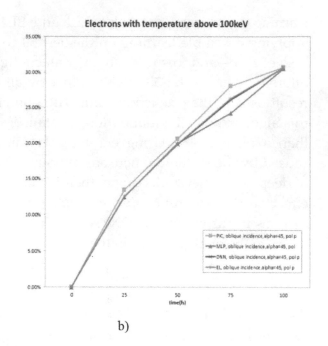

a)   b)

Figure 6. The variation in the percentage of electrons that exceed 100 keV, for interaction conditions consistent to Scenario 2 and Scenario 4. (a) Refers to Scenario 2 while (b) refers to Scenario 4.

EL3 was obtained by applying arithmetic averaging over a number of 100 predictions coming from the best 100 different DNN configurations that have been tested out of 478. Examining the curves, several conclusions can be drawn. Firstly, the DNN and the EL curves are very close, nearly superimposed. Secondly, the values predicted by DNN3 and EL3 are closer to the ones obtained from PIC simulations and more distanced from the predictions of the MLP. To the extent to which the PIC calculations are closer to real measurements, it can be confirmed that DNN and EL predictions are better than the MLP ones.

Since the obtained results were encouraging, further trials have been performed in the deep learning area, namely the deep neural networks were replaced with convolutional ones. CNNs are mostly reputed for their high suitability for applications dedicated to visual recognition from images. Therefore, in a way, CNNs' architectures make the explicit assumption that the inputs are images but this is not an incommoding aspect as—prior to being fed to a CNN—the values in the training and test data sets can be reorganized within an input volume formed out of laser parameters, plasma characteristics and yielded high order harmonics' characteristics just as images are normally structured. Consequently, I found a convenient way to organize the interaction information for the supervised training by making each entry in the training set a $20 \times 20 \times 20$ volume, in conjunction with a look-up table technique (LUT). The first dimension of each cube contains a reference in a LUT regarding the information on the incident laser's parameters, the second one includes references to the plasma characteristics (including electron and ion temperatures) while the last dimension has the references to high order harmonics spectra and to hot electrons' temperatures and percentages. The very nature of the CNN facilitates the incorporation of more features within the training and test sets. What distinguishes CNNs from DNNs is the fact that all of its layers have neurons arranged in three dimensions: width, height, depth. A second major difference concerns the connectivity. Within a DNN, all units are connected to all other neurons in the previous as well as in the next layer. As the number of layers rises, the number of connections grows exponentially, thus impacting dramatically on the computational resources. The CNNs bring a major change. The neurons in a layer are only connected to a small region in the layer before it. The output layer is the smallest in dimensions, as inherently, by the end of the network, the full input is reduced to a single vector of class scores arranged along the depth dimension. Three main types of layers exist within the architecture: convolutional layer, pooling layer and the fully connected layer and these are stacked together to form a CNN. The input is fed firstly to one or more subsequent convolutional layers. This layer is the core building block of the network and it performs all the heavy computations. More specifically, it calculates the output of neurons that are connected to local regions in the input, each of the neurons computing a dot product between its weights and a small region it is connected to in the input volume. The convolutional layer has as parameters a set of learnable filters, defined by the user. Every filter is small spatially (along the width and height dimensions), but extends through the full depth of the input volume (what in this particular case is the high orders harmonics spectra). Moreover, each of the filters is looking for a different thing in the input. During the forward pass, each filter is slid (convolved) across the width and height of the input volume and dot products between the entries of the filter and the input at any position are hence calculated. As the filter is slid, a bi-dimensional activation map is produced, that gives the responses of that filter at every spatial position. These activation maps are stacked along the depth dimension and produce the output volume which is next fed either to a pooling layer, either to a second convolutional layer. Intuitively, the network will learn filters that activate when they see some type of feature such as an increased number of high order harmonics or very intense ones on the first layer, or, eventually, an entire rich spectra on the higher layers of the network. The pooling layers perform a downsampling operation along the spatial dimensions (width, height), resulting in smaller volumes. Most commonly, they are periodically inserted in-between successive convolutional layers as they progressively reduce the spatial size of the representation in order to lower the amount of parameters and ease up the computational load in the network. But more importantly, pooling layers mitigate overfitting. The pooling layer operates independently on every input slice, most of the time by using the "max" operation. In addition to max pooling, average pooling or L2-norm pooling may be encountered. Historically, average pooling used to be the most popular but recently it has been progressively replaced by the max pooling as the latter was demonstrated to work better in practice. The fully-connected layer computes the class scores and packs them in a vector, each class score representing a high order harmonic with particular features. This is the only layer within which neurons are connected just as in a DNN. Their activations can hence be computed with a matrix multiplication followed by a bias offset. Basically, both the fully connected layer and the convolutional layer perform the convolution but the neurons in the convolutional layer are connected only to a local region in the input, and many of them share parameters in order to save computational resources.

As with the previous case of the DNNs, about 600 different CNNs have been generated and searched through with the aid of the grid search algorithm. To generate the configurations, several operations have been applied. Firstly, the number of convolutional and pooling layers was varied, as well as their position. For example, I constructed networks containing a pooling layer after each convolutional layer or a pooling layer after each two or three convolutional layers. In some network versions, pooling layers were absent except for a single one, just before the fully connected layer. Secondly, within each convolutional layer, the number of filters was modified in order to observe what happens if the layer is sensitive to more features or if it is sensitive to features that are not relevant for all the types of HHG experiments. Thirdly, several pooling methods have been tested for the pooling layers in each network, namely, the classical max pooling, the average pooling and the stochastic pooling. Last but not least, the dropout and constructive learning algorithms were applied on the fully connected layer, resulting in more CNN configurations. For efficiency purposes, regularization methods such as L2 [119] and elastic net regularization [120] were applied to all the convolutional layers and to the fully connected layer when some of the weights were observed to peak excessively. The objective was to force the layers of the CNN to make use of all of their inputs at the same rate (as much as possible) rather than to use portions of their inputs preferentially. However, the risk is ending up in having a network layer with neuron weights that are "diffuse" and rather small. Elastic net regularization—a combination between L1 and L2 types—proved to be more efficient than either of the two. Ensemble learning was also deployed, just as before, averaging over either the predictions offered by all networks, either by applying the average on the best performing 10% of the configurations. The best performing three configurations are labeled CNN1, CNN2 and CNN3, respectively. All the networks take the same input size, namely the $20 \times 20 \times 20$ volume described above and were exposed to the elastic net regularization. Their configurations are as follows. CNN1 has four convolutional layers. The first one has 128 filters and a filter size of $5 \times 5 \times 20$, the second and third convolutional layers have 256 filters but a smaller filter size, more precisely $3 \times 3 \times 20$. Finally, the fourth convolutional layer has 512 filters and the same filter size as the latter two. After the first and the third layers, a pooling layer was introduced. The pooling layers use stochastic pooling. The network's architecture ends with a fully connected 3D cubic layer with 1024 units. It can be noticed that when applying a cubic root to this value, the resulting number of units on each dimension is not an integer. This is because, dropout and constructive learning were applied to the fully connected layer resulting in either vacancies, either insertion of neurons into the volume and in an overall addition of 24 units. The training of CNN1 was done in batches of 512 examples per gradient step with stochastic gradient descent used for the cost function optimization along with the bespoke backpropagation of errors. CNN2 has five convolutional layers, also optimized with elastic net regularization, the first four ones being identical to CNN1's. The fifth layer has, 512 filters, a filter size of $3 \times 3 \times 20$ and it is followed by the sole pooling layer of CNN2. This pooling layer also employs stochastic pooling. The network's architecture ends with two fully connected 3D cubic layers with 1024 units each but with different configurations of neurons within the layers' volumes. This is again due to dropout and constructive learning applied to the fully connected layers. The training of CNN2 was done in the same way but the cost function optimization was achieved via Levenberg–Marquardt. Last but not least, CNN3 has also five convolutional layers (elastic net regularization was applied to the weights), with the first layer having 126 filters and the same $5 \times 5 \times 20$ filter size. The second and the third layers have 252 filters, the second having a $5 \times 5 \times 20$ filter size and the third a $3 \times 3 \times 20$. The fourth and the fifth have 504 filters with the same filter size as the previous one. CNN3 has just one pooling layer in between the fourth and the fifth layers, which makes use of max pooling. The last convolutional layer is followed by two fully connected 768 units layers that were subject to dropout and constructive learning. The training was done also in batches, the stochastic gradient descent being employed with the AdaDelta adaptive learning method [121]. CNN1 and CNN2 use a stride of one for all the convolutional layers while CNN3 uses a stride of 2 for the first and the fourth convolutional layers. This is a consequence of compromising based on the memory constraints that, at some point, bottleneck the GPUs. EL4 and EL5 are ensemble learning yields. EL4 averages over the best performing 10% of the CNNs while EL5 averages over all. For HHG Scenarios 1 and 2 discussed in the previous subsection, the last rows of **Table 1** feature the predictions obtained with the CNNs, EL4 and EL5.

For predicting the temperatures of the electrons within the plasma along with the corresponding percentages, it was found that the performances of CNN1, CNN2, CNN3, EL4 and EL5 were roughly identical and very close to those of DNN3 and EL3. In terms of running times, the convolutional neural networks take less time to train than the deep networks, the order being 50 hours less, on average. Prior to applying ensemble learning, the GPU Inference Engine (GIE) was used in the test phase to optimize the trained networks for run-time performance. Layer optimizations are attainable through GIE to the extent to which layers with unused output are eliminated in order to save computation time or layers may be fused for better overall performance.

One last comment concerns the libraries Theano, TensorFlow, Keras and Caffe. All four of these libraries have been alternatively used to implement both the DNNs and the CNNs. Running code written in TensorFlow was found to have the lowest running times, followed by those written in Caffe, Theano and Keras which took the most time to complete (taking 23 more minutes to complete). However, the differences are not that disturbing so perhaps this is due to some less optimal code. In terms of user friendliness, I found that the easiest to work with was Theano, followed by Caffe, TensorFlow and Keras. Again, this ranking is subjective since Theano was the first library I started working with. There is still a lot of work to be done and more room for improvements especially towards building recommender systems, hence prescriptive analytics, by combining CNNs with reinforcement learning policies. This would be of particular interest since such a system would issue a precise recommendation on how to adjust the interaction conditions in order to optimize a particular laser-plasma interaction experiment.

4. Conclusion

Technological advances in the field of laser -plasma interaction and diagnostics have provided the scientific community with lots of data. Within the last few years we have been experiencing a continuously upraising accessibility, not only to storage space and increased computer power, but also to a multitude of readily-built and easily modifiable open-source software libraries. It is thus becoming less and less problematic to exploit and explore this already available information in ways that have never been attempted before.

This paper proposes an alternative to the classical plasma kinetics simulations. Acknowledging the potential innovative technologies like cloud computing, big data, machine learning and, ultimately, the deep learning have for science, the author showed how these can be used for predictive modeling of laser-plasma interaction scenarios, with a focus on high harmonics generation. The deployment of the presented systems has the potential of yielding better predictive analytics and hence optimized laser-plasma interaction experiments, by offering a fair estimation of interaction conditions or insights on different phenomena occurring during the laser-plasma interaction.

Acknowledgements

The author would like to acknowledge support from the National Authority for Scientific Research and Innovation under Program NUCLEU, project PN1647 LAPLAS IV.

Author details

Andreea Mihailescu

Address all correspondence to: andreea.mihailescu@inflpr.ro

Lasers Department, National Institute for Lasers, Plasma and Radiation Physics, Bucharest-Magurele, Romania

References

[1] Yanovsky V et al. Ultra-high intensity—300-TW laser at 0.1 Hz repetition rate. Optics Express. 2008;**16**:2109-2114

[2] Texas Petawatt Laser [Internet]. 2015. Available from: texaspetawatt.ph.utexas.edu/overview.php

[3] Vulcan Laser Facility [Internet]. 2015. Available from: www.clf.stfc.ac.uk/CLF/Facilities/Vulcan/12248.aspx

[4] Astra Gemini Facility [Internet]. 2015. Available from: www.clf.stfc.ac.uk/CLF/Facilities/Astra/12254.aspx

[5] PHELIX Laser Facility [Internet]. 2015. Available from: https://www.gsi.de/en/start/research/forschungsgebiete_und_experimente/appa_pni_gesundheit/plasma_physics phelix/phelix.htm

[6] Apollon Laser [Internet]. 2015. Available from: http://www.apollon-laser.fr/

[7] Kneip S et al. Bright spatially coherent synchrotron X-rays from a table-top source. Nature Physics. 2010;**6**:980

[8] McKinnie I, Kapteyn H. High-harmonic generation: Ultrafast lasers yield x-rays. Nature Photonics. 2010;**4**:149

[9] PIC Codes and Methodology [Internet]. 2015. Available from: http://plasmasim.physics.ucla.edu/codes

[10] Pfund RE et al. LPIC++ a parallel one-dimensional relativistic electromagnetic particle-in-cell code for simulating laser-plasma interaction. AIP Conference Proceedings. 1998; **426**:141

[11] Lichters R et al. Short-pulse laser harmonics from oscillating plasma surfaces driven at relativistic intensity. Physics of Plasmas. 1996;**3**:3425

[12] Verboncoeur JP et al. An object-oriented electromagnetic PIC code. Computer Physics Communications. 1995;**87**:199

[13] Burau H et al. PIConGPU: A fully relativistic particle-in-cell code for a GPU cluster. IEEE Transactions on Plasma Science. 2010;**38**(10):2831

[14] Brady C et al. EPOCH, an open source PIC code for high energy density physics, user manual for the EPOCH PIC codes version 4.3.4, University of Warwick, collaborative computational project in plasma. Physics. 2015

[15] Vsim [Internet]. 2016. Available from: https://www.txcorp.com/vsim

[16] Fonseca RA et al. OSIRIS: A three-dimensional, fully relativistic particle in cell code for modeling plasma based accelerators. In: Computational Science-ICCS 2002, Series Lecture Notes in Computer Science. Vol. 2331. Berlin/Heidelberg: Springer; 2002. pp. 342-351

[17] Fonseca RA et al. One-to-one direct modeling of experiments and astrophysical scenarios: Pushing the envelope on kinetic plasma simulations. Plasma Physics and Controlled Fusion. 2008;**50**:124034

[18] Fiuza F et al. Efficient modeling of laser–plasma interactions in high energy density scenarios. Plasma Physics and Controlled Fusion. 2011;**53**:074004

[19] Huang C et al. Quickpic: A highly efficient particle-in-cell code for modeling wakefield acceleration in plasmas. Journal of Computational Physics. 2006;**217**:658

[20] An W et al. An improved iteration loop for the three dimensional quasi-static particle-in-cell algorithm: Quickpic. Journal of Computational Physics. 2013;**250**:165

[21] Tzoufras M et al. A Vlasov-Fokker-Planck code for high energy density physics. Journal of Computational Physics. 2011;**230**:6475

[22] Tzoufras M et al. A multi-dimensional Vlasov-Fokker-Planck code for arbitrarily anisotropic high-energy-density plasmas. Physics of Plasmas. 2013;**20**:056303

[23] Owens JD et al. A survey of general-purpose computation on graphics hardware. Computer Graphics Forum. 2007;**26**:80-113

[24] Owens JD et al. GPU computing, graphics processing units-powerful, programmable and highly parallel—are increasingly targeting general-purpose computing applications. Proceedings of the IEEE. 2008;**96**:879

[25] Fatahalian K, Houston M. A closer look at GPUs. Communications of the ACM. 2008;**51**(10): 50

[26] GPU Applications: Hundreds of Applications Accelerated [Internet]. 2017. Available from: http://www.nvidia.com/object/gpu-applications.html

[27] Tesla GPU Accelerators for Servers [Internet]. 2017. Available from: http://www.nvidia.com/object/tesla-servers.html

[28] Decyk VK, Singh TV. Particle-in-cell algorithms for emerging computer architectures. Computer Physics Communications. 2014;**185**:708

[29] Suzuki J et al. Acceleration of PIC simulation with GPU. Plasma and Fusion Research. 2011;**6**:2401075

[30] Lu Q, Amudson J, Synergia CUDA. GPU-accelerated accelerator modeling package. Journal of Physics Conference Series. 2014;**513**:052021

[31] Decyk VK. Skeleton particle-in-cell codes on emerging computer architectures. Computing in Science & Engineering. 2015;**17**:47

[32] Abreu P et al. PIC codes in new processors: A full relativistic PIC code in CUDA-enabled hardware with direct visualization. IEEE Transactions on Plasma Science. 2011;**39**:675

[33] Decyk VK, Singh TV. Adaptable particle-in-cell algorithms for graphical processing units. Computer Physics Communications. 2011;**182**:641

[34] Germaschewski K et al. The plasma simulation code: A modern particle-in-cell code with patch-based load balancing. Journal of Computational Physics. 2016;**318**:305

[35] Abreu P et al. Streaming the Boris pusher: A CUDA implementation. AIP Conference Proceedings. 2009;**1086**:328

[36] Yang C et al. Fast weighing method for plasma PIC simulation on GPU-accelerated heterogeneous systems. Journal of Central South University of Technology. 2013;**20**:1527

[37] Stantchev G et al. Fast parallel particle-to-grid interpolation for plasma PIC simulations on the GPU. Journal of Parallel and Distributed Computing. 2008;**68**:1339

[38] Rossinelli D et al. Mesh-particle interpolations on graphics processing units and multicore central processing units. Philosophical Transactions of the Royal Society A. 2011;**369**:2164

[39] Wang P et al. A parallel current deposition method for PIC simulation on GPU. In: Proceedings of IEEE International Vacuum Electronics Conference (IVEC2015), IEEE, IEEE XPlore Digital Library; 2015. p. 7224036

[40] Kong X et al. Particle-in-cell simulations with charge—conserving current deposition on graphic processing units. Journal of Computational Physics. 2011;**230**:1676

[41] Rossi F et al. Towards robust algorithms for current deposition and dynamic load-balancing in a GPU particle-in-cell code. AIP Conference Proceedings. 2012;**1507**:184

[42] The ALaDyn PIC Suite [Internet]. 2015. Available from: http://www.physycom.unibo.it/aladyn_pic/

[43] FBPIC (Fourier-Bessel Particle-in-Cell Code) [Internet]. 2016. Available from: https://fbpic.github.io/index.html

[44] Kirchen M, Lehe R. Accelerating a Spectral Algorithm for Plasma Physics with Python/Numba on GPU, talk given at GPU Technology Conference GTC 2016. p. IDS6353

[45] Apache Hadoop [Internet]. 2017. Available from: https://hadoop.apache.org

[46] MapReduce Tutorial. Apache Hadoop 2.7.4 [Internet]. 2017. Available from: https://hadoop.apache.org/docs/stable/hadoop-mapreduce-client/hadoop-mapreduce-client-core/MapReduceTutorial.html

[47] Apache Mahout. An environment for quickly creating scalable performant machine learning applications [Internet]. 2017. Available from: https://mahout.apache.org

[48] Lyubimov D, Palumbo A. Apache Mahout: Beyond MapReduce. Distributed Algorithm Design; 2016. ISBN-13: 978-1523775781

[49] Theano [Internet]. 2017. Available from: http://deeplearning.net/software/theano/

[50] TensorFlow [Internet]. 2017. Available from: https://www.tensorflow.org/

[51] Keras [Internet]. 2017. Available from: https://keras.io/

[52] Caffe [Internet]. 2017. Available from: http://caffe.berkeleyvision.org/

[53] Krizhevsky A et al. Imagenet classification with deep convolutional neural networks. Advances in Neural Information Processing Systems. 2012;**1**:1097-1105

[54] Opitz D, Maclin R. Popular ensemble methods: An empirical study. Journal of Artificial Intelligence Research. 1999;**11**:169-198

[55] Polikar R. Ensemble based systems in decision making. IEEE Circuits and Systems Magazine. 2006;**6**(3):21-45

[56] Rokach L. Ensemble-based classifiers. Artificial Intelligence Review. 2010;**33**(1–2):1-39

[57] Bergstra J, Bengio Y. Random search for hyper-parameter optimization. The Journal of Machine Learning Research. 2012;**13**:281

[58] Bao Y, Liu Z. A fast grid search method in support vector regression forecasting time series, intelligent data engineering and automated learning-IDEAl 4224 of the series. Lecture Notes in Computer Science. 2006;**4224**:504-511

[59] Srivastava N et al. Dropout: A simple way to prevent neural networks from overfitting. Journal of Machine Learning Research. 2014;**15**(1):1929-1958

[60] Hinton G et al. Improving neural networks by preventing co-adaptation of feature detectors [Internet]. 2012. Computing Research Repository (CoRR) abs/1207.0580. Available from: https://arxiv.org/abs/1207.0580

[61] Baldi P, Sandowski P. The dropout learning algorithm. Artificial Intelligence. 2014;**210**:78-122

[62] Baldi P, Sandowski P. Understanding dropout. In: Proceedings of Advances in Neural Information Processing Systems (NIPS 2013). Neural Information Processing Systems Foundation, Inc; 2013. p. 4878

[63] Grochowski M et al. constructive neural network algorithms that solve highly non-separable problems. In: Franco L et al. editors. Constructive Neural Networks. Berlin: Springer-Verlag; 2009. pp. 49-70

[64] Campbell C. Constructive learning techniques for designing neural networks systems. In: Leondes CT, editor. Neural Network Systems, Techniques and Applications. San Diego: Academic Press; 1997. pp. 1-54

[65] Fahlman SE, Lebiere C. In: Touretzky DS, editor. The Cascade-Correlation Learning Architecture, Advances in Neural Information Processing Systems. Los Altos, CA: Morgan Kaufmann Publishers; 1990. pp. 524-532

[66] Littmann E, Ritter H. Learning and generalization in cascade network architectures. Neural Computation. 1996;**8**:1521-1539

[67] Kwok TY, Yeung DY. Constructive algorithms for structure learning in feedforward neural networks for regression problems. IEEE Transactions on Neural Networks. 1997;**8**(3):630-645

[68] Apache Spark [Internet]. 2015. Available from: https://spark.apache.org

[69] ROOT Data Analysis Framework [Internet]. 2015. Available from: https://root.cern.ch

[70] Computing at CERN [Internet]. 2015. Available from: http://home.cern/about/computing

[71] LeCun Y et al. Deep learning. Nature. 2015;**521**:436

[72] Bengio Y. Learning deep architectures for AI. Foundations and Trends in Machine Learning. 2009;**2**(1):1-127

[73] Goodfellow I et al. Deep learning. In: Dietterich T, Bishop C, Heckerman D, Jordan M, Kearns M, editors. Adaptive Computation and Machine Learning Series. Cambridge, MA: MIT Press; 2016

[74] Schimdhuber J. Deep leaning in neural networks: An overview. Neural Networks. 2015;**61**:85

[75] Argonne Leadership Computing Facility: Project Magellan: Cloud Computing for Science [Internet]. 2016. Available from: http://www.alcf.anl.gov/magellan

[76] Zhang H et al. In-memory big data management and processing: A survey. IEEE Transactions on Knowledge and Data Engineering. 2015;**27**(7):1920-1948

[77] Apache Impala [Internet]. 2017. Available from: https://impala.apache.org/

[78] Apache Kudu [Internet]. 2017. Available from: https://kudu.apache.org/

[79] Mohri M et al. Foundations of Machine Learning. Cambridge, MA: MIT Press; 2012

[80] Bishop CM. Neural Networks for Pattern Recognition. 3rd ed. Oxford: Oxford University Press; 1995

[81] Fine TL. Feedforward Neural Network Methodology. 3rd ed. NewYork: Springer-Verlag; 1999

[82] Haykin S. Neural Networks: A Comprehensive Foundation. 2nd ed. New York: Macmillan College Publishing; 1998

[83] Bishop CM. Pattern Recognition and Machine Learning. New York: Springer-Verlag; 2006

[84] Kohonen T. Self-organized formation of topologically correct feature maps. Biological Cybernetics. 1982;**43**(1):59

[85] Kangas JA et al. Variants of self-organizing maps. IEEE Transactions on Neural Networks. 1999;**1**(1):93-99

[86] Cortes C, Vapnik V. Support-vector networks. Machine Learning. 1995;**20**(3):273

[87] Ben-Hur A et al. Support vector clustering. Journal of Machine Learning Research. 2001;**2**:125-137

[88] Apache Spark MLib: Scalable machine learning library [Internet]. 2016. Available from: https://spark.apache.org/mlib

[89] Geman S et al. Neural networks and the bias/variance dilemma. Neural Computation. 1992;**4**:1

[90] Sarle WS. Stopped training and other remedies for overfitting. In: Proceedings of the 27th Symposium on the Interface of Computing Science and Statistics. VA, Fairfax: Interface Foundation of North America; 1995. pp. 352-360

[91] Weigend A. On overfitting and the effective number of hidden units. In: Mozer MC, Smolensky P, Touretzky DS, Elman JL, Weigend AS, editors. Proceedings of the 1993 Connectionist Models Summer School. Hillsdale, NJ: Erlbaum Associates; 1994. pp. 335-342

[92] Ghahramani Z. Unsupervised learning. Vol. 3176. In: Bousquet O, von Luxburg U, Ratsch G, editors. Advanced Lectures on Machine Learning, Lecture Notes in Computer Science. Berlin, Heidelberg: Springer-Verlag; 2004. pp. 72-112

[93] Duda RO et al. Unsupervised learning and clustering. In: Pattern Classification. 2nd ed. New York: John Wiley and Sons; 2001. pp. 517-600. ISBN: 0-471-05669-3

[94] Hinton G, Sejnowski TJ. Unsupervised Learning: Foundations of Neural Computation. Cambridge: MIT Press; 1999. ISBN: 0-262-58168-X

[95] In-memory MapReduce [Internet]. 2017. Available from: https://ignite.apache.org/features/mapreduce.html

[96] Apache HBase [Internet]. 2017. Available from: https://hbase.apache.org/

[97] Apache Hive [Internet]. 2017. Available from: https://hive.apache.org/. 2015

[98] Satish N et al. Designing efficient sorting algorithms for manycore GPUs. In: IPDPS 2009 IEEE International Symposium on Parallel & Distributed Processing. IEEE, IEEE XPlore Digital Library; 2009. pp. 1-10

[99] He B et al. Mars: A MapReduce framework on graphics processors. In: Proceedings of the 17th International Conference on Parallel Architectures and Compilation Techniques. New York: ACM; 2008. pp. 260-269

[100] Mihailescu A. Stepping up theoretical investigations of ultrashort and intense laser pulses interacting with overdense plasmas. Combining particle-in-cell simulations with machine learning and big data. In: Proceedings of Grid, Cloud & High Performance Computing in Science (ROLCG), Conference. IEEE, IEEE Xplore Digital Library; 2015. p. 7367424

[101] Mihailescu A. A new approach to theoretical investigations of high harmonics generation by means of fs laser interaction with overdense plasma layers. Combining particle-in-cell simulations with machine learning. Journal of Instrumentation. 2016;11:C12004

[102] Apache Oozie [Internet]. 2017. Available from: http://oozie.apache.org/

[103] Azkaban Workflow Engine [Internet]. 2016. Available from: https://azkaban.github.io/

[104] Luigi Workflow Engine [Internet]. 2016. Available from: http://luigi.readthedocs.io/en/stable/api/luigi.contrib.sge.html

[105] Airflow Workflow Engine [Internet]. 2016. Available from: https://airflow.incubator.apache.org/

[106] Kepler [Internet]. 2016. Available from: https://kepler-project.org/

[107] Apache Yarn [Internet]. 2017. Available from: https://hadoop.apache.org/docs/r2.7.2/hadoop-yarn/hadoop-yarn-site/YARN.html

[108] Docker [Internet]. 2017. Available from: https://www.docker.com/

[109] Apache Tez [Internet]. 2017. Available from: https://tez.apache.org/

[110] Bulanov SV et al. Interaction of an ultrashort, relativistically strong laser pulse with an overdense plasma. Physics of Plasmas. 1994;1:745-757

[111] Brunel F. Not-so-resonant, resonant absorption. Physical Review Letters. 1987;59:52-55

[112] Kruer WL, Estabrook K. JxB heating by very intense laser light. Physics of Fluids. 1985;**28**:430

[113] Quere F et al. Coherent wake emission of high-order harmonics from overdense plasmas. Physical Review Letters. 2006;**96**:125004

[114] Hornik K. Approximation capabilities of multilayer feedforward networks. Neural Networks. 1991;**4**(2):251

[115] Rumelhart DE et al. Learning representations by back-propagating errors. Nature. 1986;**323**:533

[116] LeCun Y et al. Efficient BackProp. In: Orr G, Muller K, editors. Neural Networks: Tricks of the Trade. Berlin/Heidelberg: Springer; 1998

[117] Rumelhart DE, Zipser D. Feature discovery by competitive learning. Cognitive Science. 1985;**9**(1):75-112

[118] Ahalt S et al. Competitive learning algorithms for vector quantization. Neural Networks. 1990;**3**(3):277-290

[119] McCaffrey J. Test-Run, L1 and L2 regularization for machine learning, Microsoft Magazine, Issues and Downloads [Internet]. 2015. Available from: https://msdn.microsoft.com/en-us/magazine/dn904675.aspx

[120] Zou H, Hastie T. Regularization and variable selection via elastic net. Journal of the Royal Statistical Society. 2005;**67**(2):301-320

[121] Zeiler M. ADADELTA: An adaptive learning rate method [Internet]. 2012. Available from: https://arxiv.org/abs/1212.5701

10

Machine Learning Algorithm for Wireless Indoor Localization

Osamah Ali Abdullah and Ikhlas Abdel-Qader

Abstract

Smartphones equipped with Wi-Fi technology are widely used nowadays. Due to the need for inexpensive indoor positioning systems (IPSs), many researchers have focused on Wi-Fi-based IPSs, which use wireless local area network received signal strength (RSS) data that are collected at distinct locations in indoor environments called reference points. In this study, a new framework based on symmetric Bregman divergence, which incorporates k-nearest neighbor (kNN) classification in signal space, was proposed. The coordinates of the target were determined as a weighted combination of the nearest fingerprints using Jensen-Bregman divergences, which unify the squared Euclidean and Mahalanobis distances with information-theoretic Jensen-Shannon divergence measures. To validate our work, the performance of the proposed algorithm was compared with the probabilistic neural network and multivariate Kullback-Leibler divergence. The distance error for the developed algorithm was less than 1 m.

Keywords: fingerprinting, indoor localization, Wi-Fi, Jensen-Bregman divergence, probabilistic neural network, multivariate Gaussian distribution

1. Introduction

Automatically, identifying the location of a user has recently become a hot topic in research. The study in [1] estimated that the global indoor localization market is expected to grow from its value of \$935.05 million in 2014 to approximately \$4.42 billion in 2019, corresponding to an estimated compound annual growth rate (CAGR) of 36.5%. The estimation of mobile locations has an important role in many computing applications. The global positioning system (GPS) is one of the most common location-based systems, but it cannot be used inside buildings as a direct line of sight (LOS) is required between the GPS receiver and the satellite to identify the user's location. Therefore, a large number of technologies, such as Bluetooth, radiofrequency identification (RFID), wireless local area network (WLAN or Wi-Fi), magnetic field variations, ultrasound, Zigbee, and light-emitting diode (LED) light bulbs, have been developed to create high-accuracy indoor positioning systems (IPS), with Wi-Fi being the most commonly used technology. Most smartphones can obtain received signal strength (RSS) from the access points (APs) of WLANs because of the low cost and existing WLAN infrastructure [2, 3]

The IPS algorithm that uses RSS-based indoor localization can be classified into two main types: log-distance propagation model (PM) algorithms based on the signal and fingerprinting indoor localization based on the data collected. IPS based on signal propagation is divided into lateration and angulation. The main idea of lateration estimation is to calculate the distance between the smartphone and AP using geometry and signal measurement information, such as the time of arrival (TOA), time difference of arrival (TDOA), and angle of arrival (AOA), of the incoming signals from APs. In general, propagation signals suffer from non-line-of-sight (NLOS) multipath signals due to the presence of walls and furniture and the movement of people. In addition, the signal accuracy decreases if one or more AP coordinates are not accurately calculated. All of these drawbacks have made it difficult to estimate an object's position using signal propagation [4]. Thus, fingerprinting-based localization systems have been proposed as an alternative technology [5] as they do not require infrastructure. Instead, they use the existing WLAN in the building and the smartphone, which relies on the spectrum of the RSS from the APs to the location to estimate the user's location coordinates.

The fingerprint-based technique is divided into offline and online phases. In the offline phase, the entire area of interest is divided into a rectangular set of grid points, and at each point, a site survey is taken by recording the RSS from APs, which is then stored in a database called the radio map [6–10]. In the online phase, the smartphone collects the RSS from the APs and sends it to the server to compare the predefined fingerprint of the offline phase with the RSS in the online phase in order to estimate the location on the grid map, as shown in **Figure 1**.

The k-nearest neighbor (kNN) algorithm is one of the simplest ways to estimate location; it depends upon the Euclidean distance to measure the similarity/dissimilarity between the offline and online phases. Even though this algorithm is easy to implement, it has low accuracy. Other methods such as statistical learning and Bayesian modeling have also been used to estimate the location of an object. Accuracy is one of the most important requirements of IPS.

Mean distance error is typically used as the performance metric and is calculated as the average Euclidean distance between the actual location and the estimated location.

Recently, an important issue was raised about the variation of signal propagation, namely, the question of how signals are able to propagate over time in the same place in the presence of multiple factors, such as physical obstructions, radiofrequency (RF) equipment, and the presence of human bodies. These factors can lead to attenuation and multipath issues, thereby causing gradual changes in the signal that can reduce the accuracy of the localization system [11]. The values stored in fingerprint maps represent the mean value of the received signal strength indicator (RSSI). Some approaches presume that the RSSI distribution is Gaussian

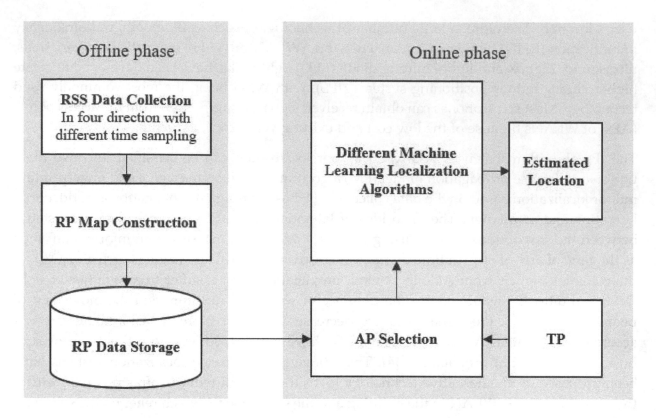

Figure 1. The offline and online stages of location Wi-Fi-based fingerprinting architecture.

[12], whereas others assume a non-Gaussian distribution, such as those described in [13]. Using Wi-Fi localization systems to estimate the location of an object has many advantages compared with other technologies, such as availability and low cost. However, because the RSSI signal uses both offline and online phases, hardware variance can significantly degrade the positional accuracy of these systems. Some studies have investigated this variance; for example, it was reported in [11] that when using different smartphones to collect RSSI data at the same time and same location, some phones consistently had higher RSSI values than others. The orientation of the user can also contribute to the variance of the RSSI signal because the human body can be a significant attenuator.

This hardware variance problem in Wi-Fi localization has also been noticed in Cisco location systems [11]; some signals were found to be omitted when a different device was used in the online phase compared with the offline phase.

This chapter presents the following:

- We propose the use of Jensen-Bregman divergence (JBD) as a WLAN-based method and a Kullback-Leibler multivariate Gaussian (KL_{MVG}) model. The matching stage was performed using probability kernels as a regression scheme.

- We propose a procedure with high characterization distribution. The RSS values were taken from four different orientations (45, 135, 225, and 315°) to prevent body-blocking effects, with a scan performed for 100 s in each direction to reduce the effects of signal variation.

- JBD and KL_{MVG} outperformed the probabilistic neural network (PNN) and kNN with respect to the accuracy and the average error distance, indicating that the proposed combination scheme is more effective in the sensitive environments of WLAN-based positioning systems.

2. Related work

Global navigation satellite systems (GNSS) such as GLONASS (Russia's version of GPS), GALILEO, and GPS work well in outdoor environments, but their accuracy can significantly decrease in indoor environments due to many factors, such as penetration loss, refraction, multipath propagation, and absorption. Therefore, it is important to develop a system that can work in indoor environments with high accuracy. To this end, many techniques have been proposed for IPS in the last decade. In model-based techniques, the location is estimated based on a geometrical model, such as the log-distance path loss (LDPL) model, in which a semi-statistical function is built on the relationship between the RF propagation function and the RSS value. Several approaches have been proposed that are trade-offs between accuracy and cost, such as TOA, TDOA, AOA, and multidimensional scaling (MDS). MDS is a set of statistical techniques that are used to visualize the information in order to find similarities/dissimilarities in the data. The matrix in MDS begins with item-item dissimilarities, and AP-AP distances are determined by a radio attenuation model [9]. The fingerprinting-based technique depends on matching algorithms (e.g., kNN) that have been used in RADAR [14], which is one of the first Wi-Fi signal strength-based IPS and is considered the basis of WLAN fingerprinting IPS. Many developed kNN algorithms have been proposed for determining the similarity/dissimilarity in metrics, which is usually done using the Manhattan or Euclidean distance, such as in [11–18]. Ref. [19] proposed a new version of kNN that is more efficient than the probabilistic methods, neural networks, and traditional kNN, as it relies upon the decision tree of the training phases and takes into account the average of reference point (RP) measurements instead of needing the entire dataset to estimate the object's location. Ref. [20] performed a modified deterministic kNN technique with Mahalanobis, Manhattan, and Euclidian distances and found the Manhattan distance to be the most accurate. Recently, the use of probabilistic distribution measurements in many IPS applications has increased. The authors in [21] pioneered the use of the probabilistic distribution measurement in IPS and proposed a probabilistic framework by using the Bayesian network to estimate the location. In [22] the authors used a modified probability neural network (MPNN) to estimate the coordinates of the object and found that it outperformed the triangulation method. In [23], a kernel method was proposed to estimate the object's location using a histogram of the RSSI at the unknown location. In [24], the probability density function (PDF) was estimated using the Kullback-Leibler divergence (KLD) framework for composite hypothesis testing between the fingerprinting database and the test point, whereas in [25], the authors assumed that the RSSI distribution was multivariate Gaussian and used the KLD to estimate the impacts of the RPs on the test point in order to estimate the probability of the closest one and to identify the coordinates of the test point.

In [26], the RSS-based Bluetooth low-energy localization technique was used to establish the fingerprint, after which the KLD was used in probabilistic kernel regression to estimate the object's location. The results showed this method to be accurate to approximately 1 m in an office environment. In general, the KLD kernel regression performs better in a multimodal distribution. In [27], the KLD was used to estimate the probabilistic kernel of both Gaussian and non-Gaussian distributions in order to compare them and to determine their limitations.

3. Overall structure of indoor positioning system

We begin with a typical WLAN scenario in which a person carries a smartphone device with WLAN access and takes RSS measurements from different APs within the College of Engineering and Applied Sciences (CEAS) at Western Michigan University (WMU). It is commonly assumed that the RSSI from multiple APs is distributed as a multimodal signal, as noted in [16]. However, in our study, the recorded signal-to-noise ratio for a single device varied significantly at any one location, with the values differing by as much as 10 dBm. Specifically, the signal-to-noise values were recorded for 35 min during rush hour for a single AP and in the same location.

There are many parameters that can affect the shape of the signal, such as reflection, diffraction, and pedestrian traffic. In this study, we sought to find a scenario that would lead to a better distribution of the Wi-Fi signal. During the offline phase, a realistic scenario was created that took into account the variation of the signal. However, because the effects of the body of the person holding the phone as well as pedestrian traffic can change the variation of the signal, a recording of the RSS was taken in four directions (45, 135, 225, and 315°) to reduce these variations. At each RP, a raw set of RSS data were collected as a time sample from the APs in the area of interest, denoted as $\left\{ q_{i,j}^{(\circ)}(\tau), \tau = 1, \ldots, t, t = 100 \right\}$, where t represents the number of time samples and $(^\circ)$ is the orientation direction. Next, the average and covariance matrix of the RSS were obtained from the four different directions and ten scans used to create the fingerprinting database, known as the Radio Map, represented by $Q^{(\circ)}$ [28]:

$$Q^{(\circ)} = \begin{pmatrix} q_{1,1}^{(\circ)} & q_{1,2}^{(\circ)} & \cdots & q_{1,N}^{(\circ)} \\ q_{2,1}^{(\circ)} & q_{2,2}^{(\circ)} & \cdots & q_{2,N}^{(\circ)} \\ \vdots & \vdots & \ddots & \vdots \\ q_{L,1}^{(\circ)} & q_{L,2}^{(\circ)} & \cdots & q_{L,N}^{(\circ)} \end{pmatrix} \tag{1}$$

where $q_{i,j}^{(\circ)} = \frac{1}{q} \sum_{\tau=1}^{t} q_{i,j}^{(\circ)}(\tau)$ and t = 10, which were randomly chosen from the 100 time samples. This allowed us to obtain the average of the RSS samples over time for different APs, $i = 1, 2, \ldots L, j = 1, 2, \ldots N$, where N represents the number of RPs and L is the number of APs. The variance vector of each RP can be defined as

$$\Delta_j^{(\circ)} = \left[\Delta_{1,j}^{(\circ)}, \Delta_{2,j}^{(\circ)}, \Delta_{3,j}^{(\circ)}, \ldots \ldots \Delta_{L,j}^{(\circ)} \right] \qquad (2)$$

where

$$\Delta_{i,j}^{(\circ)} = \frac{1}{t-1} \sum_{\tau=1}^{t} \left(q_{i,j}^{(\circ)}(\tau) - q_{i,j}^{(\circ)} \right)^2 \qquad (3)$$

where $\Delta_{i,j}^{(\circ)}$ is the variance for AP i at RP j with orientation $(\circ)$; thus, the database table of the Radio Map is $(x_j, y_j, q_j^{(\circ)}, \Delta_j^{(\circ)})$ with $q_j^{(\circ)}$ defined as

$$q_j^{(\circ)} = \left[q_{1,j}^{(\circ)}, q_{2,j}^{(\circ)}, q_{3,j}^{(\circ)}, \ldots \ldots \ldots, q_{L,j}^{(\circ)} \right] \qquad (4)$$

During the online phase, the RSS measurement is denoted as

$$p_r = \left[p_{1,r}, p_{2,r}, \ldots \ldots, p_{L,r} \right] \qquad (5)$$

4. The Kullback-Leibler multivariate Gaussian (KLMvG) model

Another approach, specifically the KLMvG model, has recently been used in fingerprinting-based methods to estimate the position of the objects. This model exploits the interdependencies between the RPs, such as the signal model and the geometry that can be quantified to find the correlations among the RPs. Milioris [29] proposed a KLMvG model to measure the similarity between the RSS measurements of test points and the RPs, defined as

$$KL_{MVG}\left(p \| q_j^{(\circ)} \right) = \frac{1}{2} \left(\left(\mu_{q,j}^S - \mu_p^S \right)^T \left(\Sigma_{j,q}^s \right)^{-1} \left(\mu_{q,j}^S - \mu_p^S \right) + tr \left(\Sigma_R^s \left(\Sigma_{j,q}^s \right)^{-1} - I \right) - \ln \left| \Sigma_p^s \left(\Sigma_{j,q}^s \right)^{-1} \right| \right) \qquad (6)$$

where S represents the matrix of RSS values from the different APs at specific locations and j represents the cell of the fingerprint location where

$$S_j^{(\circ)} = \left\{ \mu_j^{(\circ)}, \Sigma_j^{(\circ)} \right\} \qquad (7)$$

$\mu_j^{(\circ)}$ is the mean of Jth column of the RSS measurement and $\Sigma_j^{(\circ)}$ represents the covariance matrix, where $|\Sigma|$ is the determinant of Σ. Now, using a KLMvG model, we can formulate a probability kernel-based approach. The kernel regression scheme allows us to estimate the PDF of the training datasets and the true positives (TPs) from the online phase that are used to estimate the location of the object. The KL_{MVG} model is used to measure the distance between the likelihood of the input sample and the RPs in order to determine which class it belongs to. The RSS distribution can be defined as

$$D(p, q_\ell) = \exp \left(-\frac{KL_{MVG}\left(p \| q_j^{(\circ)} \right)}{2\sigma^2} \right) \qquad (8)$$

where σ is the kernel smoothing factor. The probability will be equal to 1 if p = q, and the output will decrease when the difference between p and q becomes larger.

Algorithm 1. The Kullback-Leibler multivariate Gaussian positioning method.

---

1. During the offline phase, RSS measurements are taken at different known locations, and 10 scans with 10 second time delays are used to generate the Radio Map.
2. During the online phase, RSS measurements are taken at unknown locations of the smartphone.
3. During the online phase, the following steps are performed:
    *   A database for each RP is set using RSS measurements from different locations.
    *   The RSS measurements from the APs of smartphones from unknown locations are set in the same way as the database of the offline phase with respect to the similar media access control (MAC) address.
    *   The minimum KLMvG is estimated using Eq. 8.
    *   The previous step is repeated for different APs until the minimum distance is obtained.
4. The maximum outputs to the output layer are transferred.

---

5. Bregman divergence algorithm formulation

In recent times, approaches that measure the distortion in classes have become more common, instead of depending on a single distance. Indeed, the analysis of distortion is being used in many applications of machine learning, computational geometry, and IPS. Using Bregman divergence to measure the similarity/dissimilarity has recently become an attractive method because it encapsulates both information-theoretic relative entropy and the geometric Euclidean distance, which is a meta-algorithm [30]. The Bregman distance D_φ between two sets of convex space data, p = (p_1, ..., p_d) and q = (q_1, ..., q_d), that is associated with φ (defined as a strictly convex and differentiable function) can be defined as

$$D_\varphi(p,q) = \varphi(p) - \varphi(q) - \langle \nabla\varphi(p), p - q \rangle \tag{9}$$

where $\langle .,. \rangle$ denotes the dot product:

$$\langle p,q \rangle = \sum_{i=1}^{d} p^{(i)} q^{(i)} = p^T q \tag{10}$$

and $\nabla\varphi(p)$ denotes the gradient decent operator:

$$\nabla\varphi(p) = \left[\frac{\partial\varphi}{\partial p_1} \cdots \frac{\partial\varphi}{\partial p_d}\right]^T \tag{11}$$

The Bregman divergence unifies the statistical KLD with the squared Euclidean distance by defining the distortion measurement in classes:

*   The Euclidean distance is obtained from the Bregman divergence by considering the convex function as $\varphi(p) = \sum_{i-1}^{d} p_i^2 = \langle p,p \rangle$, which is the parabolic potential function in **Figure 2**.

- The KLD is also a Bregman divergence if the convex function used is $\varphi(p) = \sum_{i-1}^{d} p_i \log p_i$, which is defined as negative Shannon entropy. The KLD is defined for two discrete distributions as

$$KL(p\|q) = \sum_s p(S=s)\log\left(\frac{p(S=s)}{q(S=s)}\right) \tag{12}$$

In information theory, the Shannon differential entropy measures the amount of uncertainty of a random variable:

$$H(p) = p\log\frac{1}{p} \tag{13}$$

The KLD is equal to the cross entropy of two discrete distributions minus the Shannon differential entropy [31]:

$$KL(p\|q) = \sum_s H^x(p(S=s)\|(q(S=s) - H((p(S=s)) \tag{14}$$

where H^x is the cross-entropy:

$$H^x\left(p(S=s)\|\left(q(S=s)\right) = \sum_s p(S=s)\log\frac{1}{q(S=s)} \tag{15}$$

and S is the set of vectors of the RSS. In general, the Bregman divergence is not symmetrical, but it can symmetrize as follows:

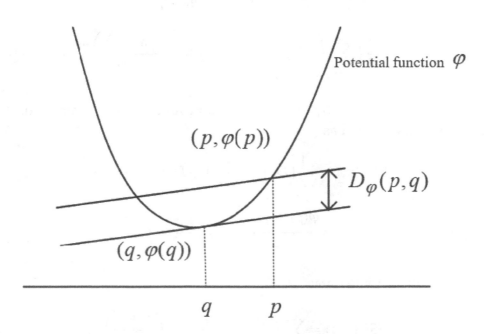

Figure 2. The Bregman divergence represents the vertical distance between the potential function and the hyperplane at q.

$$SD_\varphi(p,q) = \frac{D_\varphi(p,q) + D_\varphi(q,p)}{2} \qquad (16)$$

$$= \frac{1}{2} \langle p - q, \nabla\varphi(p) - \nabla\varphi(q) \rangle \qquad (17)$$

In the same manner, Jeffreys' divergence symmetrizes the oriented KLD as follows:

$$J(p,q) = KL(p\|q) + KL(q\|p) \qquad (18)$$

$$= H(p\|q) + H(q\|p) - (H(p) + H(q) \qquad (19)$$

$$= \sum_s \left((p(S=s) - q(S=s))\log\left(\frac{p(S=s)}{q(S=s)}\right) \right. \qquad (20)$$

Such information-theoretic divergence has two major drawbacks: first, the output can be undefined if q = 0 and p ≠ 0, and second, the J-divergence is not bound by terms of metric distance. To avoid these drawbacks and avoid the log(0) or to divide by 0, the authors in [32] proposed a new divergence called K-divergence:

$$K(p\|q) = KL\left(p, \frac{p+q}{2}\right) \qquad (21)$$

By introducing the K-divergence, [30] produced the Jensen-Shannon divergence (JSD) as follows:

$$JSD(p\|q) = \frac{1}{2}\left(KL\left(p, \frac{p+q}{2}\right) + KL\left(q, \frac{p+q}{2}\right)\right) \qquad (22)$$

$$= \frac{1}{2}\left(H\left(p\|\frac{p+q}{2}\right) - H(p) + H\left(q\|\frac{p+q}{2}\right) - H(q)\right) \qquad (23)$$

$$= \frac{1}{2}\left(\sum_{i=1}^{L}\left(p_i\log\frac{p_i}{\frac{1}{2}q_i + \frac{1}{2}p_i} + q_i\log\frac{q_i}{\frac{1}{2}q_i + \frac{1}{2}p_i}\right)\right) \qquad (24)$$

The JSD can be defined, bound by an L1-metric, and finite. In the same vein, the Bregman divergence can be symmetrized as

$$SD_\varphi(p,q) = \frac{1}{2}\left(D_\varphi\left(p, \frac{q+p}{2}\right) + D_\varphi\left(q, \frac{q+p}{2}\right)\right) \qquad (25)$$

$$= \frac{\varphi(p) + \varphi(q_j)}{2} - \varphi\left(\frac{p+q_j}{2}\right) \qquad (26)$$

for d-dimensional multivariate data:

$$SD(p,q) = \sum_{i=1}^{L}\frac{\varphi(p_i) + \varphi(q_i)}{2} - \varphi\left(\frac{p_i+q_i}{2}\right) \qquad (27)$$

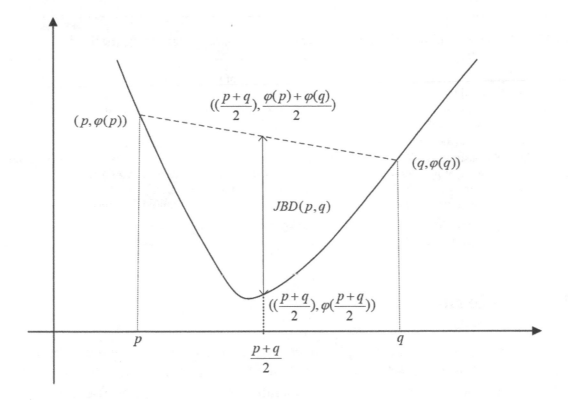

Figure 3. Interpreting the Jensen-Bregman divergence.

where q represents the fingerprint dataset and p, which is the dataset of the test points, represents the APs that the mobile device received. Because φ is a strictly convex function and $SD(p, q)$ equals zero if and only if p = q, this family of distortions is termed JSD. The geometric interpretation is represented in **Figure 3**, where divergence represents the vertical distance between $\left(\left(\frac{p+q}{2}\right), \varphi\left(\frac{p+q}{2}\right)\right)$ and the midpoint of the segment $[(p, \varphi(p)),$ $(q, \varphi(q))]$.

In general, for a positive definite matrix, the Jensen-Bregman divergence contains the generalized quadratic distance, which is known as the Mahalanobis distance:

$$
\begin{aligned}
SD(p, q) &= \frac{\varphi(p) + \varphi(q)}{2} - \varphi\left(\frac{p+q}{2}\right) \\
&= \frac{2\langle Qp, p \rangle + 2\langle Qq, q \rangle - 2\langle Q(p+q), p+q \rangle}{4} \\
&= \frac{1}{4}\left(\langle Qp, p \rangle + \langle Qq, q \rangle - 2\langle Qp, q \rangle\right) \\
&= \frac{1}{4}\langle Q(p-q), p-q \rangle \\
&= \frac{1}{4}\|p-q\|_Q^2
\end{aligned}
\tag{28}
$$

To improve accuracy, we present Algorithm 2:

Algorithm 2. The Kullback-Leibler multivariate Gaussian positioning method

---

1. During the offline phase, RSS measurements are taken at different known locations, and 10 scans with 10 second time delays are used to generate the Radio Map.
2. During the online phase, RSS measurements are taken from unknown locations of the smartphone.
3. During the online phase, the following steps are performed:
    - A database for each RP is set using RSS measurements from different locations.
    - The RSS measurements from the APs of smartphones from unknown locations are set in the same way as the database of the offline phase with respect to the similar media access control (MAC) address.
    - The minimum symmetric Bregman divergence is estimated using Eq. 27.
    - The previous step is repeated for different APs until the minimum distance is obtained.
4. The maximum outputs are transferred to the output layer.

---

6. Performance analysis

The proposed algorithm evaluations will be presented in the subsequent subsections; the algorithms were implemented on the first floor of the CEAS at WMU. To collect the data sample, a Samsung S5 smartphone with operating system 4.4.2 was used. The proposed algorithms were implemented on an HP Pavilion using Java software with an Eclipse framework. Cisco Linksys E2500 Advanced Simultaneous Dual-Band Wireless-N Routers were used in the area of interest. Most of this work discounted the variation of the RSS from the APs.

To evaluate the performance of the different fingerprinting techniques, the localization error was computed as the Euclidean distance between the actual reported coordinates of the test points and the coordinates of the mobile user during the online phase. The number of RSS of the APs and the number of nearest neighbors were noted, as they can affect the accuracy of the algorithms. The number of APs can play an important role in the accuracy of the distance error, which can distinguish near RPs from those further away.

To evaluate the performance of the different fingerprinting techniques, the localization error was computed as the Euclidean distance between the actual reported coordinates of the test points and the coordinates of the mobile user during the online phase. The number of RSS of the APs and the number of nearest neighbors were noted, as they can affect the accuracy of the algorithms. The number of APs can play an important role in the accuracy of the distance error, which can distinguish near RPs from those further away.

In order to measure the impact of the APs on the accuracy, we used a specific number of nearest neighbors with a variety of APs. However, that resulted in a longer RSS scanning interval, which slowed the process down. As a result, the online phase comprised five time samples, which took 1 s for Wi-Fi scanning on the device. To investigate the accuracy of our proposed algorithm, different algorithms were used, such as PNN and KNN, and compared with our proposed algorithm. Different numbers of nearest neighbors were used to estimate the location of the object and to evaluate the performance of our system framework.

Figure 4 shows the impact of different APs when five nearest neighbors were used. The lowest localization error was obtained when 22 APs were used: 0.98 m for kJBD, 1.12 m for kJSD, 1.16 m for KLMvG, 1.34 m for PNN, and 1.38 m for kNN. Greater accuracy was obtained when more nearest neighbors were used, as illustrated in **Figure 5**.

The lowest localization accuracy was also obtained when 22 APs were used: 0.92 m for kJBD, 1.01 m for kJSD, 1.02 m for KLMvG, 1.097 m for PNN, and 1.19 m for kNN. More improvements in system accuracy were noticed when 80 nearest neighbors were used: 0.865 m for kJBD, 0.96 m for kJSD, 0.99 m for KLMvG, 0.995 m for PNN, and 1.12 m for kNN, as shown in **Figure 6**.

Figure 7 illustrates the corresponding cumulative probability distributions of the localization error for the three methods. In particular, the median errors for kJBD were 0.89 m, 0.98 m for kJSD, and 1.02 m for KLMvG. Furthermore, an accuracy of 90% was achieved at 2.13 m for KLMvG and 1.93 m for kJSD, with the best accuracy obtained at 2.13 m for kJSD.

To validate our work, a comparison was made between the proposed algorithms with other algorithms from prior works, such as kNN [14], compressive sensing [28], and the kernel-based method [33], as illustrated in **Table 1**.

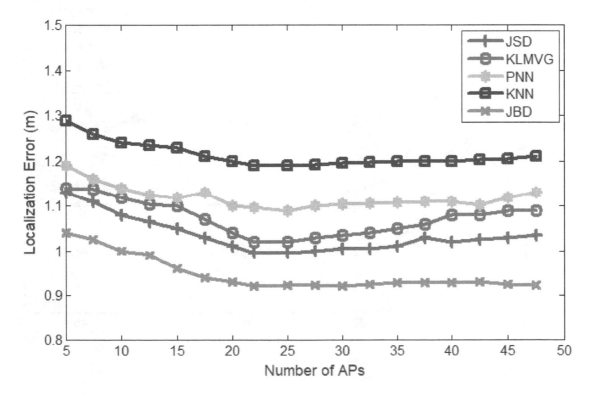

Figure 4. Error distance estimation with respect to APs with five nearest neighbors.

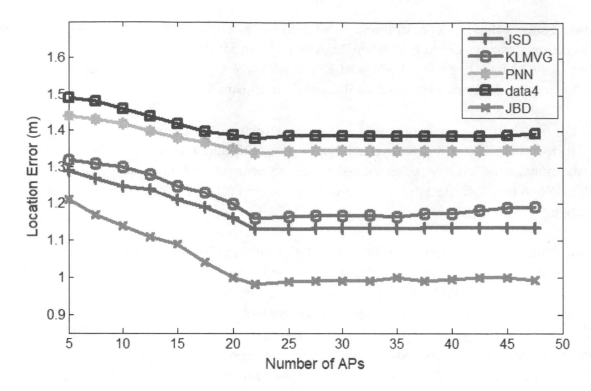

Figure 5. Error distance estimation with respect to APs with 20 nearest neighbors.

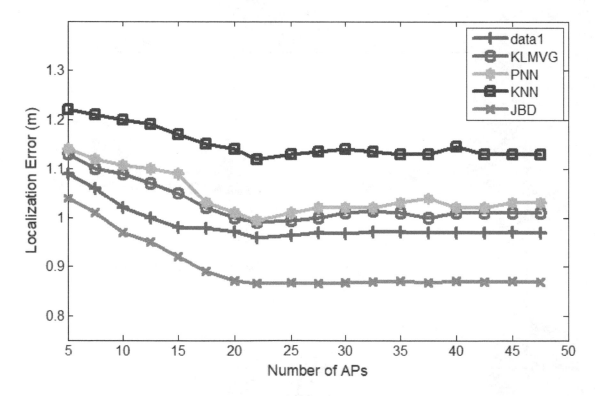

Figure 6. Error distance estimation with respect to APs with 80 nearest neighbors.

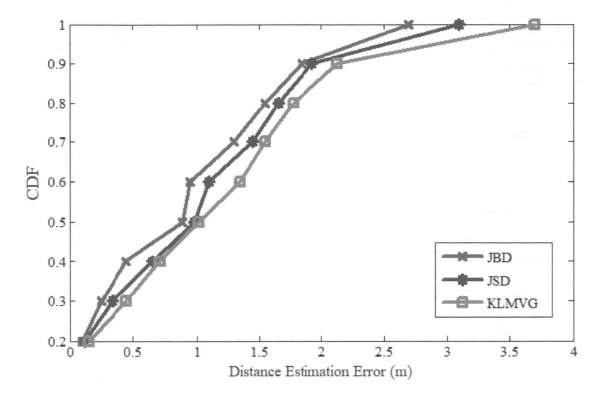

Figure 7. Experiment results: the CDF of localization error when using 80 nearest neighbors.

Technique	Median [m]	Accuracy 90% [m]
kNN [10]	1.8	3.7
Kernel-based [28]	1.6	3.6
CS-based [27]	1.5	2.7
KL$_{MVG}$	1.02	2.13
kJSD	0.98	1.93
kJBD	0.89	1.85

Table 1. Position error statistic.

7. Conclusion

IPS incorporates the power of GPS and indoor mapping and has many potential applications, for example, by emergency healthcare services, by people with impaired vision, and for navigating unfamiliar complex buildings where it is easy to get disoriented or lost (e.g., malls, airports, subways). A fingerprint map was created for a segment of the CEAS in order to utilize the relationship between different RSS readings. Different algorithms were used and compared using different approaches, including kNN and PNN, and their performances assessed for a number of APs. The results were quite adequate for the indoor environment with an average error of less than 1 m. The kJBD had the highest accuracy when there were 80 nearest neighbors with 22 APs. We are currently in the process of investigating position prediction error distributions and quantifying the localization variation of Wi-Fi signal distribution in space

Author details

Osamah Ali Abdullah* and Ikhlas Abdel-Qader

*Address all correspondence to: osamah.abdullah@wmich.edu

Electrical and Computer Engineering Department, Almamoon University College, Kalamazoo, Michigan USA

References

[1] Markets & Markets. Indoor Localization Market by Positioning Systems, Map and Navigation, Location Based Analysis, Monitoring and Emergency Services-Worldwide Market Forecasts and Analysis (2014–2019). Technical Report; 2014

[2] Torres-Sospedra J, Montoliu R, Trilles S, Belmonte O, Huerta J. Comprehensive analysis of distance and similarity measures for Wi-Fi fingerprinting indoor positioning systems. Expert Systems with Applications. 2015;42(23):9263-9278

[3] Jiang P, Zhang Y, Fu W, Liu H, Su X. Indoor mobile localization based on Wi-Fi fingerprint's important access point. International Journal of Distributed Sensor Networks. 2015;11(4):429104

[4] Shchekotov M. Indoor localization methods based on Wi-Fi lateration and signal strength data collection. In: 2015 17th Conference of. Open Innovations Association (FRUCT); Yaroslavl; 2015

[5] Swangmuang N, Prashant K. An effective location fingerprint model for wireless indoor localization. Pervasive and Mobile Computing. 2008;4(6):836-850

[6] Abdullah O, Abdel-Qader I, Bazuin B. A probability neural network-Jensen-Shannon divergence for a fingerprint based localization. In: 2016 Annual Conference on Information Science and Systems (CISS). Princeton, NJ; 2016

[7] Abdullah O, Abdel-Qader I. A PNN-Jensen-Bregman divergence symmetrization for a WLAN indoor positioning system. In: 2016 IEEE International Conference on Electro Information Technology (EIT). Grand Forks, ND; 2016

[8] Abdullah O, Abdel-Qader I, Bazuin B, Fingerprint-based technique for indoor positioning system via machine learning and convex optimization. In: 2016 IEEE 7th Annual Ubiquitous

Computing, Electronics & Mobile Communication Conference (UEMCON). New York, NY; 2016

[9] Abdullah O, Abdel-Qader I, Bazuin B. K-means-Jensen-Shannon divergence for a WLAN indoor positioning system. In: 2016 IEEE 7th Annual Ubiquitous Computing, Electronics & Mobile Communication Conference (UEMCON). New York, NY; 2016

[10] Abdullah O, Abdel-Qader I, Bazuin B. Convex optimization via Jensen-Bregman divergence for WLAN indoor positioning system. International Journal of Handheld Computing Research (IJHCR). 2017;8(1):29-41. DOI: 10.4018/IJHCR.201701010

[11] Sharma P, Chakraborty D, Banerjee N, Banerjee D, Agarwal SK, Mittal S. KARMA: Improving WiFi-based indoor localization with dynamic causality calibration. In: Eleventh Annual IEEE International Conference on Sensing, Communication, and Networking (SECON). Singapore; 2014

[12] Hähnel B, Dirk B, Fox D. Gaussian processes for signal strength-based location estimation. In: Proceedings of Robotics: Science and Systems; 2006

[13] Mirowski P, Steck H, Whiting P, Palaniappan R, MacDonald M, Ho TK. KL-divergence kernel regression for non-Gaussian fingerprint based localization. In: Proceedings of the International Conference on Indoor Positioning and Indoor Navigation; 2011

[14] Bahl P, Padmanabhan VN. RADAR: An in-building RF-based user location and tracking system. In: Nineteenth Annual Joint Conference of the IEEE Computer and Communications Societies. Proceedings. IEEE. Tel Aviv, INFOCOM; 2000

[15] Yang Z, Wu C, Liu Y. Locating in fingerprint space wireless indoor localization with little. In: Mobicom; 2012

[16] Youssef M, Agrawala A. The Horus WLAN location determination system. In: MobiSys; 2005

[17] Ni LM, Liu Y, Lau YC, Patil AP. LANDMARC: Indoor location sensing using active RFID. Wireless Networks. 2004;10(6):701-710

[18] Sen S, Radunović B, Choudhury RR, Minka T. You are facing the Mona Lisa: Spot localization using PHY layer information. In: MobiSys'12—Proceedings of the 10th International Conference on Mobile Systems, Applications, and Services; 2012

[19] Yim J. Introducing a decision tree-based indoor positioning technique. Expert Systems with Applications: An International Journal. 2008;34(2):1296-1302

[20] Farshad A et al. A microscopic look at WiFi fingerprinting for indoor mobile phone localization in diverse environments. In: Indoor Positioning and Indoor Navigation (IPIN); 2013

[21] Castro P et al. A probabilistic location service for wireless network environments. In: Ubiquitous Computing; September 2001

[22] Chen C, Chen Y, Yin L, Hwang R. A modified probability neural network indoor positioning technique. In: Information Security and Intelligence Control (ISIC), International Conference; 2012

[23] Roos T et al. A probabilistic approach to WLAN user location estimation. International Journal of Wireless Information Networks. 2002;**3**:7

[24] Wen Tsui A, Chuang Y, Chu H. Unsupervised learning for solving RSS hardware variance problem in WiFi localization. Mobile Networks and Applications. 2009;**14**(5):677-691

[25] Milioris D, Kriara L, Papakonstantinou A, Tzagkarakis G. Empirical evaluation of signal-strength fingerprint positioning in wireless LANs. In: ACM International Conference on Modeling, Analysis and Simulation of Wireless and Mobile Systems; 2010

[26] Mirowski P et al. KL-Divergence Kernel Regression for Non-Gaussian Fingerprint Based Localization. In: 2011 International Conference on Indoor Positioning and Indoor Navigation; 2011

[27] Mirowski P et al. Probability kernel regression for WiFi localisation. Journal of Location Based Services. 2013;**6**(2):81-100

[28] Feng C et al. Received-signal-strength-based indoor positioning using compressive sensing. IEEE Transactions on Mobile Computing. 2012;**11**(12)

[29] Dimitris M et al. Low-dimensional signal-strength fingerprint-based positioning in wireless LANs. Ad Hoc Networks. 2014;**12**:100-114

[30] Nielsen F, Nock R. Skew Jensen-Bregman Voronoi Diagrams. In: Gavrilova ML, Tan CJK, Mostafavi MA, editors. Transactions on Computational Science XIV. Lecture Notes in Computer Science. Berlin, Heidelberg: Springer; 2011;6970

[31] Nielsen, F. A family of statistical symmetric divergences based on Jensen's inequality. Clinical Orthopaedics and Related Research, vol. abs/1009.4004, (2010)

[32] Lin J. Divergence measures based on the Shannon entropy. IEEE Transactions on Information Theory. 1991;**37**(1):145-151

[33] Kushki A, Plataniotis KN, Venetsanopoulos AN. Kernel-based positioning in wireless local area networks. IEEE Transactions on Mobile Computing. 2007;**6**(6):689-705

11

Machine Learning Approaches for Spectrum Management in Cognitive Radio Networks

Ahmed Mohammed Mikaeil

Abstract

Cognitive radio (CR) provides a better way for utilization of spectrum resource by introducing an opportunistic usage of the frequency bands that are not heavily occupied by a licensed spectrum user or a primary user (PU). In cognitive radio, the detection and estimation of PU channel availability (unoccupied spectrum) are the key challenges that need to be overcome in order to prevent the interference with licensed spectrum user and improve spectrum resource utilization efficiency. This chapter focuses on developing new ways for detecting and estimating primary user channel availability based on machine-learning (ML) techniques.

Keywords: machine learning, spectrum sensing, spectrum management, channel state estimation, cognitive radio

1. Introduction

In this chapter, we study the problem of detection of unoccupied primary user spectrum (i.e., spectrum hole). We also introduce the methods for estimating the time when primary user channel state is available, so that the secondary spectrum user can adjust their transmission strategies accordingly.

The chapter is organized in two parts. The first part of the chapter focuses on the problem of detecting the unoccupied spectrum left by the primary user. In this part, we introduce the usage of machine-learning (ML) techniques as a fusion algorithm in cooperative spectrum sensing based on energy detector [1, 2]. In particular, we train a machine-learning classifier (i.e., K-nearest neighbor (KNN), support vector machine (SVM), Naive Bayes (NB), and Decision tree (DT)) over a set containing energy test statistics of PU channel frames along with their corresponding decisions about the presence or absence of PU transmission in the channel. Then, we use the trained classifier to predict the decisions for newly unseen PU channel frames [3]. The second part focuses on estimating the near future of PU channel state. In the literature, there are many proposals that have studied the problem of estimating PU channel state in cognitive radio (CR) [4–6]. However, most of these studies focused on predicting PU channel state in frequency domain by converting the received digital signals into frequency domain using fast Fourier transform (FFT). This increases the system complexity due to the FFT computations process. In the second part of the chapter, we introduce a new time-domain approach for PU channel state prediction based on time series prediction with some machine-learning prediction model. In particular, a time series is used to capture PU channel state detection sequence (PU channel "idle" or "occupied") in time domain. Then, prediction models such as the hidden Markov model (HMM) and Markov switching model (MSM) are used to predict the behavior of the time series that used capture PU channel state [7].

2. Machine-learning fusion-based cooperative spectrum sensing

In this part, we, first, define the system model for energy detection-based spectrum sensing; then, we present the method of calculating the thresholds for energy detector with different fusion rules. Second, we formulate a machine-learning classification problem and present four machine-learning classifiers to solve it. Then, we evaluate the performance of these classifiers with simulation experiments.

2.1. Energy detection-based cooperative spectrum sensing

Figure 1 shows a block diagram of the system model used for energy detection cooperative spectrum sensing based on machine-learning fusion rule. In this model, we consider a cooperative CR network with K cooperative nodes. Each node uses N samples for energy detection,

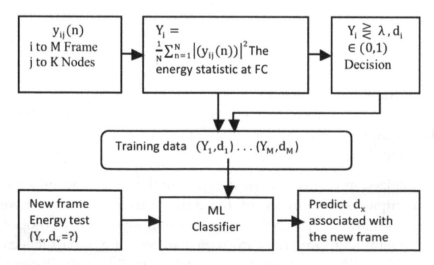

Figure 1. Block diagram of machine-learning-based fusion rule spectrum sensing.

while M frames are used for training the machine-learning (ML) classifier. The received signal of i_{th} frame at the j_{th} cooperative node $y_{ij}(n)$, $1 \leq n \leq N$, $1 \leq i \leq M$, $1 \leq j \leq K$ is given by

$$y_{ij}(n) = \begin{cases} w_{ij}(n) & H0 \\ \sqrt{\gamma_{ij}} \; s_{ij}(n) + w_{ij}(n) & H1 \end{cases} \tag{1}$$

where $s_{ij}(n)$ is the PU signal which is assumed to follow Gaussian i.i.d random process (i.e., zero mean and σ_s^2 variance), $w_{ij}(n)$ is the noise which is also assumed to follow Gaussian i.i.d random process (zero mean and σ_u^2 variance) because $s_{ij}(n)$ and $w_{ij}(n)$ are independent. Due to the fact that all K nodes are sensing the same frame at a given time, the global decision about PU channel availability will be made at the fusion center only. Thus, the energy statistic for the i_{th} frame at the j_{th} cooperative node Y_{ij} can be represented by the energy test statistic of the i_{th} frame at the fusion center which is given by

$$Y_i = \frac{1}{N} \sum_{n=1}^{N} \left| \left(y_{ij}(n) \right) \right|^2, \qquad 1 \leq i \leq M \tag{2}$$

Y_i is a random variable that has chi-square distribution probability density function (2N degrees of freedom for complex value and with N degrees of freedom for real value case). If we assume that the channel remains unchanged during the observation interval and there are enough number of samples observed ($N \geq 200$) [8], then we can approximate Y_i using Gaussian distribution as follows:

$$Y_i = \begin{cases} \left(\sigma_{ij}^2, 2\sigma_{ij}^4/N \right) & H0 \\ \left(\sigma_{ij}^2 \left(1 + \gamma_{ij} \right), 2\sigma_{ij}^4 \left(1 + \gamma_{ij} \right)^2/N \right) & H1 \end{cases} \tag{3}$$

where σ_{ij}^2, is the standard deviation of noise samples $w_{ij}(n)$, and γ_{ij} is the observed signal-to-noise ratio (SNR) of the i_{th} frame sensed at the j th cooperative node. Assuming that the noise variance and the SNR at the node remain unchanged for all M frames, then $\gamma_{ij} = \gamma_j$ and $\sigma_{ij}^2 = \sigma_j^2$. For a chosen threshold λ_j for each frame in the probability of the false alarm, P_f as given in [9] can be written as

$$P_f(\lambda_j) = \Pr(Y_i > \lambda_j | H0)$$

$$= \frac{1}{\sqrt{2\pi}\sigma_j} \int_{\lambda_j}^{\infty} e^{-(\lambda_j - \sigma_j)^2/\sqrt{2}\sigma_j^2}$$

$$= Q\left(\frac{\lambda_j}{\sigma_j^2} - 1 \right) \tag{4}$$

and the probability of detection P_d is given by

$$P_d(\lambda_j) = \Pr(Y_i > \lambda_j | H1)$$

$$= Q\left(\left(\frac{\lambda_j}{\sigma_j^2(1+\gamma_j)} - 1\right)\sqrt{\frac{N}{2}}\right) \tag{5}$$

where $Q(.)$ is the complementary distribution function of Gaussian distribution with zero mean and unit variance. To obtain the optimal threshold λ for K cooperative sensing nodes, data fusion rules are used. The calculation of the thresholds for single user and other fusion rules is presented in subsections 2.1.1 and 2.1.2.

2.1.1. The detection threshold for single-user-based sensing

For single user, sensing the number of the cooperative nodes is one (i.e., K = 1, $\sigma_j^2 = \sigma_u^2$, $\gamma_j = \gamma_u$. From Eq. (4) and for a given probability of false alarm P_f, the single-user threshold can be written as

$$\lambda_{single} = \left(\sqrt{\frac{2}{N}}Q^{-1}(P_f) + 1\right)\sigma_u^2 \tag{6}$$

where $Q^{-1}(.)$ is the inverse of the $Q(.)$ function, and the probability of the detection $P_{dsingle}$ can be written as

$$P_{dsingle} = Q\left(\left(\frac{\lambda_{single}}{\sigma_u^2(1+\gamma_u)} - 1\right)\sqrt{\frac{N}{2}}\right) \tag{7}$$

2.1.2. The detection threshold for data fusion-based sensing

In a data fusion spectrum sensing scheme, K nodes cooperate in calculating the threshold that is used to make the global sensing decision. There are many fusion rules used to calculate the global sensing decision threshold, which are divided into: hard fusion rules including AND, OR, and majority rule and soft fusion rules including maximum ratio combining (MRC), equal gain combining (EGC), and square law selection (SLS).

2.1.2.1. AND fusion rule

The AND rule decides that the signal is present if all users have detected the signal. For a system with K cooperative nodes with the same false alarm probability P_f cooperating using AND rule, the fusion center threshold can be expressed as

$$\lambda_{AND} = \left(\sqrt{\frac{2}{N}}Q^{-1}\left(P_f^{\frac{1}{k}}\right) + 1\right)\sigma_u^2 \tag{8}$$

And the detection probability P_{dAND} can be written as

$$P_{dAND} = \left(Q \left(\left(\frac{\lambda_{AND}}{\sigma_u^2 (1 + \gamma_u)} - 1 \right) \sqrt{\frac{N}{2}} \right) \right)^K \tag{9}$$

2.1.2.2. OR fusion rule

The OR rule decides that a signal is present if any of the users detect a signal. The fusion center threshold for K cooperative nodes cooperate using OR fusion rule which can be expressed as

$$\lambda_{OR} = \left(\sqrt{\frac{2}{N}} Q^{-1} \left((1 - (1 - P_f)^{\frac{1}{k}}) + 1 \right) \sigma_u^2 \tag{10}$$

And the detection probability P_{dOR} is

$$P_{dOR} = \left(1 - (1 - Q \left(\left(\frac{\lambda_{OR}}{\sigma_u^2 (1 + \gamma_u)} 1 \right) \sqrt{\frac{N}{2}} \right) \right)^K \tag{11}$$

2.1.2.3. Maximum ratio combination (optimal MRC) fusion rule

In soft combination fusion K, cooperative nodes with noise variances $\{\sigma_{11}^2, \sigma_{22}^2, ..., \sigma_{MK}^2\}$ and instantaneous SNRs $\{\gamma_{11}, \gamma_{22}, ..., \gamma_{MK}\}$ send their i_{th} frame energy test statistics $Y_{ij} = \frac{1}{N} \sum_{n=1}^{N} |(y_{ij}(n))|^2, 1 \leq j \leq K$ to the fusion center. The fusion center, weighs and adds them together after receiving these energy statistics as follows:

$$Ys_i = \sum_{j=1}^{K} w_j Y_{ij} \qquad , 1 \leq i \leq M \tag{12}$$

An assumption is made that SNRs and noise variances at the sensing node will remain unchanged for all the frames during the training process (i.e., $\gamma_{ij} = \gamma_j$, $\sigma_{ij}^2 = \sigma_j^2$). For soft optimal linear combination, we need to find the optimum weight vector w_j that maximizes the detection probability. For additive white Gaussian noise (AWGN) channels, the fusion threshold for MRC fusion rule is written as

$$\lambda_{MRC} = \left(\sum_{j=1}^{K} w_j \sigma_j^2 \right) Q^{-1} [P_f] + \sum_{j=1}^{K} w_j \sigma_j^2) \tag{13}$$

And the detection probability P_{dMRC} is given by

$$P_{dMRC} = Q \left(\left(\frac{\lambda_{MRC}}{\sum_{j=1}^{K} (1 + \gamma_j) w_j \sigma_j^2} - 1 \right) \sqrt{\frac{N}{2}} \right) \tag{14}$$

where the weighting coefficient vector $w_j\{w_1, w_2 \ldots w_K\}$ can be obtained by:

$$w_j = \text{sign}(g^T w_0)\, w_0$$

where

$$w_0 = \frac{L_{H1}^{-1/2}\left[L_{H1}^{-1/T}\right]^T g}{\left\| L_{H1}^{-1/2}\left[L_{H1}^{-1/2}\right]^T g \right\|}$$

where

$$L_{H1} = 2\,\text{diag}\left(\sigma_1^4(1+\gamma_1)^2, \ldots\ldots \sigma_k^4(1+\gamma_K)^2\right)/N$$

$$g = \left[\sigma_1^2\gamma_1, \sigma_2^2\gamma_2, \sigma_3^2\gamma_3, \sigma_4^2\gamma_4, \ldots\ldots, \sigma_K^2\gamma_K\right]^T$$

2.1.2.4. Equal gain combination (EGC) fusion rule

Equal weight linear combining employs straightforward averaging of the received soft decision statistics. In the equal gain combination, the received energies are equally weighted and then added together. The calculation of the threshold λ_{EGC} and the detection probability $P_{d\text{EGC}}$ follow Eqs. (13) and (14), respectively; the weighting vector is $\{w_j = w_1, \ldots w_K\}$ where $w_1 = w_2 = w_3 \ldots = w_K = 1/\sqrt{K}$ [10].

2.1.2.5. Square law selection (SLS) fusion rule

Here, the fusion center selects the node with the highest SNR $\gamma_{SLS} = \text{MAX}\left(\gamma_1, \gamma_2, ..\gamma_k\right)$ and considers the noise variance σ_{SLS}^2 associated with that node. Then the fusion center threshold is calculated as follows:

$$\lambda_{SLS} = \left(\sqrt{\frac{2}{N}}Q^{-1}\left(1 - (1 - P_f)^{\frac{1}{k}}\right) + 1\right)\sigma_{SLS}^2 \qquad (15)$$

And the detection probability P_{dSLS} is

$$P_{dSLS} = 1 - \left((1 - Q\left(\left(\frac{\lambda_{SLS}}{\sigma_{SLS}^2(1+\gamma_{SLS})} - 1\right)\sqrt{\frac{N}{2}}\right)\right)^K \qquad (16)$$

2.2. Machine-learning classification problem formulation

The i_{th} frame energy test statistic (Y_i for hard fusion or Ys_i for soft fusion rule) given in Eq. (2) or (12) is compared to the sensing threshold to calculate the decision d_i associated with i_{th} frame in the training data set as follows:

$$d_i = \begin{cases} 1 & Y_F \geq \lambda \\ -1 & Y_F < \lambda \end{cases} \quad 1 \leq i \leq M \qquad (17)$$

where $\lambda \in (\lambda_{single}, \lambda_{and}, \lambda_{OR}, \lambda_{MRC}, \lambda_{EGC}, \lambda_{SLS})$, $Y_F \in \{Y_i, Y_{si}\}$, M is the number of frames in the training set and "−1 " represents the absence of primary user on the channel, and "1" represents the presence of the primary user transmission on the channel. The output of Eq. (17) gives a set of pairs $(Y_i, d_i), i = 1, 2...M, d_i \in (-1, 1)$ that represent frame energy test statistics and their corresponding decisions. If we want to detect the decision (i.e., the class label) d_x associated with a new frame energy test statistic Y_x, we can use one of the following machine-learning classifiers to solve this classification problem.

2.2.1. K-nearest neighbors (KNN) classifier

For K-nearest neighbors classifier, K nearest points to Y_x are used to predict the class label d_x which corresponds to Y_x [11]. For $K = 1$, the Euclidian distance d_{st} between Y_x and the training data points can be computed as

$$d_{st}(i) = \sqrt{(Y_x - Y_i)^2} = |Y_x - Y_i| \quad i = 1, 2...M \qquad (18)$$

and, the new Y_x is classified with the label $d_x = d_{in}$, where d_{in} is the point that achieves the minimum Euclidian distance between d_{st} and Y_x.

2.2.2. Naïve Bayes classifier

Under the assumption that $d_i = -1$ and $d_i = 1$ are independent, the prior probabilities for $d_i = -1$ and $d_i = 1$ given training example $(Y_i, d_i), i = 1, 2, ..., M$ can be calculated, and the class-conditional densities (likelihood probabilities) can also be estimated from the set $[Y_1, Y_2, ..., Y_k].[Y_1, Y_2, ..., Y_k]$ in which the new Y_x is expected to fall in. And, the probability that the new Y_x to be a member of either $d_i = -1$ or $d_i = 1$ class is calculated using Naïve Bayes assumption and Bayes rule [12] as follows:

$$class(Y_x) = \underset{d_i}{argmax} \Pr(d_i) \prod_{j=1}^{k} \Pr(Y_j/d_i) \qquad (19)$$

where the prior probabilities are given to

$$\Pr(d_i = -1) = \frac{number\ of\ Y_i\ with\ class\ label^{"}1^{"}}{total\ number\ of\ class\ labels}$$

$$\Pr(d_i = 1) = \frac{number\ of\ Y_i\ with\ a\ class\ label^{"}0^{"}}{total\ number\ of\ class\ labels}$$

Whereas the class-conditional densities "likelihood probabilities" can be estimated using Gaussian density function by:

$$\Pr(Y_j/d_i) = \frac{1}{\sigma_j \sqrt{2\pi}} e^{\frac{-(Y-\mu_j)}{2\sigma_j}}, \quad Y_1 < Y < Y_k, \sigma_j > 0,$$

where μ_j, σ_j are mean and variance of the set $[Y_1, Y_2, ..., Y_k]$. Eq. (19) means that Naïve Bayes classifier will label the new Y_x with the class label d_i that achieves the highest posterior probability.

2.2.3. Support vector machine (SVM) classifier

For a given training set of pairs (Y_i, d_i), $i = 1, 2...M$, where $Y_i \in R$, and $d_i \in (+1, -1)$, the minimum weight w and a constant b that maximize the margin between the positive and negative class (i.e., $w Y_i + b = \pm 1$) with respect to the hyper-plane equation $w Y_i + b = 0$ can be estimated using support vector machine classifier by performing the following optimization [13].

$$\min_{w, b} \left(\frac{\|w\|^2}{2} \right), \quad where \; \|w\|^2 = w^T w \tag{20}$$

subject to $d_i(w Y_i + b) \geq 1 \quad i = 1, 2, ..., M.$

The solution of this quadratic optimization problem can be expressed using Lagrangian function as

$$L(w, b, \alpha) = \frac{\|w\|^2}{2} - \sum_{i=1}^{M} \alpha_i (d_i(w Y_i + b) - 1), \alpha_i \geq 0 \tag{21}$$

where $\alpha = (\alpha_1, \alpha_2, ..., \alpha_M)$ is the Lagrangian multipliers. IF we let $L(w, b, \alpha) = 0$, we can get $w = \sum_{i=1}^{M} \alpha_i d_i Y_i$ and $\sum_{i=1}^{M} \alpha_i d_i = 0$, and by substituting them into Eq. (21), the dual optimization problem that describes the hyper-plane can be written as

$$\min_{\alpha} \left(\frac{1}{2} \sum_{i=1}^{M} \sum_{j=1}^{M} d_i d_j (Y_i \; Y_j) \alpha_i \alpha_j - \sum_{i=1}^{M} \alpha_j \right), \alpha_j \geq 0 \tag{22}$$

From expression (22), we can assess α and compute w using $w = \sum_{i=1}^{M} \alpha_i d_i Y_i$. Then by choosing $\alpha_i > 0$, from the vector of $\alpha = (\alpha_1, \alpha_2, ..., \alpha_M)$ and calculating b from $b = d_j - \sum_{i=1}^{M} \alpha_i d_i (Y_i \; Y_j)$, we classify the new instance Y_x using the following classification function

$$class(Y_x) = \text{sign} \left(\sum_{i=1}^{M} \alpha_j d_j (Y_i \; Y_x) + b \right) \tag{23}$$

which means that the classification of new Y_x can be expressed as dot product of Y_x and the support vectors.

2.2.4. Decision tree (DT) classifier

For the training of a set of pairs of sensing decision (Y_i, d_i), $i = 1, 2, ..., M$, $d_i \in (-1, 1)$, the decision tree classifier creates a binary tree based on either impurity or node error splitting rule in order to split the training set into separate subset. Then, it repeats the splitting rule recursively for each subset until the leaf of the subset becomes pure. After that, it minimizes the error in each leaf by taking the majority vote of the training set in that leaf [14]. For classifying a new example Y_x, DT classifier selects the leaf where the new Y_x falls in and classifies the new Y_x with the class label that occurs most frequently among that leaf.

2.3. Performance discussion

Figure 2 shows the receiver operating characteristic (ROC) curves for single-user soft and hard fusion rules under Additive White Gaussian Noise (AWGN) channel. In order to generate this figure, we assume a cognitive radio system with 7 cooperative nodes (i.e., K = 7) operate at SNR γ_u = −22 dB. The local node decisions are made after observing1000 samples (i.e., energy

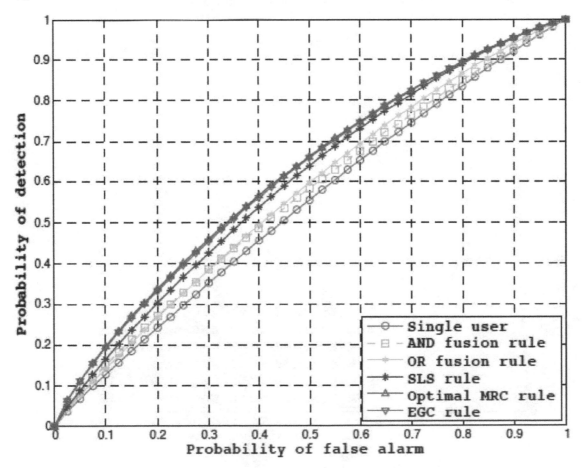

Figure 2. ROC curves for the soft and hard fusion rules under the case of AWGN receiver noise, $\sigma_u^2 = 1$, $\gamma_u = -22$ dB, K = 7 users and energy detection over N=1000 samples.

detection samples $N = 100$). For soft fusion rules, the SNRs γ_j for the nodes are equal to $\{-24.3, -21.8, -20.6, -21.6, -20.4, -22.2, -21.3\}$ and the noise variances σ_j^2 are $\{1,1,1,1,1,1,1\}$. We use a false alarm probability P_f varied from 0 to 1 increasing by 0.025. The simulation results show that soft EGC and optimal MRC fusion rules perform better than other soft and hard fusion rules even though that soft EGC fusion rule does not need any channel state information from the nodes.

Figure 3 shows the ROC curve depicting the performance of SVM classifier in classifying 1000 new frames after training it over a set containing $M = 1000$ frames. The thresholds used for training SVM classifier (i.e., single-user threshold, AND, OR, MRC, SLS, and EGC fusion rule threshold) are obtained numerically by considering the cognitive system used to generate **Figure 2**; however, here, we set the false alarm probability to $P_f = 0.1$.

From **Figure 3** and **Table 1**, we can notice that when training SVM classifier with anyone of the following thresholds: single user, OR, MRC, SLS, or EGC, it can detect 100% positive classes. We can also notice that training with EGC threshold can provide 90% precession in classifying the positive classes with 10% harmful interference, whereas training SVM with AND threshold can precisely classify the positive classes by 97.8%. **Table 1** shows the classification accuracy of

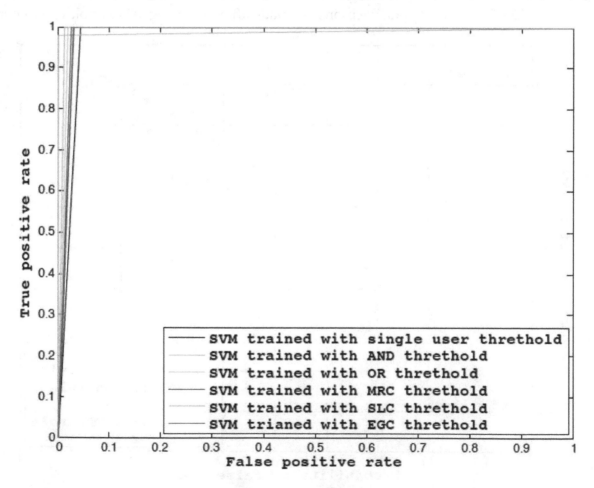

Figure 3. ROC curves shows the performance of SVM classifier in predicting the decisions for 1000 new frames after training it over a set containing1000 frames when single user, AND, OR, MRC, SLS, and EGC thresholds are used for training process.

Threshold	Single user (%)	AND rule (%)	OR rule (%)	MRC rule (%)	SLS rule (%)	EGC rule (%)
SVM						
Accuracy	96.1	98.3	98.1	97.6	98.9	98.0
Precession	77.7	100	53.7	89.4	74.4	90.1
Recall	100	97.8	100	100	100	100

Table 1. The accuracy, precession and the recall of SVM classifier.

SVM classifier (i.e., the proportion of all true classifications over all testing examples) and the precession of classification (i.e., proportion of true positive classes over all positive classes) as well as the recall of classification (i.e., the effectiveness of the classifier in identifying positive classes).

Figure 4 shows ROC curves showing the comparison of four machine-learning classifiers: K-nearest neighbor (KNN), support vector machine (SVM), Naive Bayes and Decision tree when used to classify 1000 frames after training them over a set containing 1000 frames with single-user threshold (Note: the same system used to generate the simulation of **Figure 3**. is considered

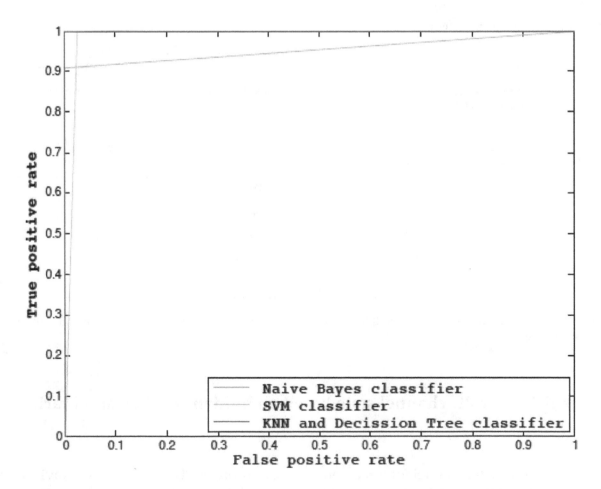

Figure 4. ROC curves shows a comparison of four machine learning classifiers: KNN, SVM, naive Bayes, and decision tree in classifying 1000 frames after training them over a set with 1000 frames using single user scheme threshold.

for computing the single-user threshold). We can notice from both **Figure 4**. and **Table 2** that KNN and decision tree classifier perform better than Naïve Bayes and SVM classifier in terms of the accuracy of classifying the new frames.

Table 3 shows the accuracy, precession, and the recall for decision tree classifier when used to classify 3000 frames after training it over a set containing 1000 frames for the same cognitive system used to generate **Figure 3**. The single-user threshold is used for training the classifier. The simulation was run with different number of samples for energy detection process. It is clear from the table that decision tree can classify all of the 3000 frames correctly or achieve 100% detection rate using only 200 samples for the energy detection process. And, due to the fact that the sensing time is proportional to the number of samples taken by energy detector, a less number of samples used for energy detection leads to less sensing time. Thus, when we use machine-learning-based fusion, such as decision tree or KNN, we can reduce the sensing time from 200 to 40 μs for 5 MHz bandwidth channel as an example, while we still achieve 100% detection rate of the spectrum hole.

Classifier	Accuracy (%)	Precession (%)	Recall (%)
KNN	100	100	100
Decision Tree	100	100	100
Naïve Bayes	98.9	100	91.2
SVM	97.6	83.9	100

Table 2. The accuracy, precession and recall of KNN, SVM, NB, and DT classifiers used in classifying 1000 new frames after being trained with 1000 frames.

Number of samples	Accuracy (%)	Precession (%)	Recall (%)
200	100	100	100
400	100	100	100
600	100	100	100
800	100	100	100
1000	100	100	100

Table 3. The accuracy, precession, and recall for decision tree classifier used in classifying 3000 frames for different number of samples.

3. Prediction of PU channel state based on hidden Markov and Markov switching model

In this part, the system model for forecasting the near future of PU channel state is divided into three models: (1) the model detecting the PU channel state (i.e., PU signal present or PU signal) which follows the conventional single-user energy detection (i.e., fusion techniques mentioned in Section 2.1 can also be considered here); (2) the model that generates a time series to capture PU channel state based on the detection sequence; and (3) the model for predicting the generated time series used to capture PU channel state based on hidden Markov model (HMM) and Markov switching model (MSM). The block diagram in **Figure 5.** illustrates these three models.

The PU channel state detection model can be written using Eq. (4); by giving probability of false alarm P_f, the detection threshold for single-user energy detector can be written as:

$$\lambda = \left(\sqrt{\frac{2}{N}} Q^{-1}(P_f) + 1 \right) \sigma_u^2 \tag{24}$$

where $Q^{-1}(.)$ is the inverse of the $Q(.)$ function.

And the decision of the sensing (i.e., PU detection sequence) over the time can be written as follows:

$$D_t = \begin{cases} \text{``0''} & \text{PU absent} & Y_t < \lambda \\ \text{``1''} & \text{PU present} & Y_t \geq \lambda \end{cases} \quad 1 \leq t \leq T \tag{25}$$

3.1. Time series generation model

Given PU channel state detection sequence over the time (i.e., PU absent, PU present), if we denote the period that the PU is inactive as "idle state," and the period that PU is active as "occupied state," our goal now is to predict when the detection sequence D_t will change from one state to another (i.e., "idle" to "occupied "or vice versa) before that happens so that the secondary user can avoid interfering with primary user transmission. For this reason, we generate a time series z_t to map each state of the detection sequence D_t (i.e., "PU present" and "PU absent") into another observation space using two different random variable distributions for each state (i.e., $z_t \in \{v_1, v_2...v_L\}$ represents PU absent or idle state and $z_t \in \{v_{L+1}....v_M\}$ represents PU occupied or present), the time series z_t can be written as

$$z_t \in \begin{cases} \{v_1, v_2, ..., v_L\} & Y_t < \lambda \\ \{v_{L+1}, ..v_M\} & Y_t \geq \lambda \end{cases} \quad 1 \leq t \leq T \tag{26}$$

Now, supposing that we have given observations value $O = \{O_1, O_2, O_t, ...O_T\}$, $O_t \in \{v_1, v_2...v_M\}$ and a PU channel state at time step t, $X_t \in s_i$, $i = 1, 2....K$, $s_i \in \{0, 1\}$ (i.e., 0 for

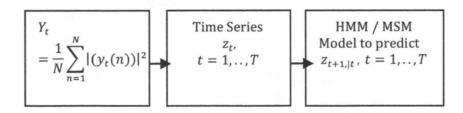

Figure 5. Block diagram of PU channel state prediction model.

PU idle and 1 PU occupied state), and we want to estimate the channel state at one time step ahead of the current state X_{t+1}. We can solve this problem using hidden Markov model Viterbi algorithm [15].

3.2. Primary users channel state estimation based on hidden Markov model

The generic HMM model can be illustrated by **Figure 6.—in this figure,** $X = \{ X_1, X_t, ... X_T\}$ represents the hidden state sequence, where $X_t \in \{s_1, s_2, ..., s_K\}$, K represents the number of hidden states or Markov chain and $O = \{ O_1, O_t, ..., O_T\}$ represents the observation sequence where $O_t \in \{ v_1, v_2, ..., v_M\}$ and M is the number of the observations in the observation space. A and B represent the transition probabilities matrix and the emission probabilities matrix, respectively, while π denotes the initial state probability vector. HMM can be defined by $\theta = (\pi, A, B)$ (i.e., the initial state probabilities, the transition probabilities, and emission probabilities) [15].

Initial state probabilities for HMM can be written as

$$\pi = (\pi_1, \pi_2, \pi_i.... \quad \pi_K)$$

$$\pi_i = P(X_1 = s_i), \quad i = 1, 2, ..., K \tag{27}$$

For a HMM model with two hidden states $i = 2$,

$$\pi = (\pi_1 \pi_2)$$

And the transition probabilities can be written as,

$$A = \left(a_{ij} \right)_{K \times K}$$

$$a_{ij} = P\left(X_{t+1} = s_j | X_t = s_i \right), i, j = 1, ..., K \tag{28}$$

where a_{ij} is the probability that next state equal s_j when current state is equal to s_i. For HMM model with two states, the matrix A can be written as

$$A = \begin{pmatrix} a_{00} & a_{01} \\ a_{10} & a_{11} \end{pmatrix}$$

The emission probabilities matrix for HMM model is written as

$$B = \left(b_{jm} \right)_{K \times M}$$

$$b_j(m) = P(O_t = v_m | X_t = s_j) \triangleq b_j(O_t), \quad j = 1...K, m = 1, ...M \tag{29}$$

B and b_j represent the probability that current observation is v_m when current state is s_j. For example, in an HMM model with $M = 6$ and $K = 2$, B is written as

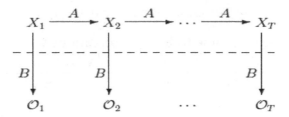

Figure 6. Hidden Markov model.

$$B = \begin{pmatrix} b_{11} & b_{12}\, b_{13} & b_{14} & b_{15}\, b_{16} \\ b_{21} & b_{22}\, b_{23} & b_{24} & b_{25}\, b_{26} \end{pmatrix}$$

Now, for the problem we describe in subsection (3.1), if we assume that HMM parameters $\theta = (\pi, A, B)$ and the observations value $O = \{ O_1, O_2\ O_t, ...O_T\}$ are given. If we assume that the maximum probability of state sequence t that end at state i to be equal to $\delta_t(i)$ where

$$\delta_t(i) = \max_{X_1, ..., X_{t-1}} \{P(X_1, ..., X_t = s_i; O_1, ..., O_t | \theta)\} \tag{30}$$

And we let $\psi_t(i)$ to be a vector that stores the arguments that maximize Eq. (30), we can write Viterbi algorithm to solve the problem mentioned in subsection (3.1) as follows:

1) step 1 initializes $\delta_t(i)$ and $\psi_t(i)$.

$$\delta_t(i) = \pi_i b_i(O_1)$$

$$\psi_t(i) = 0, \quad i = 1, ..., K \tag{31}$$

2) step 2 iterates to update $\delta_t(i)$ and $\psi_t(i)$.

$$\delta_t(j) = \max_{1 \le i \le K} \big[\delta_{t-1}(i)a_{ij}\big] b_j(O_t) \quad , t = 2, ..., T, \quad j = 1, ..., K \tag{32}$$

$$\psi_t(j) = \underset{1 \le i \le K}{\text{argmax}} \big[\delta_{t-1}(i)a_{ij}\big] \quad , t = 2, ..., T, j = 1, ..., K \tag{33}$$

3) step 3 terminates the update and calculates the likelihood probability P^* and the estimated state $q_T{}^*$ at time T as

$$P^* = \max_{1 \le i \le K} [\delta_T(i)] \tag{34}$$

$$q_T{}^* = \underset{1 \le i \le K}{\text{argmax}} [\delta_T(i)] \tag{35}$$

In the above case, HMM parameters $\theta = (\pi, A, B)$ are unknown and need to be estimated. We estimate these parameters statistically using Baum-Welch algorithm [16].

3.2.1. Hidden Markov model parameters estimation using Baum-Welch algorithm

If we assume that we have given some training observations with length L $\{O_1, O_2\ O_t, ...O_L\}$ and want to approximate HMM parameters $\theta = (\pi, A, B)$ from them, we can use maximum likelihood estimation. In order to do that, we define $\gamma_t(i)$ to be the probability of being in state s_i at time t, given t O_t ,t $= 1, 2...L$. $\gamma_t(i)$ is written as

$$\gamma_t(i) = P(X_t = s_i \mid O_1, ..., O_L, \theta) \tag{36}$$

We also define $\zeta_t(i, j)$ to be the probability of being in state s_i at time t and transiting to state s_j at time $t + 1$, given O_t ,t $= 1, 2...L$. $\zeta_t(i, j)$ is written as

$$\zeta_t(i, j) = P\big((X_t = s_i; X_{t+1} = s_j \mid O\ O_1, ..., O_L, \theta\big) \tag{37}$$

Given $\gamma_t(i)$ and $\zeta_t(i, j)$, the anticipated number of transitions from state s_i during the path is written as

$$E\big(\gamma_t(i)\big) = \sum_{t=1}^{L-1} \gamma_t(i) \tag{38}$$

and the anticipated number of transitions from state s_i to state s_j during the path is written as

$$E(\zeta_t(i, j)) = \sum_{j=1}^{L-1} \zeta_t(i, j) \tag{39}$$

Given $E(\zeta_t(i, j))$ and $E(\gamma_t(i))$, we can extract the model parameters $\theta = (\pi, A, B)$ from the training sequence as given in [16] using the step listed below

1- for $i = 1, 2, 3...K$, let $\widehat{\pi}_i =$ expected frequency in state s_i at time $(t = 1)$

$$\pi_i = \gamma_1(i) \tag{40}$$

2- for $i = 1, 2, 3...K$ and $j = 1, 2, 3...K$, compute

$$\widehat{a}_{ij} = \frac{\text{Expected number of transitions from state } s_i \text{ to state } s_j}{\text{Expected number of transitions from state } s_i}$$

$$= \frac{E(\zeta_t(i, j))}{E(\gamma_t(i))} = \frac{\sum\limits_{j=1}^{L-1} \zeta_t(i, j)}{\sum\limits_{t=1}^{L-1} \gamma_t(i)} \tag{41}$$

3- for $i = 1, 2, 3...K$ and $j = 1, 2, 3...K$, compute

$$\widehat{b}_i(m) = \frac{\text{Expected number of times in state } s_j \text{ and observing } v_m}{\text{Expected number of times in state } s_j}$$

$$= \frac{\sum_{\substack{t=1 \\ O_t = v_m}}^{L} \gamma_t(i)}{\sum_{t=1}^{L} \gamma_t(i)} \qquad (42)$$

The estimation algorithm can be summarized in the following steps:

1. Get your observations $O_1\, O_2,\, \ldots O_L$,

2. Set a guess of your first θ estimate $\theta\,(1), k = 1$

$$\text{Update } k = k + 1$$

3. Compute $\theta\,(k)$ based on $O_1\, O_2,\, \ldots O_L$ and

$$\gamma_t(i), \zeta_t(i,j) \quad \forall 1 \leq t \leq L, \quad \forall 1 \leq i \leq K, \forall 1 \leq j \leq K$$

4. Compute $E\big(\gamma_t(i)\big)$ and $E(\zeta_t(i,j))$ from Eqs. (38) and (39)

5. Compute according to 5 the new estimate of $a_{ij}, b_i(k), \pi_i$, and call them $\theta\,(k+1)$

6. Go to 3 if not converged.

The prediction for a one-step ahead PU channel state can be done based on the trained parameters $\{\pi, A, B\}$ with the help of Eqs. (31), (34), and (35) by setting $T = 1$.

3.3. Primary users channel state estimation based on Markov switching model

An alternative way to estimate PU channel state is to use Markov switching model (MSM). For the time series in Eq. (26), we assume that z_t obeys two different Gaussian distributions $N \sim (\mu_{z0}, \sigma_{z0}^2)$ or $N \sim (\mu_{z1}, \sigma_{z1}^2)$ based on the sensed PU channel state "PU channel idle" or "PU occupied." We can rewrite Eq. (26) as follows:

$$z_t \sim \begin{cases} (\mu_{z0}, \sigma_{z0}^2) & Y_t < \lambda \\ (\mu_{z1}, \sigma_{z1}^2) & Y_t \geq \lambda \end{cases} \quad 1 \leq t \leq T \qquad (43)$$

It is obvious that Eq. (43) represents a two-state Gaussian regime switching time series which can be modeled using MSM [17]. In order to estimate the switching time of one state ahead of the current state for this time series, we need to derive MSM regression model for the time series and estimate its parameters.

3.3.1. Derivation of Markov switching model for Gaussian regime switching time series

A simple Markov switching regression model to describe the two-state Gaussian regime switching time series is given in Eq. (43). This model can be written by following Ref [17] as

$$z_t = \mu_{s_t} + \epsilon_t \qquad \epsilon_t \sim \left(0, \sigma_{s_t}^2\right) \tag{44}$$

where μ_{s_t} is an array of predetermined variables measured at time t, which may include the lagged values of z_t, ϵ_t is the white noise process, $s_t = \{0,1\}$ is a hidden Markov chain which has a mean and standard deviation over the time equal to $\mu_{st} = \mu_0(1 - s_t) + \mu_1 s_t$ and $\sigma_{st} = \sigma_0(1 - s_t) + \sigma_1 s_t$, respectively (the state variable s_t follows first order Markov chain (i.e., two-state Markov chain as in [18])). Given the past history of s_t, the probability of s_t taking a certain value depends only on s_{t-1}, which takes the following Markov property:

$$P(s_t = j| s_{t-1} = i) = P_{ij} \tag{45}$$

where $P_{ij}(i; j = 0; 1)$ denotes the transition probabilities of $s_t = j$, given that $s_{t-1} = i$. Clearly, the transition probabilities satisfy $P_{i0} + P_{i1} = 1$. We can gather the transition probabilities P_{ij} into a transition matrix as follows:

$$P = \begin{pmatrix} P(s_t = 0| s_{t-1} = 0) & P(s_t = 0| s_{t-1} = 1) \\ P(s_t = 1| s_{t-1} = 0) & P(s_t = 1| s_{t-1} = 1) \end{pmatrix}$$

$$= \begin{pmatrix} P_{00} & P_{01} \\ P_{10} & P_{11} \end{pmatrix} \tag{46}$$

The transition matrix P is used to govern the behavior of the state variable s_t, and it holds only two parameters (P_{00} and P_{11}). Assuming that we do not observe s_t directly, we only deduce its operation from the observed behavior of z_t. The parameters that need to be estimated to fully describe the probability law governing z_t are the variance of the Gaussian innovation σ_0, σ_1, the expectation of the dependent variable μ_0, μ_1, and the two-state transition probabilities P_{00} and P_{11}.

3.3.2. Markov switching model parameters estimation via maximum likelihood estimation

There are many ways to estimate the parameters for the Markov switching model. Among these ways are Quasi-maximum likelihood estimation (QMLE) and Gibbs sampling. In this section, we focus on maximum likelihood estimation (MLE).

If we denote $\psi_{t-1} = \{z_{t-1}, z_t, z_{t+1}...z_1\}$ to be a vector of the training data until time $t - 1$ and denote $\theta = \{\sigma_0, \sigma_1, \mu_0, \mu_1, P_{00}, P_{11}\}$ to be the vector of MSM parameters, then $\psi_L = \{z_{t-1}, z_t, ..., z_L\}$ to a vector of the available information with the length L sample (see **Figure 7**.). In order to evaluate the likelihood of the state variable s_t based on the current trend of z_t, we need to assess its conditional expectations $s_t = i$, $(i = 0, 1)$ based on ψ and θ. These conditional expectations include prediction probabilities $P(s_t = i|\psi_{t-1}; \theta)$, which are based on the information prior to time t, the filtering probabilities $P(s_t = i|\psi_t; \theta)$ which are based on the past and current information, and finally the smoothing probabilities $P(s_t = i|\psi_L; \theta)$ which are based on the full-sample information L. After getting these probabilities, we can obtain the log-likelihood function as a byproduct, and then we can compute the maximum likelihood estimates.

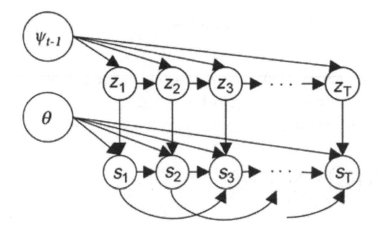

Figure 7. Markov switching model.

Normally, the density of z_t conditional on ψ_{t-1} and $s_t = i$, $(i = 0, 1)$ is written as

$$\mathcal{F}\left(z_t \middle| s_t = i, \psi_{t-1}; \theta\right) = \frac{1}{\sqrt{2\pi}\sigma_{s_t}} e^{-\frac{\left(z_t - \mu_{s_t}\right)^2}{2\sigma_{st}^2}} \tag{47}$$

where $\mathcal{F}$ represent the probability density function. Given the prediction probabilities $P\left(s_t = i \middle| \psi_{t-1}; \theta\right)$, the density of z_t conditional on ψ_{t-1} can be obtained from

$$\mathcal{F}\left(z_t \middle| \psi_{t-1}; \theta\right) =$$

$$= P\left(s_t = 0 \middle| \psi_{t-1}; \theta\right) \mathcal{F}\left(z_t \middle| s_t = 0\ \psi_{t-1}; \theta\right)$$

$$+ P\left(s_t = 1 \middle| \psi_{t-1}; \theta\right) \mathcal{F}\left(z_t \middle| s_t = 1\ \psi_{t-1}; \theta\right) \tag{48}$$

For $i = 0; 1$, the filtering probabilities of s_t are given by:

$$P\left(s_t = i \middle| \psi_t; \theta\right)$$

$$= \frac{P\left(s_t = i \middle| \psi_{t-1}; \theta\right) \mathcal{F}\left(z_t \middle| s_t = i\ \psi_{t-1}; \theta\right)}{\mathcal{F}\left(z_t \middle| \psi_{t-1}; \theta\right)} \tag{49}$$

The prediction probabilities are:

$$P\left(s_{t+1} = i \middle| \psi_t; \theta\right)$$

$$= P\left(s_t = 0, s_{t+1} = i \middle| \psi_t; \theta\right) + P\left(s_t = 1, s_{t+1} = i \middle| \psi_t; \theta\right)$$

$$= P_{0i}\ P\left(s_t = 0 \middle| \psi_t; \theta\right) + P_{1i}\ P\left(s_t = 1 \middle| \psi_t; \theta\right) \tag{50}$$

where $P_{0i} = P\left(s_{t+1} = i \middle| s_t = 0\right)$ and $P_{1i} = P\left(s_{t+1} = i \middle| s_t = 1\right)$ are the transition probabilities. By setting the initial values as given in [19] assuming the Markov chain is presumed to be ergodic:

$$P\left(s_0 = i\middle|\psi_0\right) = \frac{1 - P_{jj}}{2 - P_{ii} - P_{jj}}$$

we can iterate the Eqs. (49) and (50) to obtain the filtering probabilities $P\left(s_t = i\middle|\psi_t; \theta\right)$ and the conditional densities $\mathcal{F}\left(z_t\middle| s_t = 0\ \psi_{t-1}; \theta\right)$ for $t = 1, 2, \ldots T$. Then we can compute the logarithmic likelihood function using

$$\log\left(L\left(\hat{\theta}\right)\right) = \sum_{t=1}^{T} \sum_{i=1}^{2} \log(\mathcal{F}\left(Z_t\middle| S_t = i, \psi_{t-1}; \theta\right) \times P\left(S_t = i\middle|\psi_t; \theta\right)) \qquad (51)$$

where $L\left(\hat{\theta}\right)$ is the maximized value of the likelihood function. The model estimation can finally be obtained by finding the set of parameters $\hat{\theta}$ that maximize the Eq. (51) using numerical-search algorithm. The estimated filtering and prediction probabilities can then be easily calculated by plugging $\hat{\theta}$ into the equation formulae of these probabilities. We adopt the approximation in Ref [20] for computing the smoothing probabilities $P\left(s_t = i\middle|\psi_L; \theta\right)$

$$P\left(s_t = i\middle| s_{t+1} = j, \psi_L; \theta\right) \approx P\left(s_t = i\middle| s_{t+1}, \psi_t; \theta\right)$$

$$= \frac{P\left(s_t = i, s_{t+1}\middle|\psi_{t-1}; \theta\right)}{P\left(s_{t+1} = j\middle|\psi_t; \theta\right)}$$

$$= \frac{P_{0i}\ P\left(s_t = i\middle|\psi_t; \theta\right)}{P\left(s_{t+1} = j\middle|\psi_t; \theta\right)}$$

And, for $i; j = 0; 1,$ smoothing probabilities is expressed as:

$$P\left(s_t = i\middle|\psi_L; \theta\right)$$

$$= P\left(s_{t+1} = 0\middle|\psi_L; \theta\right) P\left(s_t = 1\middle| s_{t+1} = 0, \psi_L; \theta\right)$$

$$+ P\left(s_{t+1} = 1\middle|\psi_L; \theta\right) P\left(s_t = i\middle| s_{t+1} = 1, \psi_L; \theta\right)$$

$$= P\left(s_t = i\middle|\psi_t; \theta\right) \times \left(\frac{P_{i0}\ P\left(s_{t+1} = 0\middle|\psi_L; \theta\right)}{P\left(s_{t+1} = 0\middle|\psi_t; \theta\right)} + \frac{P_{i1}\ P\left(s_{t+1} = 1\middle|\psi_L; \theta\right)}{P\left(s_{t+1} = 1\middle|\psi_t; \theta\right)}\right) \qquad (52)$$

Using $P\left(S_L = i\middle|\psi_L; \theta\right)$ as the initial value, we can iterate the equations regressively for filtering and prediction probabilities along with the equation above to get the smoothing probabilities for $t = L - 1, \cdots, k + 1.$

3.4. Results and discussions

Figure 8 shows the training detection sequence which we generate as a training observation using randomly distributed PU channel state "idle and occupied" over T = 250 ms simulation

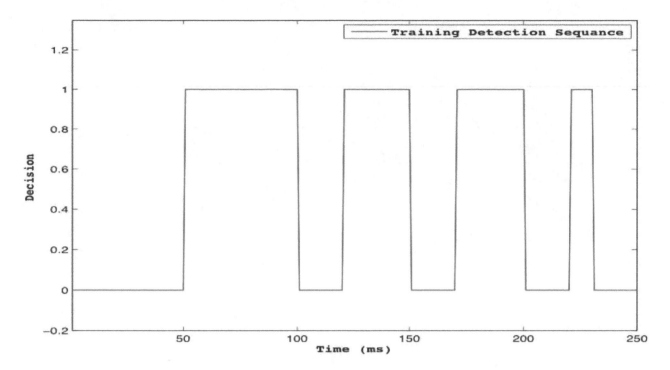

Figure 8. The training detection sequence for HMM and MSM.

time. We use this training observations to train *Baum-Welch algorithm* in order to estimate HMM model parameters $\theta = (\pi, A, B)$, assuming that the first estimate of θ (1) is:

$$\pi_1 = \begin{pmatrix} 1 & 0 \end{pmatrix}$$

$$A_1 = \begin{pmatrix} 0.85 & 0.15 \\ 0.10 & 0.90 \end{pmatrix}$$

$$B_1 = \begin{pmatrix} 0.17 & 0.16 & 0.17 & 0.16 & 0.17 & 0.17 & 0.17 \\ 0.60 & 0.08 & 0.08 & 0.08 & 0.08 & 0.08 & 0.08 \end{pmatrix}$$

Figure 9a shows the performance of HMM algorithm in estimating the PU channel states (i.e., PU idle or PU occupied) of the time series that capture the detection sequence for a single-user cognitive radio network. **Figure 9a** contains three plots; the top plot shows the randomly distributed PU channel states over time T = 500 ms . The middle plot shows the generated time series following the distribution $z_t \in \{1, 2, 3\}$ for idle states and $z_t \in \{4, 5, 6\}$ for occupied states (note: we can construct the observation space from these two distributions as $O_t \in \{1, 2, 3, 4, 5, 6\}$, t = 1, 2...500 ms). The bottom plot shows performance of HMM algorithm in forecasting the time series generated to capture PU detection sequence.

Figure 9b shows the performance of MSM algorithm in predicting the switching process between the two PU channel states for the same PU detection sequence given in **Figure 9a** T = 500 ms . The top graph in **Figure 9b** shows the generated time series with the following distribution $z_t \sim (0.1, 0.5)$ for idle states and $z_t \sim (0.01, 0.2)$ for occupied states and the bottom graph shows the prediction performance using MSM. As it is clear from the figure, the prediction performance is smoother than HMM approach.

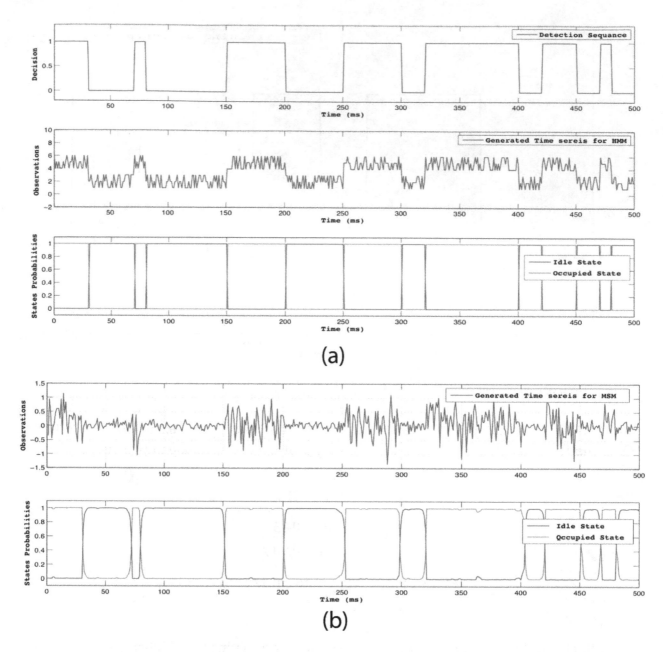

Figure 9. (a) Shows the performance of HMM algorithm in predicting the generated time series to capture PU channel state detection sequence. (b) Shows the performance of MSM algorithm in predicting the generated time series to capture the same PU detection sequence in **Figure 8**.

4. Conclusions

In this chapter, we have presented a per-frame decision-based cooperative spectrum sensing based on machine-learning classifier-based fusion approach. The simulation and numerical results have shown that the machine-learning classifier-based fusion algorithm performs same as conventional fusion rules in terms of sensing accuracy with less sensing time, overheads, and extra operations that limit achievable cooperative gain among cognitive radio users. In addition, we have also studied the problem of primary user channel state prediction in cognitive radio network and introduced Markov model and Markov Switching Model to solve this problem. We finally showed by the means of simulation that both hidden Markov model and Markov switching model perform very well in predicting the time series that capture the actual primary user channel state.

Acknowledgements

I gratefully acknowledge the funding received from Shanghai Jiao Tong University to undertake my PhD. I also thank Prof. Bin Guo for his encouragement and help on the topic.

Author details

Ahmed Mohammed Mikaeil

Address all correspondence to: ahmed_mikaeil@yahoo.co.uk

Department of Electronic Engineering, School of Electronic Information and Electrical Engineering, Shanghai Jiao Tong University, Shanghai, China

References

[1] Teguig D, Scheers B, Le Nir V. Data fusion schemes for cooperative spectrum sensing in cognitive radio networks. Communications and Information Systems Conference (MCC), 2012 Military. IEEE; 2012

[2] Zhai X, Jianguo P. Energy-detection based spectrum sensing for cognitive radio. 2007:944-947

[3] Mikaeil AM, Guo B, Bai X, Wang Z. Machine learning to data fusion approach for cooperative spectrum sensing. 2014 International Conference on Cyber Enabled Distributed Computing and Knowledge Discovery(CyberC), Shanghai,13–15 October 2014, 429-434

[4] Zhe C, Qiu RC. Prediction of channel state for cognitive radio using higher-order hidden Markov model. IEEE SoutheastCon 2010 (SoutheastCon), Proceedings of the IEEE. 2010

[5] Zhe C et al. Channel state prediction in cognitive radio, part II: Single-user prediction. Proceedings of IEEE Southeast Con. 2011

[6] Chang-Hyun P et al. HMM based channel status predictor for cognitive radio." Microwave Conference, 2007. APMC 2007. Asia-Pacific. IEEE, 2007

[7] Mikaeil AM, Guo B, Bai X, Wang Z. Hidden Markov and Markov switching model for primary user channel state prediction in cognitive radio. IEEE 2nd International Conference on Systems and informatics (ICSAI). 2014:854-859

[8] Kieu-Xuan T, Koo I. A cooperative spectrum sensing scheme using fuzzy logic for cognitive radio networks. KSII Transactions on Internet and Information Systems (TIIS). 2010; **4**(3):289-304

[9] Khaira ND, Bhadauria P. Cooperative spectrum sensing and detection efficiency in cognitive radio network. International Journal of Electronics and Computer Science Engineering (IJECSE, ISSN: 2277–1956)1. 2012;**01**:64-73

[10] Qin Q, Zhimin Z, Caili G. A study of data fusion and decision algorithms based on cooperative spectrum sensing. Fuzzy Systems and Knowledge Discovery, 2009. FSKD'09. Sixth International Conference on. Vol. 1. IEEE, 2009

[11] Bermejo S, Cabestany J. Adaptive soft k-nearest neighbor classifiers. Pattern Recognition. 2000;**33**(12):1999-2005

[12] Metsis V, Androutsopoulos I, Paliouras G. Spam filtering with naive bayes-which naive bayes? CEAS. 2006

[13] Thilina KM et al. Pattern classification techniques for cooperative spectrum sensing in cognitive radio networks: SVM and W-KNN approaches. Global Communications Conference (GLOBECOM), 2012 IEEE, 2012

[14] Barros RC et al. A survey of evolutionary algorithms for decision-tree induction. Systems, Man, and Cybernetics, Part C: Applications and Reviews, IEEE Transactions on. 2012; **42**(3):291-312

[15] Rabiner L. A tutorial on hidden Markov models and selected applications in speech recognition. Proceedings of the IEEE. 1989;**77.2**:257-286

[16] Welch LR. Hidden Markov models and the Baum-Welch algorithm. IEEE Information Theory Society Newsletter. 2003;**53**(4):10-13

[17] Frühwirth-Schnatter S. Finite Mixture and Markov Switching Models: Modeling and Applications to Random Processes. Springer; 2006

[18] Kuan C-M. Lecture on the Markov switching model. Institute of Economics Academia Sinica. 2002 available at homepage.ntu.edu.tw/~ckuan/pdf/Lec-Markov_note.pdf

[19] Hamilton JD. Time Series Analysis. Vol. 2. Princeton: Princeton university press; 1994

[20] Kim C-J. Dynamic linear models with Markov-switching. Journal of Econometrics. 1994; **60.1**:1-22

Permissions

List of Contributors

Sherrene Bogle
University of Technology, Jamaica, Kingston, Jamaica

W. David Pan
Department of Electrical and Computer Engineering, University of Alabama in Huntsville, Huntsville, AL, USA

Yuhang Dong and Dongsheng Wu
Department of Mathematical Sciences, University of Alabama in Huntsville, Huntsville, AL, USA

Ibtehal Talal Nafea
College of Computer Science and Engineering (CCSE), Taibah University, Medina, Kingdom of Saudi Arabia

Dandibhotla Teja Santosh
School of Technology, GITAM, Rudraram, Patancheru, Sanga reddy, Hyderabad Campus, India

Bulusu Vishnu Vardhan
JNTUHCEM, Manthani, India

Li Du and Yuan Du
Hardware Architecture Research Engineer, Kneron Inc., Research Scientist, UCLA, Los Angeles, USA

Yves Rybarczyk
Intelligent & Interactive Systems Lab (SI2 Lab), Universidad de Las Américas, Quito, Ecuador
Department of Electrical Engineering – CTS/UNINOVA, Nova University of Lisbon, Monte de Caparica, Portugal

Rasa Zalakeviciute
Intelligent & Interactive Systems Lab (SI2 Lab), Universidad de Las Américas, Quito, Ecuador

Suhuai Luo
School of Electrical Engineering and Computing, The University of Newcastle, Callaghan NSW, Australia

Samar M. Alqhtani
College of Computer Science and Information Systems, Najran University, Najran, Saudi Arabia

Jiaming Li
Quantitative Imaging Research Team, CSIRO Data61, NSW, Australia

Noureddine Bouhmala, Kjell Ivar Øvergård and Karina Hjelmervik
Department of Maritime Technology and Innovation, SouthEast University, Norway

Andreea Mihailescu
Lasers Department, National Institute for Lasers, Plasma and Radiation Physics, Bucharest-Magurele, Romania

Osamah Ali Abdullah and Ikhlas Abdel-Qader
Electrical and Computer Engineering Department, Almamoon University College, Kalamazoo, Michigan USA

Ahmed Mohammed Mikaeil
Department of Electronic Engineering, School of Electronic Information and Electrical Engineering, Shanghai Jiao Tong University, Shanghai, China

Index

CPSIA information can be obtained
at www.ICGtesting.com
Printed in the USA
BVHW011244270822
645617BV00003B/131